Metadata Management for Information Control and Business Success

For a listing of recent titles in the *Artech House Computing Library*,
turn to the back of this book.

Metadata Management for Information Control and Business Success

Guy Tozer

RECEIVED

DEC 13 2000

MINNESOTA STATE UNIVERSITY LIBRARY
MANKATO MN 56001 6062

Artech House
Boston • London

Library of Congress Cataloging-in-Publication Data

Tozer, Guy V.
    Metadata management for information control and business success /
Guy Tozer.
        p.   cm.—(Artech House computing library)
    Includes bibliographical references and index.
    ISBN 0-89006-280-3 (alk. paper)
    1. Database management.   2. Metadata   I. Title.
QA76.9.D3T6863   1999
005.74—dc21   99-16539
                                                      CIP

QA
76.9
.D3
T6863
1999

British Library Cataloguing in Publication Data

Tozer, Guy V.
    Metadata management for information control and business
    success. — (Artech House computing library)
    1. Metadata   2. Management information systems
    I. Title
    658.4'038011
    ISBN 0-89006-280-3

Cover design by Elaine Donnelly

© 1999 Artech House, Inc.
685 Canton Street
Norwood, MA 02062
All rights reserved

All rights reserved. Printed and bound in the United States of America. No part of this book
may be reproduced or utilized in any form or by any means, electronic or mechanical, including photocopying, recording, or by any information storage and retrieval system, without permission in writing from the publisher.

    All terms mentioned in this book that are known to be trademarks or service marks have
been appropriately capitalized. Artech House cannot attest to the accuracy of this information. Use of a term in this book should not be regarded as affecting the validity of any trade-
mark or service mark.

International Standard Book Number: 0-89006-280-3
Library of Congress Catalog Card Number: 99-16539

10 9 8 7 6 5 4 3 2 1

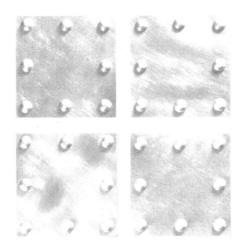

Contents

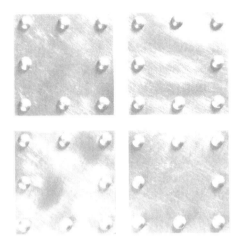

Preface

THE TERM *metadata,* according to the standard and somewhat unsatisfactory definition, is "data about data." A more useful perspective is gained by seeing metadata as the means by which the *structure* and *behavior* of data is recorded, controlled, and published across an organization. Examples of the questions that metadata might help to answer include the following:

- What is a product group?

- What values can be assigned to currency codes and what does each value signify?

- How often is sales data transferred from the order processing system to the general ledger and under what conditions?

- Who assigns new customer codes and sets credit limits?

These questions are wide-ranging and are likely to be of interest to diverse groups within the organization. *Systems designers, application users, management, data owners,* and *database administrators* all have a vested interest in controlling and understanding the metadata relevant to their roles. In essence, nearly all employees within an organization will be affected by the quality of data and the "rule book" or *metadata* that defines how the data are captured and manipulated.

If it is going to be possible to provide these diverse groups with accurate and consistent answers to their questions, then the metadata must be managed at an enterprise level, rather than being treated as by-products of application development. Accordingly, a new approach to data management must be defined.

The importance attached to capturing and exchanging information in the modern commercial world cannot be overstated. If any single factor characterizes the changes in business over the last 25 years it is the explosive increase in the availability of, and reliance on, data. As a result, information technology has come to be seen as the cornerstone upon which commercial progress depends.

In many organizations, a great emphasis is placed on the need to treat information as a corporate asset. Despite good intentions, few companies understand how to achieve this and very often confuse the ability to deliver large quantities of data with controlling their quality.

My previous work, *Information Quality Management* (NCC-Blackwell, 1994) described the problems that occur when data quality is not managed effectively and how an organization can be set up to avoid them. In the course of writing this book, it became clear that the lack of a formal structure for data control hindered the effectiveness of the methods proposed and that further consideration should be given to understanding the business rules that constrain the data. It seemed that the IT community had come to accept that data quality was a matter of common sense, whereas the evidence from real-world experience was that the sense required was very far from common!

If information is truly an asset to be valued by an organization, then it should be managed actively—for the common good. Data must be shareable in a transparent fashion across the organization and be under *corporate ownership*, rather than serving vested interests. This requires the implementation of cultural changes and a framework for ongoing data management. Unfortunately, very little has been done to establish a formal methodology behind the establishment of such a control framework.

Metadata Management for Information Control and Business Success has been written to bridge this gap and to establish a common understanding of the issues faced by all information consumers.

Of course, the production and consumption of information is not a new feature of human behavior. In a preliterate society, information was gathered by observation. Each individual relied on his or her senses to determine what was happening. Where their immediate experience was insufficient, they learned to ask questions of others whose knowledge may have been broader or more closely applicable to the problem in hand. Later, widespread literacy enabled experiences and observations to be shared between people or groups who were remote from each other.

With the advent of the computer, data became far easier to access and available in exponentially larger quantities, leaving us with the impression that the world is totally awash with information. We must recognize, however, that whether information is transferred orally, in written form, or via computer the same tests should be applied to determine whether its inherent usefulness is preserved.

Information should, of course, be accurate. This underpins any real value that may be given to data and, as such, is fundamental to the usefulness of the data. It must also be complete, timely, and understood by the user. If some information is missing or out-of-date, or the user of the information is incapable of interpreting it, then it will not be truly useful either.

Accuracy should, of course, lie at the heart of any information-provision activity. If someone asks a question or looks in a book or computer system for an answer to some issue, the assumption must be that the information provided will be accurate, at least within some acceptable and recognized margins for error. The responsibility to provide accurate information is generally very well understood and accounted for by information providers, be they the recognized wise members of prehistoric tribes, authors of books, or the people constructing and populating information systems. Unfortunately, the contribution to usefulness of data made by the other factors mentioned (consistency, timeliness, and clarity of purpose) has been largely ignored as modern technology is deployed.

The basic concept of information quality underlies many of the successes (and failures) of the so-called information age. It is by understanding the establishment and control of data quality that much of the frustration and complexity of using IT can be avoided.

In the earliest commercial computer applications, information quality reflected little more than the ability to control the correctness of data. If an article was priced at $10, then this was, indeed, the price at which it should be sold. This provided some degree of robustness, since most of the systems in use were *functionally isolated.*

Each application was designed with a specific, tightly bounded purpose in mind. The inputs received and the outputs produced were closely specified, and together with the processing required to convert one into the other formed the entire specification for the computer application. For instance, an invoicing system (often self-built by the organization for which it was used) would be concerned solely with the production of sales invoices based on the data within the sales order and delivery files.

As the commercial use of IT developed and became more sophisticated, it became clear that systems would need to communicate with each other. At a basic level, this meant that *interfaces* would need to be built to allow formally structured messages to be sent back and forth between systems.

An implicit but often ignored effect of this was the need to ensure that the definition of data within each system was consistent. Each system had to be seen as part of a larger picture, with intersystem transfers of data being designed and controlled explicitly with this picture in mind. Any two systems that interacted needed to have a consistent view of what the data were and what constraints or business rules were to be applied to these data. There are three broad categories of approaches that can be adopted to achieve this.

The first, and still by far the most common, involves building specific conversions and restructuring logic into the interfaces between systems. This appears to be the simplest method, at a tactical level, since it focuses on the immediate problem and allows (relatively) easy adaptation of older systems. It does, however, lead to considerable wasted effort. Many conversion activities will need to be repeated as further interfaces are built, and much rework will be done as the assumptions that were used for applications A and B are proved to be insufficient for application F, at some future stage. The overall effect of adopting this approach in the long term is that the applications will be linked by a poorly controlled and costly to manage "spiderweb" of interfaces.

The second approach is to ensure that the databases for different applications are *integrated*. This approach is fundamental to the design of so-called enterprise resource planning (ERP) systems, such as SAP R/3, Baan, and PeopleSoft. It relies on the implementation of large, broad-scope systems, usually provided by third parties. All application areas within an ERP system have been designed to fit a cohesive, integrated data structure. The customer data within the sales and distribution area can be relied upon to be consistent with the customer data within the accounts receivable subsystem.

This approach has clear advantages over the ad hoc interface building method in design effort saved and reusability. It does, however, have the drawback of being costly and time-consuming to implement. It relies on the robustness of a third-party design, and it also assumes that a very large proportion of the organization's activity can be automated using the same system (since anything left out of the ERP scope will still face the consistency problems previously described). The underlying problem is to control the behavior of data in a consistent, predictable manner across the target system, which brings us to the subject of this book, namely *metadata*.

The third approach—the only approach that will ensure long-term, universal control of all of the characteristics that contribute to making the data usable—is based on an organization-wide, *architected* approach to metadata.

In this architected environment, the nature and behavior of customer data, for instance, would be managed to ensure that each system could understand the data captured and manipulated by each other system. It would also provide a formal, neutral definition of all business rules associated with the customer data and allow all interested parties to access and understand these rules.

Metadata Management for Information Control and Business Success has been written to provide a road map for all potential users of metadata. It explains the ways in which an organization can be set up to manage metadata, provides examples of the data structures that will be required, and defines the particular issues relevant to metadata in the context of the Internet, and data warehousing. Furthermore, the book examines each aspect of metadata management in detail and builds a cohesive picture of the ways in which metadata can be recorded, manipulated, and accessed across the enterprise.

Part One explains the basics of metadata, familiarizing readers with the terminology and concepts required to understand metadata management. It explores the need to control metadata and examines the ways in which robustness can be achieved within IT applications without sacrificing flexibility. In addition, it describes the types of problems that occur when metadata are poorly controlled and considers the downstream effects of such problems. The reason why a strategic, rather than a tactical, approach to data management is required is developed to enable readers to see their own data-related problems in the broader context. Part One also introduces a common basic metamodel, defining a formal backbone for the structure of metadata, upon which extensions will be built to support distinct user requirements.

Part Two explores some specific business areas that benefit directly from improved metadata management. In addition, it discusses recent developments in the use of business intelligence (BI) software, data warehouses, and the Internet. Each of these hot topics has brought with it new issues related to data quality. Accordingly, Part Two describes the role of metadata in ensuring that these problems are avoided and the state of the art for metadata control in each case.

Part Three examines the way in which management of the overall set of metadata can be separated into autonomous but overlapping areas of activity. Each area relates to a component of the IT architecture, defining such factors as the business view of data, the IT applications, the technical platforms, and the people and other resources, and is supported by a so-called metamodel. Example structures for each metamodel are provided to assist readers in understanding the concept and to provide a blueprint for the resources that may be required in the readers' organization.

Ultimately, it is only by managing the metadata that the data in an organization can be managed. Proper data management allows the information base to be exploited in a cost-effective and flexible manner. Too often in the past, IT has failed to deliver on its promises, not because of inherent design flaws in the software, but because of the lack of a binding force to control information across the organization. Effective enterprise-wide metadata control can fulfill this role, and this book aims to explain how such control can be achieved.

Part I

The Concept of Metadata

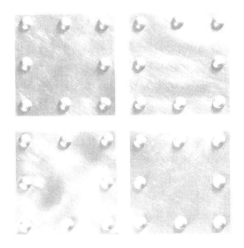

1

Background

1.1 Information in business—an overview

For most IT departments in commercial enterprises, the key measures of success focus on engineering precision and financial efficiency. The service levels maintained on machines that provide the raw computing power, containment of costs in application development and support activities, and the degree to which it can be proven that the provision of computer systems reduced the overall costs of the business all play a significant part.

At a tactical level, these measures contribute to good stewardship of resources devoted to IT activities. However, the needs of business users for information are becoming more sophisticated. Management is used to the idea of information on demand, and the emphasis has shifted toward IT delivering the widest possible scope of data in a manner that is highly consistent and that allows it to be analyzed by nonspecialists in a simple yet useful fashion.

The pressure that these requirements are putting on IT departments, coupled with their often contradictory nature, is forcing many into a radical rethinking of their roles and a restructuring of the skill base of many of their staff. Far from making the business more appreciative of their technical skills, IT professionals are finding that these new roles are highlighting just how ill-prepared they are to take on new tasks such as managing data warehouses or becoming "data miners" or "object custodians."

Very few business people would deny that the availability of good information is a critical factor to the success of their commercial activities. Much has been written about the profound effect that IT has had on the efficiency, effectiveness, and profitability of business in general. Everyone now recognizes that the way in which knowledge is controlled and disseminated around an enterprise is critical to the ultimate success of an endeavor. If information about the operation of a business, the market within which it operates, and the world at large is not available in an appropriate form, then the business is severely handicapped and stands a much greater chance of being one of the first casualties in times of economic constraint.

Accordingly, business people have come to accept, albeit reluctantly, that very large amounts of money sometimes need to be spent on computer technology, in order to sustain their organization's appetite for information. Whether referred to as data processing, IT, information management (IM), or whatever, most companies have devoted a sizeable proportion of their resources to the support and development of computer systems.

What is often overlooked by those directly involved is that, despite having words like data and information used prominently in their titles, most of the effort and expense around these activities is not directed at managing data at all but on deploying and controlling technology.

As increasing emphasis is placed on the widespread availability of data across the enterprise and the need for flexibility in the way this data can be processed, IT departments need to adopt a more commercial, customer-focused approach to their role within the organization.

Specifically, the commercial reality for most IT departments is that they are responsible for the provision of high-quality data for the use of *information consumers* in other parts of their organization. Producers of any goods can be split into two groups—those to whom the production process is of prime importance and those who emphasize the product itself. In general, companies in the latter group have thrived better in an increasingly competitive world.

Unfortunately, this lesson has yet to be applied in a thorough and considered way to the typical IT department. Management of the infrastructure is still seen as the overriding aim, at the expense of ensuring the flow of good quality information through that infrastructure. The production process is managed for its own sake, rather than being seen as a means to an end.

So much effort is expended in the process of tinkering with the hardware/software mix and trying to keep the old application infrastructure going that very little is left to devote to the product itself. Data processing managers do not worry about data; they worry about machines and programs. Far from being, as they are often perceived, at the forefront of the technological revolution, many of them spend most of their working lives fighting to avoid being choked by the legacy of the past.

Most IT managers are conscious of their internal role as providers of a product to the rest of the organization. It is true that, at least in the more enlightened environments, they strive hard to ensure that this product has been provided to a high quality. The real problem is that the product required by the business has changed. A reliable, robust systems infrastructure with user-friendly interfaces is now taken very much for granted. The value-added portion of IT activity, as perceived by the rest of the business (the customer), has shifted toward the provision of information. IT departments' success in doing this is judged, not on the sheer quantity of data, nor the aesthetics of the means of delivery, but the basic *usefulness* of the information made available. Unfortunately, at the same time that business management is becoming increasingly obsessed with the importance of information to the success of their ventures, the IT departments are becoming less and less capable of delivering this information in the form it is required.

1.2 Common factors affecting data quality

In many companies, this leads to a situation where mutual misunderstanding between the systems department and information consumers is rife. Technological advance is providing a steady stream of tools with which to build and run computer systems. Yet for many computer users, the lack of responsiveness of the IT infrastructure to the changing demands of the business is causing the gap between the "virtual" and "real" organizations to widen, with the resulting perception that computers are failing to deliver the goods.

The underlying message that data should be considered as the life-blood of any modern commercial enterprise is not new, and yet, just how many organizations really understand what the implications are of keeping data under control? How many IT managers have a good notion of how to provide high-quality information? Of these, how many have any practical means of measuring the quality of the information they deliver to their organizations?

In those companies that have managed to gain such understanding, the key factors that enable this high level of quality to be maintained include the following:

1. Accuracy (whether the value of each item of data is correct);

2. Timeliness (whether the data are up-to-date);

3. Consistency (whether the data in one part of the database have a common, appropriate set of controls to related concepts stored elsewhere);

4. Transparency of meaning (whether the context for the data—the circumstances under which data can be used to derive information—is clearly and commonly understood by all those with a legitimate interest);

5. Availability (whether the people who need the data can actually access it?).

If all of these factors are kept under control, then there is a good chance that the data within the enterprise can be considered high-quality in the sense of fulfilling its wider purpose.

However, if the data does not meet expectations in any of these areas, then the business will face potentially serious problems. If people cannot get at the data they need, if data is inaccurate, late, or unintelligible or require reinterpretation before it can be discussed by people in other departments, then the data is patently failing in its purpose.

1.3 Data flexibility and responsiveness to business change

All of these factors contribute to the provision of high-quality data in an unchanging environment. However, one further factor is becoming increasingly important as management thinking evolves. In a business environment under constantly changing commercial pressures, the need for flexibility is being stressed. Business process reengineering stresses the importance of recognizing change as a key factor in sustaining commercial success. For the business to respond to change in a fast and appropriate fashion, it is necessary for the information infrastructure of an enterprise to be capable of adaptation in a far more dynamic fashion than in the past.

In their seminal work on reengineering, Hammer and Champy [1] highlight several areas in which a consistent, well-controlled information environment is critical to the success of a reengineering approach. Specifically, reengineering places great emphasis on the need for the information infrastructure—the various computer and manual systems in place and the way in which they interact—of an enterprise to be adaptable to the changing needs of the business. If the organization is radically redesigned, and the work patterns of everyone reformed, but the flows and nature of information still follow their old pattern, then the results will be suboptimal at best and, at worst, catastrophic.

It is also important to consider the way in which information is structured and controlled and the effect it has on the behavior of the business in general. In any business, each component part has a set of formal and informal goals. The success that the organization has in achieving these goals provides a measure of their performance. In a typical case, different departments may have goals relating to such factors as maximization of revenue, minimization of cost, elimination of error, or provision of a fixed standard of service.

1.4 Active IM

Hammer and Champy also emphasize the way in which, within successful organizations, these goals are complementary to each other and to the overall goals of the enterprise. Where this is not the case, it is clear that problems will occur with the efficient operation of the business. For the performance of each department to be measured in a way that reflects its effect on other departments, and through them on the organization as a whole, a new approach is required to the management of information within the enterprise.

The activities of any organization can be arranged in the form of a hierarchical decomposition, which can be constructed in an infinite number of combinations. The ability to build a business process decomposition that reflects the most efficient division of work, while excluding activities that do not inherently add value to the business, is key to the success of reengineering exercises. Examples of such top-level business processes may include such concepts as "sell product," "manage corporate strategy," or "control manufacturing process."

Bearing in mind the need for data to be properly cared for, if an organization stands any chance of optimizing the use of its resources, a strong case can be built for including a process, which we shall call "manage information," at the top level of this hierarchy. It is vitally important not to confuse information management (IM) as a process with the classical activities of an IT or DP department.

Inevitably, IM overlaps quite heavily with these activities, but it also encompasses many factors that, in the "traditional" model, have been dealt with by the business at large, together with many that have usually not been managed at all! As the name implies, IM is concerned with the stewardship of information and the data from which it is derived. For our purposes, the term *data* refers to the "bits and bytes"—the values that are stored and manipulated by computer applications. *Information,* by contrast, generally refers to the data placed in a particular context, having a particular meaning, and thus being of value to the users of the applications. Thus, IM should include management of the technology required to control and disseminate this information and the activities of processing data. However, these activities must be considered subordinate to the major goal of managing information—providing high-quality, accurate information to those who need it in a timely and useful fashion and ensuring that it is used in a manner appropriate to its nature.

1.5   Information management processes

Broadly speaking, there are three levels upon which IM activities will be conducted:

- *Strategic:* Concerned with the optimization of information usage around the enterprise as a whole and the degree of match between the provision of information and the overall goals of the business;

- *Tactical:* Concerned with the establishment of an "infrastructure" (including working practices, hardware and software, and networking) capable of supporting this optimal information use, now and in the future;

- *Operational:* Concerned with the actual use of information and its inherent quality as it is processed in the course of executing mainstream business activities.

The process of IM can only be performed in an optimal manner if a common, objective structure is developed for the enterprise that reflects the needs and considerations of those who operate at all of these levels.

1.6   Data and metadata

To many readers concerned with more practical matters, the nature of information may appear to be a rather nebulous concept. In the chapters that follow, this idea will be explored in considerable detail. This will explain the profound effect that active IM can have on the bottom line for information-intensive business organizations. The intention is to ensure that anyone involved in the process of managing information (which, as we have shown, encompasses most of the business) has a sound understanding of the way in which information actually should be managed.

Much of this understanding depends on the ability to translate standard systems analysis techniques from the tactical to the strategic level.

To automate the solution to a business problem, it is normal for systems analysts to develop a formal model. Within this model the analyst will document the nature of each type of data that is relevant to the subject area they are analyzing and the business rules that constrain the behavior of those data (and, by implication, the people using it).

This set of business rules is the first and simplest level of metadata to be captured within the business. During the course of this book, the nature of the "IM problem" will be made clearer by developing, discussing, and refining a model of the way in which data, in general, behave and the types of *metadata* that will prove useful for management of business information.

The term metadata is intended to cover the concept of data that is, in itself, concerned with the behavior of data. This is generally assumed to include all the information that is required to manage the data at the disposal of an enterprise.

In the context of a normal commercial organization, subsets of the overall "database" can be identified that relate to the work of individual departments, work groups, or individuals. The sales department will have sales data; the purchasing department will have purchasing data; the accounts department will have financial data, and so on. Each of these subsets of the overall corporate "database" overlap, and these overlaps represent the interactions between the different departments of a company. Each of these "views" of the data can be defined and documented and are referred to as *subject-area databases*.

In such an environment, the IM department will also have responsibility for a subset of the corporate database—the information necessary for its successful operation. For the purposes of this book, we will adopt a looser definition of the term metadata to encompass all data that fall within the subject area view of a typical IM department.

In general, we can split our definition into four subcategories, each of which will be treated distinctly later on in the book:

- Data management data (concerned with managing business data— "classical metadata");

- Application management data (concerned with managing application systems as they are created, updated, and destroyed);

- IT infrastructure management data (concerned with managing machines, networks, etc.);

- IT activity management data (concerned with managing IT personnel and the work they do).

Data management data has priority at a conceptual level, since it can be used to analyze and explain the behavior of data in each of the other categories. It would be symptomatic of the most dangerous form of data bigotry, however, to emphasize this preeminence in the practical environment of a commercial IM department.

We will define metadata analysis, therefore, as being concerned with the definition, control, and evolution of all data pertinent to, and owned by, the IM department in a typical organization. In other words, metadata analysis is concerned with the imposition of a formal structure on the activities of the IM department in a way that simplifies the task of managing it and optimizes the contribution of IM to the success of the business as a whole.

1.7   Information technology—science, engineering, or black magic?

It can, of course, be argued that the task of managing the IT department is no different to that of managing any other part of the company, given a sufficiently high level of abstraction from the day-to-day process. Many readers may believe that it is only natural to assume that those who are put in charge of managing everyone else's data also have adequate control over their own.

In principle, this is a justifiable point of view. There are, however, several practical obstacles to the achievement of good control in this area that exist in most organizations of any size or complexity.

The three major causes of such problems are the following:

- Complexity of IT activities;

- Cost and complexity of introducing proper metadata control;

- Low importance attached to IM (as opposed to technology).

In fact, there is a wide diversity of activity that is seen by the "outside world" as IT, and these groups of activity are mutually dependent without being mutually understood. Because of this, the whole area is difficult to see as a single logical mechanism and is hence difficult to manage effectively.

There have been many attempts at building tools that help in the process of managing IT, but the investment required is usually great compared to the immediate benefits (at least as seen by non-IT management). In particular, many of these tools require a certain amount of reengineering of the existing IT infrastructure (or legacy system architecture, as it is sometimes known), which can, as is well-understood, be a costly and error-prone business. Both of these factors have led to a general tendency to put IT control practices and facilities at the bottom of the list, when budgets are being allocated across the spectrum of business activities.

However, this need not necessarily be the case. The first problem can be tackled in the same way that complexity in other parts of business is tackled, by members of the IT department themselves. Carefully chosen systems analysis techniques can be used to provide a formal structure to IT activities and, building upon this, to simplify the processes involved.

Once these activities are simplified, the need for complex and expensive tools to support them is also reduced. Effective control can be achieved by gaining and maintaining a clear understanding of the structure and behavior of the "metadata-base." Simple tools can be built in-house to enable management to keep a clear picture of the IT infrastructure.

These two factors will allow companies to avoid large-scale investment in such things as repository management software and hence significantly reduce resistance from non-IT management to the introduction of a metadata-centered IT management regime.

One purpose of this book, therefore, is to provide IT managers with a broad understanding of metadata behavior, enabling them to recognize how such an approach can be applied to their particular organization. It will also provide a blueprint from which a simple tool kit can be built, enabling management to control the IT infrastructure without large investment in complex facilities or disturbing the application legacy, in the short term. In addition, the book provides examples of how metadata analysis can be used at the "boundaries" of the IT subject area to assist in the process of selling the approach as something from which tangible benefits can be derived.

1.8 IT organizations and responsibilities

IT encompasses a large and diverse set of activities, technologies, techniques, and skills. There is a considerable number of people who would term themselves IT personnel, although the jobs that they actually do differ widely.

In a typical company, the IT department would include some or all of the following:

- *Operators:* Ensure that the computing facilities are running smoothly on a day-to-day basis, that any processing that is not normally initiated directly by end users is run, and that the physical machines are kept in good order;

- *Systems programmers:* Responsible for ensuring that the computer system behaves in a logically cohesive way and is optimized to make best use of the physical machine power available;

- *Database administrators:* Responsible for the structure and mechanical performance of application databases, ensuring that they meet the needs of the business and are tuned for optimum performance;

- *Application programmers:* Responsible for construction, testing, and implementation, in a computerized manner, of end-user business requirements;

- *Systems analysts:* Determine and consolidate end-user requirements, producing specifications that the programmers use to create applications;

- *Network engineers:* Ensure that the physical communications backbone is in place and operating in a satisfactory manner;

- *IT management:* Ensure that all of the above is being done in a satisfactory and consistent manner, within the financial constraints that are, in turn, imposed by upper management.

1.9   Metadata entity types

It is apparent, therefore, that a wide variety of activities take place within the authority of the IT department. These activities make use of a correspondingly wide list of data types. Some of these data types, or *entity types* as they will be referred to hereafter, are under the ownership of parts of the IT department, and some are not.

In this context, data ownership implies the right to define the usage, structure, and population of an entity. Specifically, if the IT department manager has ownership of the APPLICATION entity, which contains details of each computer application, then they are responsible for deciding the following:

- How these data should be used, and by whom (USAGE);

- Which details are relevant to their scope (STRUCTURE);

- Which applications are to be included (POPULATION).

It may be simpler to consider what each of these responsibilities entails for an ordinary business data entity, a CUSTOMER, for example.

Control of the USAGE corresponds with the need for someone to define who has access to CUSTOMER data, what type of access they require (e.g., read, write, and delete), and what business purpose the access will fulfill.

Determining the STRUCTURE of the CUSTOMER data will define the details that are required—for example, whether there is a need to capture the full customer address, the forenames of the purchasing manager within the CUSTOMER, or the VAT number.

POPULATION of the data entity will not imply that the data owner has to capture all CUSTOMER data but that he or she will have overall control of which business partners will be captured as CUSTOMERs. This may include such nuances as deciding whether a prospect who has not yet placed an order will be captured as a customer and whether "internal" customers (that is, sister companies within the group) are to be included. In a similar fashion, each metadata entity will require an owner to "take care of" it within the organization.

1.10 Introduction to the enterprise metamodel

There are many ways in which the metadata within an organization can be structured and captured. The structures defined below are intended to provide guidance on how this might be achieved, rather than being in any sense proscriptive. For our purpose then, metadata falls into four categories, corresponding to the types of data mentioned above. These categories, IT infrastructure management data, IT activity management data, IT application management data, and data management data, are discussed in Sections 1.10.1–1.10.4, respectively.

1.10.1 IT infrastructure management data

These data are used to define and manage the physical infrastructure built up around IT systems within the organization. Such data will typically be "owned" by someone with a title such as network manager or possibly computer services manager and will include entities such as the following:

- COMPUTER;
- SERVER;
- LAN (local area network);
- NETWORK NODE;
- DISK DRIVE;
- TAPE DRIVE.

1.10.2 IT activity management data

This data is used to define and manage the work that is taking place under the aegis of the IT department and the people who are doing that work. IT activity management data will typically be "owned" by someone with a title such as IT manager, although many of the entities will be owned externally to the IT department (e.g., by the personnel or human resources department). This category will include entities such as the following:

- IT EMPLOYEE;

- PROJECT;

- PROJECT PHASE;

- TASK;

- SUPERVISOR;

- PROJECT PLAN.

1.10.3 IT application management data

This data is used to define the applications that have been created to support the business as a whole and will be "owned" by someone with a title such as application development manager. Such data will include the following entities:

- APPLICATION;

- APPLICATION MODULE;

- APPLICATION RELEASE;

- APPLICATION INSTALLATION;

- SOFTWARE SUPPLIER;

- APPLICATION ENTITY.

1.10.4 Data management data

This data falls under the classical view of metadata, being data that is used to define the behavior of data. Data management data will typically not be explicitly "owned" by anyone (a major concern, which will be discussed in more detail in Chapter 4), but could be under the aegis of a database administrator, a data quality manager, or a data architect, for widely different reasons. This category will include entities such as the following:

- ENTITY;

- ATTRIBUTE;

- RELATIONSHIP;

- SUPERTYPE;

- SUBTYPE.

Each of these categories has a profound effect on the others, and upon the more general business data within the organization. The precise nature of these effects and the ways in which they can be managed will be discussed at length in Chapter 3.

1.11 The importance of metadata

If each member of an organization has a clear, precise, and authoritative view of the enterprise metamodel, three major categories of benefit will accrue, derived from the following factors:

1. Robustness, leading to stability;

2. Common structure, leading to simplification;

3. Consistency of approach, leading to efficiency.

For any sphere of activity, there is a set of data that is relevant to its execution. Some of this data will be used directly to perform the activity; other data will be used to support the infrastructure within which the activity is taking place. As we have seen, the business activities of the IT department are a complex network of subprocesses that use different, overlapping subsets of the "metadata-base" and that have profound but usually ill-defined effects on each other.

A clear understanding of the behavior of data, namely the nature of metadata, takes an individual a very long way toward a clear and comprehensive understanding of the work of an IT department. IT managers might be expected to have full control over the entities that are "owned" by the IT department. If, in addition, a company's business management maintains a clear appreciation of the effect that IT managers' actions will have on those entities "owned" by the business at large, IT managers will be able to claim, with some justification, that they are managing the computer facilities in an almost optimal manner.

There is no universally acceptable way of portraying the metamodel of an organization. This book endeavors to derive, on a step-by-step basis, a metamodel template that can be refined to provide a valid structure for any organization. In deriving and using this model, a variety of people involved with the care of computer systems, among others, will gain a clear and objective insight into the scope of their responsibility. In addition, because the metamodel encompasses many interwoven strands of activity, it will provide all of an organization's employees with a context-specific insight into the effects that their areas of responsibility have on those of others.

The third major benefit of a metadata-driven approach is that of *consistency*. It enables the various suborganizations not just to understand each other at a conceptual level but to have a shared management view on a day-to-day basis. By enforcing consistency of approach, terminology, data identification, and structure, great efficiencies can be gained in the operation of an enterprise as a whole.

An environment of perfectly controlled metadata will profoundly affect the work of the following parties:

- *IT tactical management:* The capability to view and understand the operation of the IT infrastructure within the enterprise will be much enhanced, by virtue of improved quality and breadth of information around the business of IT itself, on a day-to-day basis.

- *IT strategic management:* Once the overall IT infrastructure is properly cataloged, IT managers with the responsibility for drawing up long-term plans will have a clearer view of the areas that could benefit from rationalization. This will include cases where diverse systems have been implemented to cover similar functionality and where proper data control can be implemented to avoid redundant work for system users.

- *Systems analysts:* The metamodel will provide a reference library for system designers, enabling them to pinpoint synergies with other applications through shared development, by providing a "rule book" for certain constructs and by facilitating the task of identifying potential impacts of changes to the infrastructure.

- *Methodologists:* For those concerned with how people work within the enterprise, mapping the organizational structure and the tasks performed within the organization onto the basis of the metamodel will provide a robust and consistent framework for the development of working practices in IM.

- *Systems maintainers:* Once again, those who change the systems in any way will be given a clear understanding of the impact of their proposed changes and the likelihood of adverse effects resulting from their actions will be considerably reduced.

These are generally the same goals that were targeted by those who have tried to develop repository management systems or extensible data dictionaries, or who advocated widespread use and central control of CASE tools.

Indeed, the metadata structures and models discussed at length in this book represent the type of analysis that would be used to define the database engine for a CASE tools or repository manager. Systematic application of these types of tools can make a profound difference to the levels of efficiency and productivity within an IT department. However, it should be remembered that the benefits that are brought about by use of these tools are a direct result of the metadata foundation upon which they rely, not just the tools themselves.

If a good understanding of this foundation can be achieved—and shared across the organization—then these benefits will accrue. In addition, when the operation of the metadata is clearly understood, it can be applied more effectively to the operation of each organization as developers see fit—rather than trusting a tool to impose a generic version of the rules. The difference is that the benefits can be accrued by enhanced understanding of the ways in which data behave and application of this understanding to the business of tracking IT as a process, rather than through the deployment of expensive, complex, and sometimes disruptive tools.

Reference

[1] Hammer, Michael, and James Champy, *Re-engineering the Corporation,* HarperCollins, New York, 1994.

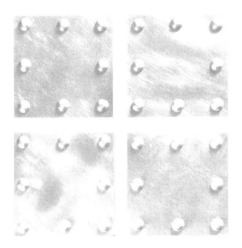

2

The Challenges of
Information Management

S OME INDIVIDUALS are obsessive—or just plain curious—enough to have scratched beneath the surface of the metadata control problem. Their most common reaction to what they find underlying this issue has been to try to develop ideas, tools, and methodologies that enable a more robust approach to be taken to the problem, occasionally making a lot of money in the process. In previous decades, such developments have included structured programming, structured analysis and design. These have been joined more recently by CASE tools, global project management methodologies, repository management, and object-oriented programming, among other contributions.

Many of these facilities have enabled significant improvements in productivity for those developing and managing computer systems, but few, if any, have addressed the root cause of the problem. Even some of the more advanced thinkers in this area still embrace the following assumptions:

1. The imprecision involved in construction of computer systems can somehow be eliminated if a sufficiently robust "engineering" approach is adopted.

2. The data that are used within an application are integral parts of that application. (They are, in fact, owned by the programming logic that is manipulating them.)

These two assumptions have led us to develop, in the first case, project-building methods that are too rigid for the purpose of dealing with real, human needs and, in the second case, systems that are inflexible and mutually contradictory. As a result, most commercial IT departments are currently facing a set of challenges that will ultimately determine their ability to deliver information to the enterprise they serve.

2.1   Challenge 1: Recognizing the fallacy of software engineering

The willingness, on the part of IT professionals, to accept the vagueness of their profession (indeed, many make a virtue out of the fact that a certain amount of black magic is required to develop good systems) has led to distrust and exasperation in many of their customers. To many outside the profession, the claim that the manipulation of data by machines should in some way be treated as an artistic or creative pursuit is often seen as a poor excuse for lack of rigor in the approach of DP professionals to problem solving.

On balance, this suspicion seems quite justified, bearing in mind the difficulty that most computer people would have in explaining just how this imprecision arises. At the lowest level, few would disagree that the machines themselves act in a highly precise manner. The processor has the ability to recognize binary digits and to compare them with each other in a variety of ways. The vagueness does not arise because of any problems at this level, nor within the machine code nor the programming of the system software (though bugs undoubtedly do exist in all cases). The assumption that the behavior of computers cannot be controlled scientifically nor observed empirically is caused by problems arising only when the "top layer" of business-specific "end-use" logic is placed on the technical foundation.

Why should this be? If we cannot blame it on some inherent defect in the computer platform, what can be identified as the root of the problem? There has been no lack of willingness nor aptitude in those charged with constructing these systems in the past. People have recognized the problem and have invented a variety of ways to counteract its effects. Clear trends have been established toward the implementation of an "engineering mentality" among software developers.

Software engineering practices have developed to allow for a much greater degree of precision in the development of systems. The intention was to provide a clear and precise methodology within which systems could be specified, developed, and evolve over time. Somewhat later, a lot of effort was spent on the semi-automation of this process. CASE tools were developed to do the "bookkeeping," ensuring that the rules defined by the analysis process were mutually consistent and providing a convenient and straightforward way of representing these rules visually.

However, the analogy that was drawn between software engineering and what we shall call real-world engineering should be subject to some close scrutiny. If physical engineering principles are to be used as the paradigm upon which a computer science is to be built, we need to understand the way in which it has been used to solve real-world problems.

Engineers develop and use a set of rules that define the way in which the physical world behaves under certain controlled circumstances. This enables them to design and construct items from particular materials and components, in a way that both satisfies their needs and ensures predictable behavior of the finished product. This need for predictability leads to a further aspect of engineering science, which takes into account the fact that, in general, the real world is not a controlled environment. Absolute predictability of all the circumstances that are likely to occur is not feasible. Engineers account for this unpredictability by developing general rules about the variability of these circumstances, analyzing the likelihood that each type of variability will occur, and predicting the result that such occurrences will have on their intended finished products. By doing this, they can build sufficient tolerance into the design to ensure that circumstances that are likely, but unpredictable, are not going to affect the performance of the product. This effectively transforms the task to which they have been assigned from an "open" problem for which it is impossible to precisely define all parameters under which the finished product will operate, into a "closed" problem—that can be solved, at least in theory, by a series of predefined, replicable steps.

In trying to extend this basic notion to software, there appear to be two areas that are likely to result in problems, described as follows:

■ *The ability of a project "client" to define its needs in precise enough terms to present the engineer or implementer with a "closed" problem:* Quite rightly, the client's language is used to describe the problem to be solved at the highest level. In software design, a business problem is described in business language, together with the constraints that exist on the solution of the problem. The scope for variability in the design process is considerable, despite the intervention of systems analysts, whose job it is to reduce such variability and present a precise yet commonly understood version of the job to be done. The systems analyst will also begin the task of decomposing the processes to be automated, to enable a translation to a machine-interpretable form. In the case of real-world engineering, the degree of precision that can be gained in this type of specification is usually sufficient for detailed design to take place, without concern for the context in which a particular component should operate. For systems, however, we are faced with the problem that separate, orthogonal views of the decomposition exist in the minds of the system client and the system provider in nearly all cases. This difference of perspective leads in turn to the second problem.

■ *The ability of engineers or implementers to break down the problem with which they are presented into atomic components:* This should be done in such a way as to optimize the design and production processes and to minimize the risk of error. It is rare for a business problem to be decomposable directly in such a way as to enable system implementers to identify the components they have to use at the lowest level. Most forms of systems engineering require that, at some stage in the decomposition, a translation is made between the users' view of the problem to be solved and the facilities available to the implementers to solve it.

In the real world, a requirement will be identified for a particular engineering job to be performed. Take the example of a chemical plant that is to be constructed from scratch. The end product of the manufacturing processes is identified, and the chemical processes through which the raw materials are transformed are identified. The components of the plant required are identified at the high level. Some are complex—subplants in themselves. Others are relatively simple—e.g., pipelines, valves, and storage vessels. The more complex components are decomposed logically until, within relatively few steps, the atomic components—nuts, bolts, valves, and sheets of metal—are identified. The specification for each of the pieces is understood within the appropriate context. The physical materials used determine their behavior, and any unpredictability is accounted for by building appropriate safety margins.

Fundamentally, real-world engineering depends on the ability to decompose hierarchically from the original requirement, to the point where the implementer is faced with a "closed" problem for each atomic component to be provided. This approach presumes that the behavior of each such component can be predicted precisely, within known tolerances, and that the way in which it interfaces with other components is predetermined and understood by the implementer. The combination of these factors means that engineering projects can be treated as scientific exercises, even though the real world is, in fact, orders of magnitude more complex than the implementers took into account. With a few extremely famous and newsworthy exceptions, this general assumption holds true in the real world.

Contrast this with the case of so-called software engineering. If, within a computer project, one starts at the top of a business process decomposition and works downward toward the atomic level, in the natural course of events he or she will end up with simple business task steps.

Depending on the level of sophistication of the development environment, the lowest level available to the implementer will be programming language syntactic elements, predeveloped parameter-driven modules, logic-driver tables, or, in more modern cases, object libraries.

These two separate decompositions cause a key problem even in the case of object-oriented environments. It is generally not possible to construct a one-to-one correspondence between elements at their respective lowest levels.

In summary, it can be argued strongly that "engineering" is not, intrinsically, the best paradigm to adopt when attempting to build a robust, scientific basis for the construction of business computer systems. The differences between building a logical framework for the automation of business processes and a physical structure in the real world are too great to ignore. There exists an unavoidable risk that context sensitivities that have not been translated correctly from the requester to the implementer will cause the system to fail in some way. When properly deployed, modern approaches such as object-oriented design do reduce this risk. They, nevertheless, do not address the problem of translation itself but simplify it by moving it further down the decomposition.

The remainder of this chapter endeavors to show the importance of a clear understanding of metadata—that is, the inherent structure describing the behavior of data in general—in the solution to this problem. By describing this behavior in a context-independent way and explaining the way it can be used to map between the two hierarchies, this book intends to provide the key to performing this translation in an effective and error-reduced manner—and at the most appropriate level of detail.

2.2 The evolution of software engineering

To understand how the "engineering view" has become dominant in computer systems development, it is important to examine the historical perspective. It can be argued that the evolution of IT over the last couple of decades reflects two overriding trends.

In the first place, there has been a great deal of emphasis placed on the provision of more information to more people than ever before. At all levels within commercial organizations and society at large, data is being supplied on a wider variety of subjects more completely and more cheaply than was possible in the past. The widespread popularity of public information sharing services shows that this explosion on the supply side for information is seeking to fulfill a genuine demand. Aside from the obvious leisure-related uses to which the Internet, for instance, is put, it cannot be doubted that without a serious demand for information sharing, such facilities would not exist.

The second dominant trend is the way in which the tools that assist in the manipulation of data have become simpler, more visually appealing, and, occasionally, more entertaining. This can have the effect of making what could have previously been seen as tedious administrative tasks almost into a form of leisure activity! The mass-marketing of graphical user interfaces has contributed significantly to the explosion in demand for computers themselves. Without such programs as Microsoft Windows™, it is unlikely that such a large number of personal computers would have been sold for private use and that their operation would be viewed as a pleasurable activity by millions of children, adolescents, and adults throughout the world.

However, such large and rapid cultural changes can lead to un-expected—and, in some cases, undesirable—side effects. Taking the example of television, it is debatable whether society will ever come to terms in a rational manner with the cumulative effect that watching many hours of television has on children as they grow into adults. The behavioral effects of going through such a wide range of experiences early in life, albeit vicariously, and the way this reflects on individuals and society as a whole is much written about but little understood after only one generation of having televisions in the majority of homes.

In a similar way, the sudden availability of large volumes of information, and the painless way in which it can be accessed and manipulated, has not been thoroughly explored. Although the immediate sociological consequences might be less marked than those of television, there are still several serious issues that should be addressed:

- How can we ensure that information systems are built in the most efficient manner?

- How can we ensure that information systems are used in the most effective manner?

- How can we, and to what extent should we, control what information is used by whom?

- How can we ensure the quality of information in general?

- How can we ensure that information (rather than just data) is easy to provide?

These two major trends are just reflections of an ongoing shift in the economic dynamics of computer systems. Consider the four major categories of costs involved in the deployment and use of computer systems—and the way these costs have changed over the years—listed as follows:

1. The cost of processing power;
2. The cost of program logic;
3. The cost of acquiring data;
4. The cost of using data.

In three out of the four categories, the costs have been diminishing at unprecedented speed. This has led to a "virtuous circle" (at least from the point of view of those providing the appropriate goods and services), where more and more people are making direct use of computers, thus further enhancing the economies of scale. It is, however, time that some serious consideration is given to the fourth category, especially in view of its nature at the "end of the chain" as will be explained in Section 2.2.4.

2.2.1 The cost of providing adequate computing power

In the early days of computers, the real financial investment made in the system hardware needed to perform a particular task was vast. In terms of raw computing power per dollar, the trend line has been inversely exponential over the intervening years. Although there has been a certain compensating trend due to the exponential increase in system software complexity, there is still, in general, an expectation that each generation of processor will be both orders of magnitude more powerful and cheaper in real terms than its predecessor. Add to this the tendency for the generations themselves to be compressed, and we can infer that raw computing power is becoming almost insignificant in the total cost equation for computer systems, in the general case.

System software should be included in this category of costs, since it complements the hardware to provide the foundation for system development. The trend has been toward standardization of system software, certainly in the low to medium part of the market. Standard operating systems have been introduced for personal computers and local area networks. The massive increase in the actual number of installations has driven down unit costs through economies of scale, despite massive increases in sophistication. Together, these two factors have caused the cost of providing an operating environment to become an insignificant part of the overall picture.

2.2.2 The cost of developing effective application systems

Looking back a couple of decades, the economics of systems development dictated that a great deal of emphasis should be placed on ensuring that the hardware operated as close to optimally as possible. The cost of buying computing power was great, compared to the costs involved in buying programmers' time. More recently, there have been two factors that have influenced the reduction in the relative cost of system development.

First, the emphasis on efficiency has decreased at the application level to the point of insignificance. Although the programmers involved in writing operating systems, compilers, and the like still have to consider and devote effort to optimizing the performance of the machine in the execution of a particular task, this is no longer a major concern for application programmers. This means that they can devote more time to the provision of business solutions to the people who are requesting them. In principle, this enables application programmers to provide for the needs of their "primary customers" to a higher quality and in less time.

Second, there has been a significant increase in both the power and simplicity of the tools that are available for development of applications. In many cases, end users are now able to provide their own applications with minimal effort, using spreadsheets and simple-to-use desktop database tools. Even where professional expertise is still required, there has been a distinct improvement in the sophistication of compilers, code generators, and other tools available to programmers. Code libraries and the improvements in intermachine portability have also improved programmer productivity.

2.2.3 The cost of capturing or otherwise acquiring data

Yet again, the costs involved incurred in the process of getting the data into the computer have decreased significantly, both for data that is "manually" captured and for that which is obtained from external sources. The work of those involved in the manual capture of data has evolved over relatively few years from having to enter rigidly formatted data on "punched-card images" to direct online entry with contextual help screens, drop-down menus, cue cards, and other user-friendly features.

2.2.4 The cost of making effective use of information

Amongst all this good news about getting more for less money, it should not be forgotten that the main purpose of a computer application is not to use up computing power, nor is it to make life easier for the programmer or even, in the ultimate case, for the person capturing data. The main purpose of a computer application is to satisfy a business need for information. This information will only become available once the data required to service the application has been captured and processed in the appropriate manner. The needs of the *information consumer*—the eventual customer for the data—are paramount, and the costs of fulfilling these needs are becoming increasingly significant over time.

There are two very important factors to consider that apply only to this "customer-facing" cost category—factors that are, unfortunately, quite often forgotten or ignored by people involved in the provision of computing power:

1. This cost category is the only one of the four cost categories that we have discussed that has a balancing benefit figure!

2. The cost category is also the only one of the four where there has not been, at the very least, a rapid linear reduction in the size of costs involved!

Thus, to (over)simplify the current situation, we have organizations in which the following are true:

- The IT department is spending less on the provision of more "raw" computer power.

- The programmers (whether in-house or third party) are spending less time automating or re-automating what has already been done by the organization.

- The clerical staff (at least those who still have jobs) is spending less time capturing and preparing data for use.

- The real users of the data are being slightly (but not dramatically) more efficient in their manipulations and analysis. Often, the efficiencies that have been gained through having user-friendly tools at their disposal are counterbalanced by the fact that they are performing tasks that they would have delegated previously and by the complexity of wading through the sheer volume of data available to get at what they want.

The net effect of all this progress is that users' expectations are raised faster than the ability of the IT department to satisfy them.

2.3 Challenge 2: Distinguishing between data and information

Some readers might be slightly confused, at this point, about the repeated and slightly divergent use of the words data and information in the preceding discussion.

A clear separation exists between the data, which represent more or less a structured set of values that are stored within a system, and information, which is only created when the data are placed in a particular context. For instance,

John Smith; 21/06/60; United Kingdom

is a list of data elements that may be intended to mean "John Smith was born on June 21, 1960, in the United Kingdom" or "John Smith has been a resident of the United Kingdom since June 21, 1960," or "John Smith owns a car that he bought on June 21, 1960, and that was made in the United Kingdom." Without a framework within which they may be interpreted, data elements are inherently useless. Once this framework has been provided, it can be considered information. Remember that we are not concerned with the correctness of the data (a problem in itself) but the ability we have to translate it into information.

People in the organization need to perform this transformation in a manner that is the following:

- Accurate;

- Timely;

- Efficient;

- Repeatable.

Their ability to do so is mutually dependent on their ability to map from the user view of the activities performed by a computer system to the IT view. The widespread existence of such skills will be the major factor in determining whether the so-called information revolution can continue unabated. However, without a scientific basis on which this transformation activity can take place, we are in danger, if not of killing the goose that laid the golden egg, at least of keeping it on starvation rations!

Developing such a scientific basis provided another motivation for the writing of this book: To understand the ways in which the usefulness of information can be maximized, it is important to understand the behavior of the data used in its creation.

2.4   Challenge 3: Recognizing data/application independence

It is critically important to treat data as an independent issue from the construction of particular application systems. Although applications may last for many years in a normal commercial environment (often a lot longer that the original designers intended and a lot longer that those who have to support old systems would like), they do eventually get replaced. The data, on the other hand, is likely to remain useful to the business after the application has been replaced. Even in the shorter term, reorganizations of the business or changes in working practices and emphasis may lead to problems if a particular application system treats data in an idiosyncratic manner. The only certain way to avoid this type of problem is to treat the planning, design, and construction of databases as entirely separate from that of program logic. Even if, at the time of development, there is an exact correspondence between the scope boundaries for the database and the functionality of the system, this is almost never going to remain the case for long.

2.5 Challenge 4: The information overload problem

The amount of information available to individual users of computer systems has increased substantially in recent times. The rate at which this information is gathered and dispersed is itself increasing, leading, in many cases, to a significant danger of information overload. The problem for many systems users is not how to obtain the data they need to perform their job but how to sift out the subset that is useful for their particular purpose from the mass of data that is not. It is becoming increasingly difficult for them to target the information they want, to cross-reference it to information from different sources, and to analyze the results. Without some form of framework that can be used to impose order on the various sources of information available, the correspondences between them will become increasingly difficult to spot, even as their number increases.

2.6 Challenge 5: Effective classification of information

At its simplest, the concept of an *entity* provides us with the means to determine what a particular thing is (and hence what it is not). Assuming that the definition of the entity type itself is robust and accurate, then we can look at any instance of that entity and be able to say, "Yes. That thing will behave in a predictable way."

Following directly from this, we can also assume, since the definition of the ENTITY entity tells us so, that things that fall into the same entity type behave in similar ways and have similar qualities or *attributes*. Thus, once we are aware of the structure and behavior of an instance of the CUSTOMER entity we will, in general, be more likely to recognize other instances of that same entity.

All this is very well, but it assumes a very black and white picture of the real world. An instance of entity type A can be recognized from its definition. An instance of entity type B can also be recognized, and the fact that it is not an "A" determined. The concept of *affinity* between instances of the same entity type is established, by definition, but no account is taken for the fact that there are degrees of affinity between instances of different entity types.

In real life, we can recognize an instance of the entity DOG and an instance of the entity CAT. We can also, by virtue of the fact that we have been taught to recognize affinity as a relative condition, determine that a particular instance of the entity DOG is more similar to a particular instance of the entity CAT than it would be to say, the entity TRACTOR. Although the individual dog and the individual cat are instances of different entities, it is intuitively obvious to us that they are more similar than either is to a tractor.

This is not because we recognize the attributes of each dog we meet as being similar to that of each cat we meet, rather that we know that a high affinity exists between dogs and cats at the entity level. This enables us to deal with the general degree of likeness between different things rather than examining them specifically. In our discussions of the behavior of data in this section, it will become clear that in order to control all this rich diversity, the concept of *data entity classification* has a strong role to play.

It is important to recognize that there are no absolutes in the judgment of the degree of affinity between instances of different entities. It is clear that for everyday purposes, most people will consider a cat more similar to a dog than to a tractor. However, there may be peculiar instances in which this assumption is not true. If the color of a particular object is of prime importance—for instance in composing a photograph—then the fact that the dog and the tractor are both black, whereas the cat is brown, might be considered as of greater importance. As a result, the similarities between the two objects will, in this context, be considered more important than any similarities either may have to the cat.

The degree of affinity exhibited by entities of different types can be formally determined by their closeness on a *hierarchy of classification*. In the general case, if we start with a totally general entity "THING" and subdivide it, we will arrive at a point where we distinguish between cats and dogs. If, in a particular context, this distinction is made directly (i.e., on one level they are part of the same entity, and at the next split they are explicitly recognized as cats and dogs) then they may be considered as particularly close in affinity.

More commonly, this branching takes place further up the classification hierarchy. Domestic cats and dogs are distinguished at a level significantly higher than the one at which they are explicitly recognized as members of the orders *canis* and *felix*. At this point, they have been split apart from carnivores, but are not yet distinguished from lions, tigers, or wolves.

There is no right or wrong way to determine affinity, since it relies entirely on the context in which the distinction between entities of different types is made and hence on the structure of the class hierarchy to which they both belong. This can differ in many ways, described as follows:

- By missing levels, to increase the affinity of the "subtype" entities (e.g., by sub-classifying ANIMALs into DOGs and CATs, without going through intermediate levels);

- By adopting an entirely different structure (as required by the photography example above, where objects are split first and foremost by their color).

The concept of classification is by no means unique to the context of data modeling. In many different spheres of activity, a system of classification is used to record and keep control of the observed similarities and differences of groups of different entities. Two examples follow.

1. *Zoological and botanical classification:* The way in which the animal and plant kingdoms are split up into a hierarchy is a prime example of classification at work. At the top of the hierarchy, all animals or plants are part of the same group. At each level, the set

of entities is split into subsets, depending on certain observed criteria. As the number of levels increases, these distinctions become finer, and the similarities between members of different but adjacent subsets become more marked (since they may have common "grandparents" further up the classification tree, for instance). A key strength of this method is that, in general, only those criteria that are necessary to define the differences between types of animals at a particular level need be considered. Those that are used to split "higher up" can be assumed, and those that are "lower down" can be ignored. Its weakness is that a particular hierarchy can only represent a single view of the relative importance of the criteria. If, for a particular purpose, egg laying were considered more important than the split between reptiles, birds, amphibians, and insects, there would be no way of deriving this group from the standard zoological tree.

2. *Library book identification:* The Dewey classification system used in libraries also makes use of an implied hierarchy: the use of numbers to classify books by subject matter in such a way that like subjects are grouped together matches the way in which the hierarchy is used to classify animals. The similarity of two subjects is broadly in line with the closeness of their index numbers. The less significant the first digit that diverges between them, the closer they are in context (a book classified as 710.0 is less closely related to one classified as 720.0 than it is to one classified as 711.2). This does not allow a purely arithmetic approach to be made to gauging similarity, since there is very little relationship between a book classified as 699.9 to one classified as 700.01, despite the closeness of their numbers. Once again, being purely hierarchical, there is only one way of ordering the criteria upon which the sequence of the splits is made, which may result in subjects that are closely related from one person's perspective being far apart in the classification. Clearly, for data modeling purposes, which require us to be able to model the real world in ways that suit a variety of purposes, rather than just one, this hierarchical approach to classification is inadequate.

A more appropriate approach to take is based on set theory, which allows subsets, or individual items, to reside at the intersection of two sets. No superiority of one set over the other is required; it is simply acknowledgment of the fact that all items within the intersection obey the rules of membership for both parent sets. This technique, when applied to modeling the information behavior, is known as *multiple inheritance.*

When considering computer systems, this approach will allow us to express in precise, nonredundant form the behavior of particular types of data. It is possible to express this concept using basic entity-relationship diagramming, but a large part of the richness of the technique is lost. The IDEF1X methodology (together with several object-oriented analysis techniques) has a specific syntax for representation of super- and subsets, which we have adapted slightly and will be using throughout the book.

2.7 Occam's dilemma—recognizing necessary complexity

One of the oldest tenets of computing is a principle known as "Occam's Razor." This states that "entities should not be unnecessarily multiplied" and is drawn from the philosophical observations of William of Occam, a fourteenth-century scholar and theologian. It has long been regarded as particularly significant for the design and construction of work systems (and in later times, computer systems). However, if we adopt the technique of explicit subclassification, enabling multiple inheritance, large and complex data models can often result.

The assumption that an entity C is defined as being a subset of A and a subset of B enables C to inherit the properties of both A and B and to possess properties that make it unique. In this way, for a system (whether computerized or otherwise) that has been designed with this philosophy in mind, there is no need to explicitly define the behavior that C exhibits purely because it is a subtype of A. The fact of it being a subtype is, of itself, sufficient. This type of subclassification can seriously affect the complexity of work patterns, and we are placed in a position of apparently contradicting Occam's rule.

Consider the following: Assume that a requirement has been identified to build a system (not necessarily computerized) to regulate the execution of a particular process. Let us further assume that to do this, it is necessary, but not sufficient, to identify the following:

1. The subprocesses that comprise the process, in such a way that each subprocess can be treated in an "elementary" or "atomic" manner (we will conveniently leave aside just what we mean by this, for the moment);

2. All entity types (types of "things") that are involved in the execution of the process;

3. How these entity types behave, and are affected by, the execution of the process.

In general, it is recognized that these three components represent a large proportion of ordinary systems analysis effort and that each has to be correctly and precisely identified for the successful implementation of the new system.

What is left open to interpretation is the degree to which each of these should be analyzed, if we are to optimize the construction and use of the system. The first two points mentioned above represent "proliferation" in the sense that was intended by Occam. The amount of effort in the third point is determined by the extent to which the other two have been completed. In systems analysis work, Occam's razor has often been seen as a justification for a "minimalist" approach.

In the first case, what is left in doubt is the point at which process decomposition should be halted. The effect this decision can have is determined by the degree to which a "business-based" decomposition can be restructured and reinterpreted in a manner more suited to the construction of computer systems.

When we come to consider the second case, namely the extent to which an elaborate and comprehensive data model should be developed to support the design of the new system, we are faced with an apparent dilemma. If we follow the spirit of Occam's principle, we should avoid enrichment of the data model with subclassification, the introduction of entities that are not apparent in the "real" world, and the like. However, if we follow this path, we are likely (in fact, almost certain) to end up with a system that is suboptimal in the following ways:

1. The data structure employed will not be in a form that enables a "context-independent" approach to logic to be taken. The result of this is that the logic will be full of exceptional clauses to allow for the fact that the data with which it is dealing are not one type of thing but may have significant subtypes "hidden" within them.

2. The common rules pertaining to the normalization of data will not be applied. This will mean that the data structure is unlikely to match the business rules implied by the logic in a complete and sustainable manner.

3. Because simplification of the data model implies complication of the system logic, the finished product is more likely to be "bug-ridden," since differing approaches would have to have been taken to essentially the same activities, to allow for such factors as "exceptions" and context sensitivities.

Thus, the argument we have is not so much with Occam but with those who maintain that the construction of large, comprehensive data models is an activity divorced from the real-world needs of the system user. In recent years, it was the fashion in some organizations to construct "corporate data models" that sought to provide a structure within which all data entities of interest to the business could be accommodated. Many purists considered this heretical, since it seemed to imply that Occam was wrong. They also maintained that the resulting models were impossible to validate against the business because of their theoretical basis. Also, it was said that the effort of creating and maintaining such models was prohibitive, bearing in mind the benefits to be achieved, and that once constructed, they required a cadre of "gurus" to interpret them—if they were to be accessible to mere systems builders. Each point is taken in turn as follows:

1. Occam did not stand out against proliferation of entities themselves, but against unnecessary proliferation. Thus, the test to be applied when deciding whether his principle has been broken is

not to look at the size and complexity of the data model but whether such richness is needed.

2. The mistake made by some organizations was to build up their corporate data model *in vacuo*. The decision was made to set up a task force that would lock itself away for six months and produce the corporate data model. The members of this task force would often emerge after about 18 months (rather than the six originally envisaged), with a 1,000-entity data model that they would then take to be blessed by senior management. A more appropriate approach would be to build up the corporate data model over several years, as major projects are launched in particular areas of the business. If the opportunity can be taken to do this in parallel with business process reengineering activities, or similar activities, then so much the better.

3. The third point, that such large data models are difficult to construct and even more difficult to interpret and administer, leads us on to one of the major benefits of a thorough understanding of metadata. The more that people can be aware of the general behavior of data and comfortable with the conceptual models that define this, the easier it will be for them to make use of a comprehensive tool such as the corporate data model. This book endeavors to raise the level of understanding in the area of metadata to the point where the construction and use of a corporate data model is a manageable, realistic, and efficient exercise. Indeed, if the rules implied in a well-developed metadata-base are understood and followed by all those who design and develop systems within an organization, it can be argued that this bypasses the need for a corporate data model at all.

2.8   Metadata analysis

A highly developed set of principles exists to define and control the ways in which data behaves within computer systems. The craft of data analysis has been developed over the years to enable robust definitions to be made of the following:

- The structure of data records within a database;

- The way in which different types of data records are related and the dependencies they have on each other;

- The business rules implied by these constraints.

In addition to being the means by which the behavior of data in general is expressed, metadata itself represents only a peculiar type of data. Therefore, a simplified subset of the data analysis techniques will be used throughout this book to explain the behavior of metadata itself. An additional benefit of this (once the conceptual complexity is understood) is that the metadata models derived in the course of this discussion will be self-defining, in the sense that they will record the rules followed in their own construction! This should ensure that those readers who take the time to gain a thorough understanding of the early chapters will, as a result, gain a clear insight into the behavior of all types of data.

2.8.1 Tools, techniques, and syntax

This book does not intend to teach or advocate a particular modeling technique. The syntax and protocols used throughout the following pages represent an interpretation and simplification of some commonly used methods. No implied preference for these methods is made; neither is it suggested that the syntax used is in any way complete, in the sense of being rich enough for all systems analysis purposes. It does include a set of components that will enable us to describe the metamodel itself and, through it, the business as a whole.

The syntactic elements that we will make use of throughout this book are listed as follows:

- Entities;

- One-to-one relationships;

- One-to-many relationships;

- Discrete subtypes;

- Overlapping subtypes.

2.8.2 The entity concept

Each entity will be denoted by a rectangle, within which the name of the entity will usually be written, as shown in Figure 2.1. This name should be a singular noun, as relevant and descriptive as possible while remaining concise. In some cases, artificial "intersection entities" may be introduced that will not have a name, since their entire meaning and existence is dependent on their "parents." The convention of writing entity names in uppercase (e.g., CUSTOMER, PRODUCT) will be followed throughout the book to reduce confusion between formal entities and general English usage.

2.8.3 One-to-one relationships

The relationships that one entity type can have to another come in a variety of forms. The simplest case to understand is where, for every single instance of one entity, an instance of another entity exists. This will be represented as two entity boxes, connected by a single unbroken line, as shown in Figure 2.2. Although simple, these relationships rarely occur within data or metadata modeling, since this type of total mutual dependence means that the two entities are usually better represented as one.

2.8.4 One-to-zero or -one relationships

A more realistic relationship type is where an instance of the entity may or may not exist, but where it does it has an exact correspondence with the existence of an instance of a second entity. We will represent this by placing a "Z" character at the end of the relationship line that denotes

Figure 2.1 The entity.

Figure 2.2 The one-to-one relationship.

the optional entity, as shown in Figure 2.3. This example implies that a VEHICLE instance can exist without a REGISTRATION NUMBER, but the REGISTRATION NUMBER cannot exist without a corresponding VEHICLE, which must be unique for that number.

2.8.5   One-to-many relationships

The more normal real-world situation is where, for a particular entity instance, the possibility of zero, one, or several instances of a different entity exist. We will express this general case using a blocked-in arrowhead, at the "many" end of such relationships, as shown in Figure 2.4. The type of relationship—namely one-to-one; one-to-zero or -one; one-to-zero, -one, or -many—is known as its cardinality. In the case of one-to-many relationships, we will refer to the "single-end" entity as the parent entity and the "multiple-end" entity as the child entity.

2.8.6   Discrete subtypes

A particular entity can be classified according to the values of classifying attributes. These are properties of the entity, the values of which determine to which subtypes of the entity particular instances belong. We shall denote two different situations in which subtyping occurs: the discrete subtype and the overlapping subtype.

The discrete subtype represents a situation where, by examining a particular classifying attribute of an entity instance, we can determine which subtype entity it represents. In this case, it may belong to one and

Figure 2.3   The one-to-zero or -one relationship.

Figure 2.4   The one-to-many relationship.

only one of the subtypes—it is impossible for it to belong to more than one at the same time. This situation will be represented as Figure 2.5.

In Figure 2.5, it is implied that both the entity CAR and the entity BICYCLE are subtypes of the entity VEHICLE but that a vehicle cannot be both a CAR and a BICYCLE at the same time. It should be noted that this is an incomplete classification, since the subtypes do not cover the full scope of the supertype (a VEHICLE can be something other than a CAR or a BICYCLE). If the subtyping is complete, for instance splitting the PERSON entity into complementary subtypes MALE and FEMALE, it is represented as shown in Figure 2.6.

In Figure 2.6, unlike Figure 2.5, the possibility of introducing additional, as yet unknown subtypes is not allowed for, since the classification is assumed to be already *complete* (that is, all members of the PERSON set will be represented by one or the other subtype).

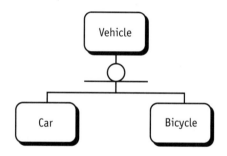

Figure 2.5   The discrete subtype.

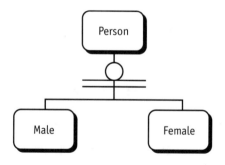

Figure 2.6   The complete discrete subtype.

2.8.7 Overlapping subtypes

In some cases, there may be more than one different subtyping activity of interest when considering a particular entity. In such cases, it might be that an instance could fall into two different subtypes of a supertype entity, rather than strictly one, as explained above. In such cases, the subtypes are separated. See Figure 2.7.

In Figure 2.7, it is implied that a BUSINESS PARTNER can be a CUSTOMER, a SUPPLIER, both, or neither. The split of the set BUSINESS PARTNER into CUSTOMER and non-CUSTOMER is independent of its split into SUPPLIER and non-SUPPLIER.

Having established the means by which the behavior of metadata as a whole will be documented and explained, we can begin to consider the basic components of the common basic metamodel. It will be necessary to make use of the concepts we have just discussed to define their own behavior at one level of abstraction removed (that is, by considering the ENTITY entity and the way it relates to other metadata entities).

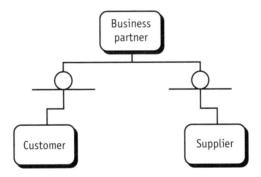

Figure 2.7   The overlapping (independent) subtype.

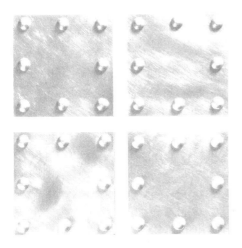

3

Establishing a Common Basic Metamodel

T HE FIRST STAGE in the construction of an effective metamodel is to define the basic building blocks of data analysis itself. This must be done in a manner that is:

1. Understandable by all those who will have access to the metamodel;

2. Extensible for all subsets of activity under consideration;

3. Universally true—in other words, not subject to riders, reservations, or exceptions limiting the scope of its "truth."

Although the concepts we will model in this chapter are relatively simple, and generally well-understood by most systems professionals, it is nevertheless a good idea to include them in our library of metamodels, due to the following:

- It will often be simpler, when discussing more complex issues, to have an accepted, simple base upon which we can rely and that has been fully documented;

- It will always be necessary to involve people without a systems analysis background in the process of systems design. Having a basic structure that can be explained relatively quickly and that is common to all other system design activity will both help them to understand the process itself and avoid unnecessary discussion on the subject.

This chapter will therefore describe the basic building blocks of systems analysis and provide example metamodels for use as a cornerstone for our metadata-base. Figures in the text define the diagramming syntax that is used throughout the book. These are particularly relevant to consideration of the formal metamodel descriptions given in the appendixes. It is recommended, therefore, that the reader becomes familiar with the syntax at an early stage, since it will become necessary to refer to these models at frequent intervals as our discussion progresses.

3.1   Entities

Entities are "types of things" that are of interest within the scope of the activities of the business. We are immediately faced with the possibility of linguistic confusion, since the first type of thing with which the metadata analyst should be familiar is the ENTITY entity itself.

We will therefore adopt the protocol that, when referring to the type of thing, we will use uppercase and reserve lowercase for normal English usage. Thus, the "type of thing" describing the set of "types of things" will be known as the ENTITY entity (i.e., in the same way that we may be interested in the CUSTOMER entity or the ACCOUNT entity). A formal definition of the ENTITY entity could be phrased as follows:

Any distinct class of things that can be associated by a set of common characteristics. These things can be concrete, real items such as vehicles or people; they can be business events, such as purchase orders or deliveries. In some cases, they can be abstract, such as an opinion or a desire for a particular commodity. (Synonyms include RECORD TYPE, TABLE, and RELATION.)

The process of normalization (and indeed common sense) dictates that, to be a distinct ENTITY, a thing must have characteristics that are in themselves distinct, either by virtue of existence or value, from those of other entities. If this is not the case, then only the common super-set of both ENTITYs is worthy of consideration, unless or until such distinguishing characteristics become of interest. For instance, if you are interested in both CORPORATE and INDIVIDUAL CUSTOMERS but are capturing exactly the same data about each and applying the same constraints, then there is no need to distinguish between them. Instead of introducing unnecessary complexity, treat both as CUSTOMERs, pure and simple.

Each individual thing within the set described by these particular characteristics is known as an ENTITY OCCURRENCE. This is defined formally as follows:

An individual member of a class defined by a particular ENTITY. (Synonyms include TUPLE, ROW, and INSTANCE.)

From this alone, we can begin to build up our metamodel, since these definitions impose two simple yet vitally important constraints on our activities:

- Metadata business rule 1: All ENTITY types that are of interest to an enterprise have a corresponding ENTITY OCCURRENCE within the ENTITY entity. From a logical perspective, this means that if a particular ENTITY (CUSTOMER, for example) is of interest, then it is a corresponding instance of the ENTITY entity that can define what CUSTOMERs in general are and how they behave.

- Metadata business rule 2: All ENTITY types that are of interest to an enterprise are subclasses (at some level) of the ENTITY entity. This is represented graphically in Figure 3.1.

3.2   Attributes

The properties of an ENTITY are known as its ATTRIBUTEs. The contents of these ATTRIBUTE fields form the real business data and represent the point at which the metadata and "real" business data views interact most heavily. Formally, we define an ATTRIBUTE as follows:

> Each ENTITY is distinguished by a set of properties that are of interest, known collectively as its ATTRIBUTEs. These have particular (but not necessarily unique) values for each instance of the ENTITY that is of interest. (Synonyms include RECORD FIELD and COLUMN.)

For the sake of simplicity, those ATTRIBUTEs that have a strong and permanent resemblance to each other and behave in a similar way no matter what ENTITY they are contained within can be grouped together. These ATTRIBUTE TYPEs can then be used as an efficient means by which the behavior and values of individual pieces of business data can be controlled.

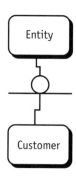

Figure 3.1   Metadata business rule 2.

3.3   Classification

One ENTITY type may be related to many others by the process of classification. The splitting of a set of ENTITY OCCURRENCEs into two or
more subsets is performed by examining the value of one or more
CATEGORIZING ATTRIBUTEs. The entity being split is referred to as
the SUPERTYPE ENTITY, and the component subsets themselves form
instances of distinct SUBTYPE ENTITYs. This may be formally defined
as follows:

> An ENTITY that wholly encompasses several other ENTITYs,
> each of which are distinguished one from the other by means of
> a CATEGORIZING ATTRIBUTE, is referred to as a SUPERTYPE
> ENTITY. Conversely, an ENTITY that defines a bounded subset of the
> instances of another ENTITY is referred to as a SUBTYPE ENTITY.
> The NON-CATEGORIZING ATTRIBUTEs of a particular SUBTYPE
> ENTITY may be shared with some or all other sibling SUBTYPE ENTI-
> TYs ("cotypes") or may be unique in themselves. In general, the
> ATTRIBUTEs (including CATEGORIZING ATTRIBUTEs) that are
> shared by all SUBTYPE ENTITYs will be kept at the SUPERTYPE
> ENTITY level.

3.4   Relationships

Relationships are the means of defining just how one ENTITY type
behaves in relation to another and how they affect each other in more
general terms. The term RELATIONSHIP is formally defined as follows:

> A RELATIONSHIP describes the properties of one ENTITY as it acts
> upon, relates to, or restricts another.

In reality, this means that RELATIONSHIPs are the prime means of
defining the business rules under which the scope of a data model will
operate. Together with classifications, they enable the data analyst to
place constraints on the nature of ENTITYs and thus the logic that may be
executed upon them.

An important feature of the definition of relationships is the cardinality. A RELATIONSHIP defines the influence that an ENTITY type brings to bear upon another. The cardinality of this RELATIONSHIP defines the number of ENTITY OCCURRENCEs that can take part in this process. It may be appropriate to a particular business that an ORDER can only be placed by one PERSON, acting for one CUSTOMER. For another company, this may not be the case. The cardinality of the relationships between these entities expresses the differing business rules and has a profound effect on how these rules will be implemented.

3.5   Domains

Consideration of DOMAINs helps us to understand the ways in which ATTRIBUTE TYPES, and through them ATTRIBUTEs of particular ENTITYs, can be restricted in the values that they take. A formal definition of the DOMAIN concept is:

> A set representing all possible values that may be taken by a particular ATTRIBUTE TYPE. A particular DOMAIN may be "bounded" or "unbounded." A BOUNDED DOMAIN can be expressed explicitly as a list of values; an UNBOUNDED DOMAIN is usually expressed as a set of restrictions on the size, format, or character of a particular ATTRIBUTE TYPE. Strictly speaking, UNBOUNDED DOMAINs are not infinite, since it would be possible to list all permissible values.

The distinction between these two types of DOMAIN is a matter of personal preference. It is clear that, for most purposes, the Boolean DOMAIN [YES, NO] is best expressed by a list of values, whereas no purpose is served by listing the set of all possible surnames. It is, of course, sensible to make a restriction on the length and composition of such names, rather than composing an explicit list.

3.6   Events

There is one further concept of which we must be aware. If the universe of ENTITYs that we are attempting to model is changing over time, then we must have the means to define and record the circumstances under which these changes take place. Therefore, we must consider the EVENT entity, which is defined as follows:

> A happening, or series of happenings, that changes either the STATE (an ENTITY occurrence is transformed into an occurrence of a different ENTITY occurrence) or the CONDITION (the value of one or more ATTRIBUTEs of an ENTITY is changed) of an ENTITY.

This leads directly to the formulation of a third business rule, the metadata business rule 3. Under this rule, an EVENT that causes a CLASSIFYING ATTRIBUTE of an ENTITY to change in a way that reclassifies it as a different SUBTYPE ENTITY is, by definition, a STATE EVENT. The formal metamodel definition relating to this is shown in Figure 3.2.

Figure 3.2 provides a shorthand representation of several business rules pertaining to the common metamodel. The same syntax will be used throughout the book, enabling complex concepts to be described in a concise manner. For this case, we will state the business rules explicitly:

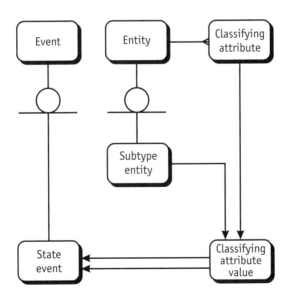

Figure 3.2   Metadata business rule 3.

1. STATE EVENT is a subtype of EVENT.

2. SUBTYPE ENTITY is a subtype of ENTITY (being the set of ENTITYs that forms subtypes of others). It is also related to ENTITY through the action of subtyping itself, although this is not represented on the diagram. In other words, each member of the set SUBTYPE ENTITY, in addition to being a member of the set ENTITY (expressed by the subtype), is also related to a different instance of the set ENTITY, being that instance that represents its superset! The significance of this multiple relationship will become clearer in time!

3. Each ENTITY has between zero and many CLASSIFYING ATTRIBUTEs (a subtype of ATTRIBUTE—not shown).

4. Each CLASSIFYING ATTRIBUTE belongs to only one ENTITY.

5. Each CLASSIFYING ATTRIBUTE can take a set of values, contained in the entity CLASSIFYING ATTRIBUTE VALUE.

6. A STATE EVENT has a relationship with exactly two CLASSIFYING ATTRIBUTE VALUE instances, one of which is the value before the EVENT itself took place; the other is the value after.

7. Each SUBTYPE ENTITY has a set of CLASSIFYING ATTRIBUTE VALUEs that define its boundaries. Strictly speaking, if the SUBTYPE ENTITY boundaries are not overlapping, then the subsets they represent must be mutually exclusive. Thus, as represented on Figure 3.2, a CLASSIFYING ATTRIBUTE VALUE can only be relevant to one SUBTYPE ENTITY.

The implication of these rules is that a STATE EVENT alters an ENTITY from one SUBTYPE ENTITY to another, by means of changing the value of a CLASSIFYING ATTRIBUTE relevant to that subclassification split.

This somewhat verbose exposition of a six-box diagram (Figure 3.2) should demonstrate the value of a modeling technique to express these concepts. The ability to define metadata constructs in these terms, and the ability to interpret them, are key to the establishment of a truly data-literate environment.

In Part II we will explore the ways in which these basic constructs build up into the separate metamodels and the ways in which these interact. In essence, this defines the extent of the management problem within IT, taken as a collection of business activities.

Part II

Metadata in the Business

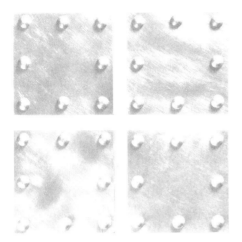

4

Managing the Metadata

4.1 The principles of metadata management

Now that a common understanding of the metamodel has been established, the practical implications of actually populating the metadata-base and keeping it accurate and complete over time should be considered. To get an idea of just what this involves, let us start by making a list of the sort of events that will have an impact on the metadata within each of our submodels. The following events will have a significant impact on the metadata-base:

- Changes to the data management metamodel;

- Refinement of subject area data models;

- Changes to existing domains;

- Changes to business rules;

- Changes to the IT management metamodel.

Clearly, change must be recognized as a factor in the management of metadata, and formal procedures must be established and followed for each type of change. There must be job roles defined to manage the changes that occur within the IT infrastructure, and these roles must be filled by competent individuals. In many cases, the changes we will examine are managed already within a well-run IT environment. It is important to recognize, however, the ways in which the various types of metadata interact with each other, such that the overall infrastructure can be managed in an efficient manner.

Generally speaking, the changes that occur should be limited to major projects and formal releases in the manner of software development. The major changes can be analyzed, controlled, and documented as part of the project effort (and should, of course, be included within the project plans and economic justification). Minor changes should, where possible, be "batched up" and implemented on a periodic basis. The metadata-base can be subject to release management on a three- or six-month cycle, allowing thorough investigation of the impacts of each change and ensuring the ongoing cohesiveness of all metadata.

This will also allow thorough testing of the changes to be made to metadata, where applicable. The actual testing of impacts will depend on the environments concerned. Each individual change will be reflected on a number of applications. The formal testing and sign-off of the change in the context of each impacted system will be performed in isolation (as unit testing), together with an integrated test procedure to ensure that all amended and nonamended applications interact appropriately.

4.1.1 Changes to the data management metamodel

In a normal business, it will not be feasible or politically acceptable to devote the staff required to building a comprehensive enterprise data model from scratch. The task itself will require the involvement of people with a comprehensive understanding of the entire business, together with significant IT resources. If an enterprise data model is to be defined at any but the most trivial level, it will require substantial effort from these people (who are, in all likelihood, seen to be very valuable elsewhere in the business).

Development of new subject area data models

Seen as a stand-alone exercise, the development of such a model can be extremely difficult to justify. In most cases, therefore, it is better to adopt an evolutionary approach, starting with a universal but very high-level model and fleshing it out in stages, as specific needs are addressed.

In most cases, what will actually happen is that those subject areas that require immediate attention—because there is a project already going on to reengineer the process or to develop a major new application system—will be identified. As a result, the portions of the enterprise model that relate to these subject areas will be defined in more detail before other, less urgent areas.

Over time, as each portion of the business becomes subject to such a major reconsideration, the enterprise model will become more complete. It is important to remember that to ensure the ongoing accuracy of this model as it evolves, it must be managed actively. For this reason, it is in everyone's interests to appoint a *data architect* (q.v.) at an early stage, to act as the custodian of the enterprise model.

When it is decided to build a new subject area database, this will have a considerable impact on the entities within the data management metamodel. An analyst (typically sourced from within the IT function) responsible for the technical construction of this new portion should be identified, and a "client" role should be filled from the business. The client will be responsible for ensuring that the model as defined by the data analyst is complete and accurate for the purposes of the business. The analyst appointed to add and document the new entities will coordinate with the data architect to ensure that the whole picture remains cohesive—in other words, that the newer portions of the model do not contradict the more established subject area submodels.

Assuming that some portion of the metamodel covering ENTITY, ATTRIBUTE, and RELATIONSHIP concepts has been constructed, the process of extending it will take on the following structure:

1. The data analyst will record a new subject area data model on the DATA MODEL meta-entity.

2. The data analyst and the client working together will determine which subset of the entities already in place in the ENTITY entity are relevant to the new subject area.

3. The data analyst should build a prototype subject area model that encompasses all the entities that were previously identified. This will include all their attributes and any relationships for which both "ends" have been included (i.e., both the "parent" and the "child" entity of a relationship are part of the new model).

4. This prototype should be analyzed by the data analyst and the client to determine which parts are irrelevant to the new subject area. Any such elements should be selectively eliminated in consultation with relevant business management.

5. The main data analysis for the subject area should now take place as a coordinated exercise between the data analyst and the "client." This will involve extending the prototype with new elements to model the business rules, in full, for the new subject area.

6. All new elements that impact the existing model (new relationships attached to existing entities, new attributes for existing entities, etc.) should be discussed and approved by the "owners" of the entities concerned to ensure that they do not conflict with the existing view of the business rules or add duplicate concepts. These *data owners* (q.v.) will normally be relatively senior business people responsible for the processes that most heavily interact with the entities concerned. For instance, a sales manager may have ownership of the CUSTOMER entity; a production manager may be responsible for the PRODUCT entity, etc.

7. Any conflicts thus identified should be resolved, in a process involving the metamodel owner, the process owner for both (or all) subject areas involved, and the analysts proposing the change.

In principle, where there is a genuine inconsistency between the existing and new view of a particular section of the enterprise model, this can be resolved in a number of ways:

■ The new rule is correct and is recognized as either a restatement or a compatible extension of the existing rules—some refinement of the new subject area model is required.

■ The new rule is incorrect, and the existing model will suffice to cover the case of the new subject area, in the context—remove the erroneous rules from the new subject area model.

■ Both rules are correct but are only partially stated, leading to an apparent contradiction. By adding further conditions to the rules—for example, stating what happens within specific departments, countries, situations, etc.—the distinction between the two rules can be elaborated and verified.

■ The new rule is correct, and the existing model is inherently flawed. This situation has very serious consequences, since it will imply that a model that has been previously developed, and may be already in use to develop an application, has errors. How precisely this should be handled will depend on the political situation, but the importance of resolving such conflicts cannot be overemphasized. If this type of inconsistency is left in place, it will undoubtedly lead to major problems between the subject area activities in the future, caused by the different, contradictory interpretations of the same situation. (Note that great care should be taken to ensure that differences in business rules really are contradictory; see Appendix A.)

Potential impact

Alterations to the data management metamodel will involve changes to some or all of the following entities:

■ DATA MODEL;

■ DATA MODEL ENTITY;

■ DATA MODEL RELATIONSHIP;

■ DATA MODEL ATTRIBUTE.

4.1.2   Refinement of subject area data models

Over time, the contents of each subject area data model will evolve to match the changing circumstances of the business and the need for greater detail. Broadly speaking, there are three types of changes that can drive the need for such evolution, described as follows:

1. Changes to the application (for instance, the computer application is extended to include business processes that were not previously automated);

2. Internally driven changes to business processes (for instance, extra controls are introduced, or existing controls are recognized as unnecessary and dropped);

3. Externally driven changes in the business environment (for instance, legislation, mergers, and acquisitions; changing market conditions; or introduction of new industry standards).

Assuming that these changes do not in themselves introduce new rules that are in contradiction with the enterprise data model (see Section 4.1.4), the issues to be taken into consideration are as follows:

- How does this change affect the operation of other applications or processes within this subject area? If a change has been made while developing or evolving one application within the subject area that will affect the operation of other applications or processes, then these changes should be analyzed to determine their impact and appropriate plans made to ensure that consistency within the subject area is maintained. Where a potential conflict occurs over the interpretation of particular rules by two applications or processes within the subject area, an arbitration procedure should be established involving the process owner, the development teams and the metadata manager (q.v.). This situation should only occur when the original change has been initiated from within one of the applications. If it is due to a change in the business, either internally or externally driven, then there is a clear responsibility for all of these applications that are in conflict to conform to the new rules, and hence to the new model, rather than retain their own inconsistent versions.

- How does the change affect other applications or processes outside this subject area that rely on the data produced within it in some way? Provided that the change remains consistent with the enterprise data model (see Section 4.1.4), then once again any changes should be analyzed to determine whether they have a material effect on other applications. Some applications so affected will fall outside the subject area (and will be sent data over interfaces or copy management facilities that are materially changed). In such cases an arbitration procedure involving the process owners, the metadata manager, and all relevant application development and support organizations should be convened.

- How does the change affect the enterprise data model? (See Section 4.1.4.)

Potential impact

Refinements to subject area data models will involve changes to some or all of the following entities:

- DATA MODEL;

- DATA MODEL ENTITY;

- DATA MODEL RELATIONSHIP;

- DATA MODEL ATTRIBUTE.

4.1.3   Extension or reduction of existing domains

A DOMAIN represents the constraints that are operating on a particular attribute or set of attributes, with regard to the values they are permitted to take. If this set of values changes, it will, in some cases, have a direct effect on existing applications and databases. This effect can take a number of forms:

- The DOMAIN can be extended, so that all values that are currently valid remain valid and some new values are allowed. In such cases, no effect will be felt on the existing systems and database, since the result represents a "pure" superset of the original case.

- The DOMAIN can be changed so that some values that were previously valid become invalid. In this case, prior to the domain change being considered "live," any instances on existing databases where the newly invalidated values are used should be identified and examined to determine whether they should be eliminated, or whether the value should be preserved after all.

- The DOMAIN can be changed in such a manner that some values that were previously valid have been replaced by others. The real need for such change should be established at the highest appropriate level and, once reinforced, all instances that make use of the existing (but soon to be incorrect) value should be identified and put through a "mapping" mechanism. This should take the form of a procedure that substitutes the original value for the new value, at a time after the new values have been included in the DOMAIN, and before the old values have been deleted. In some cases, this will be a one-for-one substitution, in which case the mapping will be relatively straightforward. In others, there will be the need for complex algorithms, involving the examination of other attributes, etc.

Potential Impact

Changes to existing domains will involve alterations to some or all of the following entities:

- DOMAIN;
- ATTRIBUTE TYPE;
- ATTRIBUTE.

4.1.4 Changes to business rules

Having established that the enterprise model represents some reasonable subset of the universal truth about the way the organization functions, it is clear that any changes to this truth need to be handled with great care. Early on in the history of an enterprise data model, it is quite possible that there will be very little overlap between the subject areas, and hence between the applications that will be affected by changes. As the enterprise model becomes more complete, it will be increasingly difficult to see how the concept of change can be managed in a way that will not lead to a breakdown of the entire premise.

In order to calm our nerves on this issue, it is worth taking a simplistic view of what can happen in such cases. Let us assume that a change has been proposed that implies that the contents of the enterprise data model (and hence the sum total of the universal truth that it embodies) will be altered in some way. This change can take one of the following forms.

1. An adjustment that is entirely compatible with the existing enterprise data model, in which case it should have no mandatory effect on existing data usage and logic;

2. An adjustment that is not compatible with the existing enterprise data model but that makes changes that are not currently embedded in existing applications (i.e., no effect is cascaded down to the subject area level). Once again, no effect should be felt outside the area during the change;

3. An adjustment that is proposed is not compatible with the existing enterprise data model and will stand in conflict with subject areas that have made use of the old version.

Put simply, these possibilities may be described as follows:

- The old version is indeed wrong, and the applications that make use of it must be changed anyway to stay in line with business requirements.

- The old version is verified as correct, in which case the change should not be made.

- They are both wrong, for whatever reason, in the new business context, in which case a new version of the rules must be developed to take account of the correct parts of each.

Potential impact

Changes to business rules will involve changes to some or all of the following entities:

- DATA MODEL;

- DATA MODEL ENTITY;

- DATA MODEL RELATIONSHIP;

- DATA MODEL ATTRIBUTE;

- ENTITY;

- RELATIONSHIP;

- ATTRIBUTE.

4.1.5   Changes to the IT management metamodel

In a similar fashion, the impacts of many types of business changes can be analyzed and managed in terms of the effects that they have on the population of a variety of metamodel entities.

Changes falling into this category include the following:

- For the application management metamodel:

  - New application releases;

  - New application module releases;

  - New application modules;

  - Changes to the user base for an application;

  - Changes to user responsibilities;

  - Redesign of user jobs;

  - Changes to address issues raised during systems audits;

  - Interaction with the software supplier;

  - Business process reengineering activities.

- For the activity management metamodel:

  - New application development projects;

  - Changes in IT personnel;

  - Project development progress;

  - Changes and refinements to project plans;

  - Corporate reorganizations.

- For the infrastructure management metamodel:

  - Installation or decommissioning of hardware;

  - Corporate restructuring (mergers and acquisitions, downsizing, outsourcing, etc.);

  - Moving location.

4.2 Metadata management roles and responsibilities

The notion that the activities within a business can be expressed as a hierarchy is clearly established. This involves determining a set of processes that optimally represent the structure of necessary work within the organization and arranging them hierarchically. As a result, during business process reengineering the decomposition that would optimize that organization's structure can be established.

As a basis for such analysis, each major process has a process owner with overall responsibility for the way in which the activities within that process are conducted and the organizational structure is used. The whole essence of business rationalization depends on the way in which these process owner roles are fulfilled.

In the past, many business processes have been conducted as if they were unique to one part of the enterprise, rather than as part of a common pattern. The responsibility for the execution of these processes has been rightly delegated to the lowest level. Problems occur when the responsibility for deciding on the nature of the process itself has been delegated as well. Rather than taking a generic model of the business processes and tailoring it to individual business units or departments, the structure of model is changed to contradict the generic rules. A classic example of this would be purchasing rules within a large organization. The controls applicable to each level of purchasing authority would be set globally and executed locally. In poorly controlled environments, the local execution could be allowed to become inconsistent with the spirit of the global rules, leading inevitably to problems within the business.

More recently, it has been recognized that a "logical centralization" of process design leads to a great deal of efficiency in the enterprise. At the cost of some (often unnecessary) flexibility, common business processes enable the following:

1. Increased flexibility in response to changes in the business circumstances (since only one process has to be adapted, rather than a variety of similar but nonidentical versions);

2. Increased mobility and flexibility of the work force (elimination of local peculiarities enable people to be moved between jobs in

different parts of the organization with greater ease and the jobs themselves to be simpler);

3. Improved systems support (with a complete, mutually consistent set of business processes, the construction of computer and other systems to support the enterprise can be achieved more quickly and robustly than before).

Ironically one of the areas to benefit least from this approach has been the management of data, which is still, in most organizations, left to the whim of a wide variety of people.

Where the concept of data quality management is understood, it is rarely implemented. Where it is implemented it is rarely effective.

Part of this is due to a "time-lag effect," where systems that were built around a "local" view of data are still in place and the way in which data is managed within them still reflects this.

The ability to manage data at an operational level in an effective and efficient manner depends on the existence of a logical, consistent framework within which such management activities take place. Such a framework is derived, implicitly or explicitly, from the metamodel for the enterprise and needs to be actively managed over time to ensure that it remains relevant and complete as the business evolves. Without explicit stewardship of this metamodel, the chances of long-term success in the management of information are not good. It is, therefore, advisable to establish *information provision* as a formal business process and to assign corporate responsibility for its management.

We have already mentioned the advantages of grouping the activities of a business into formal processes, which represent value-added, cohesive, and complete "chains" of work. The chain involved in the provision and control of information is, in itself, often considered in this manner.

As with any other business process, the "provide information" chain should define a process owner, who is, at the global level, responsible for the conduct of the entire process across the entire enterprise. This process ownership role would form part of the responsibility for a *metadata manager* within the enterprise. In our previous discussions, we have alluded to several job roles that should be defined within the enterprise to support the metadata manager in this process owner role, including the following:

- *Business process owners:* Those with responsibility for the conduct of "slices" of the business activity, the manner in which data is used within these activities, and the maintenance of a consistent approach across their boundaries. The process owners are both prime "customers" and "suppliers" to the metadata manager. They will provide the intelligence on the use of data within the enterprise that will enable the metadata manager to function effectively, while holding them responsible for the overall coordination of data usage at a corporate level. As a general rule, the business process owners will be drawn from a business background and be relatively senior in the organization. This will ensure that they have a broad perspective of the business operation, together with the necessary influence to exert global control over the execution of the process, where necessary.

- *Application architect:* This individual is responsible to the metadata manager for the construction and management of the application architecture, which is a detailed representation of the computer applications operating within the enterprise, the business processes they support, the data they use, and the manner in which they interact. This position will typically be filled by someone with a high degree of familiarity with the technical and business context for the applications deployed within the enterprise. Often, a highly experienced "business-focused" IT professional would be the ideal candidate for this role.

- *Security architect:* This individual will be responsible to the metadata manager for ensuring that the way in which people are allowed to access data and to execute processes within the context of the business are in the best interests of the enterprise and are mutually consistent. A background in internal control, audit, or IT security would provide a sound skill base for this job.

4.3 The responsibilities of the metadata manager

The existence of a single point (an individual or closely coordinated group) in the enterprise with overall responsibility for the structure and use of the metamodel provides a solid core upon which all systems development and management activities can be centered. The detailed nature of this role and the responsibilities that it entails will, of course, vary substantially from one enterprise to another. There is, however, a common structure that will be suitable for most purposes.

The metadata manager has overall responsibility for the structure, development, and use of the metamodel. This implies the stewardship of, or at the very least a strategic interest in, four different levels of abstraction, namely the following:

1. The metamodel itself;

2. The metadata-base;

3. The application (or subject area) data models;

4. The application databases.

Each level provides a structural framework for the level below and serves to populate the level above. For example, the metadata-base is structured according to the metamodel and provides structure for the application data models. The metamodel will describe the structure, or nature, of the ENTITY entity—effectively the rules for constructing data models. The metadata-base will contain records, each of which generically describes an individual entity—CUSTOMER or PRODUCT, for example—and the rules for storing business data. The application data model will define the specific constraints by which the data will be controlled within a system, and the application database will store the actual data according to those rules. The metadata manager will have responsibilities for the upkeep of the models at each of these levels, requiring a strong grasp of the operation of the business allied to a capacity for conceptual thinking.

4.3.1 The metadata manager and the metamodel

Clearly, the metadata manager has ownership of the metamodel. He or she will be responsible for the structure of the metamodel and, through it, the overall behavior of the data within the enterprise. This responsibility does not imply a large analytical overhead since the metamodel is, to a large degree, generic and stable. What it does require of the metadata manager is a clear and comprehensive understanding of the constraints or business rules that are operating within the metamodel and the ability to translate these rules from the general to the specific.

In other words, it is critical for metadata managers to understand, for instance, the relationships between the ENTITY entity and the ATTRIBUTE entity. This will enable them to visualize how these relationships reflect on actual ENTITYs and ATTRIBUTEs that are used within the applications of the enterprise and to determine how these constraints will affect the use of computer systems by the business. Of course, this can be learned and applied with practice. It is worth noting, however, that there are some individuals who appear to possess an intuitive understanding for such things. Such individuals, provided they maintain a pragmatic approach to their responsibilities, make ideal candidates for the job of metadata manager.

In practice, the role of "owner" of the metamodel implies that the metadata manager will be responsible for the construction of the model and its refinement over time. As with the owner of any mainstream business process, this means that metadata managers will be responsible for determining which business rules apply to the model and how these should be implemented. For a normal process, this means knowing how the business rules reflect on the data model for, say, manufacturing processes, and how these will be implemented as constraints on physical data structures used by a manufacturing system.

For the metadata manager, this means knowing how to adapt the structure of the metamodel to the needs of the IT activities in an enterprise (and through that to the needs of the enterprise as a whole). It also implies that metadata managers should have the ability to reflect these theoretical changes on the physical structure of the data used in running the IT department (e.g., a repository data structure or a paper-based equivalent, the internal structure of CASE tools, etc.).

4.3.2 The metadata manager and the metadata-base

Taking one step from the abstract to the concrete, the metadata manager will also be held responsible for the application of the metadata structure in reality. We will collectively refer to all such structures as the metadata-base.

In fact, this database may be physically dispersed across a variety of sources. Typically such sources might include the proprietary structures embedded in CASE tools and repository managers or tools used for database administration and optimization. It might also include the paperwork associated with project planning and management (by whichever methodology is appropriate to the enterprise), records of application support activities, and operator's incident log sheets.

The metadata manager will be responsible for ensuring that these diverse data sources can be managed as a whole. This includes ensuring the following:

- A consistent means of identifying the relevant metaENTITY(s) is in place, well-communicated, and observed;

- The business rules (i.e., the relationships between the various metaENTITYs) are imposed consistently;

- The owners and custodians of the various entities are aware of and execute their responsibilities in this context.

4.3.3 The metadata manager and the application data models

Getting closer still to the real use of data within the enterprise and to the bulk of the work conducted by the metadata manager, we will examine the role he or she plays in the development and refinement of data models for individual applications and how this role reflects on the metadata-base. First, for each new or modified system within the appropriate scope, the way in which the changes made reflect on the subject area data models should be determined. This will initially be performed by an analyst within the project team and will be brought to the metadata manager for refinement, approval, and incorporation into the corporate data model (which forms the data management subset of the metadata-base).

The way in which this is achieved is discussed in detail in Chapter 5, but it should be recognized that (at least within a relatively stable IT environment) it will form a major part of the workload for the metadata manager.

4.3.4 The metadata manager and the application databases

The degree to which the metadata manager will be involved with the actual data contained in business databases will be limited. Having established that the structure, content, and context of these databases are consistent with the wider needs of the enterprise, they will be of limited impact to the metamodel. There will, however, be some circumstances under which the appropriate business owner does not actively manage the data they contain. This will be either because they cannot be identified in the current organizational structure or because the use of an entity is so widespread that allocation of any such business ownership would be purely arbitrary. In such cases (for instance the management of the codes for units of measurement, currency, etc.) the metadata manager will act as surrogate owner and will take responsibility for ensuring that the corporate code set meets the needs of the enterprise and that all physical application code sets conform to it.

4.4 Scalability of metadata management activities

An important factor to bear in mind when considering the implementation of architected metadata management is the cost. As with any business function that is seen as a support activity, there will be strong and persistent pressure on the amount of time and money that is spent on indirect contributions to the bottom line.

It should be clear that, in time, the benefits to be accrued from consistent data management are substantial and as such any effort put in to this area should be self-justifying. There will be some need, especially in smaller organizations, to tailor the approach that is outlined in this text to match financial and organizational constraints.

In large multinationals, it is not unreasonable to expect a task force to be set up, perhaps with four or five full-time members, reporting to the data architect. This task force will define the data quality improvement program, mount an education campaign to ensure that all personnel are aware of the issues arising from poor data quality, and form the backbone of data management resources into the future. For smaller companies, however, it will likely be left to a single committed individual to spread the word.

This is likely to be someone who has a full-time role in addition to being a champion of metadata management, so it becomes critically important that the necessary activities are spread around the organization. The way in which this is done will, of course, vary with circumstances. There are, however, a few observations that are worth making about how to achieve true data quality management practices with limited resources. It is important to take the following steps:

1. Ensure that the business concentrates on management of the key data entities—typically those in the front line of business such as CUSTOMER, PRODUCT, and financial data.

2. Collect evidence of poor data management practices leading to mistakes and wasted effort in the past. This will make it easier to justify any expenses incurred in clearing the situation up for the future. Some of these examples can be anecdotal, but it is important to include a selection that will have identified, tangible costs associated with them.

3. Try to instill a culture of metadata awareness into the IT community. This may take the form of suggesting a metadata-driven approach to future software development and support activities. As can be seen, the formalization of metadata in these areas is not too far away from normal good practices anyway, so the task should not be too difficult.

4. Concentrate on the delegation of "data ownership" responsibilities into the business. The business (rather than the IT) community should bear the burden of maintaining the data according to the agreed business rules. This, once again, can be seen as simply instilling a sense of responsibility for data quality at an appropriate part of the organization. This will depend, most fundamentally, on being able to sell the concept of data belonging to the enterprise, rather than to departments or individuals.

5. Concentrate on the process of metadata management, not the selection of tools that can be used to facilitate it. This can be seen (perhaps with some justification) as the IT community being isolated from the reality of the business.

It should be possible for a single individual to coordinate all data quality responsibilities within a medium-sized organization, provided the underlying business processes are not complex. Where it is necessary to concentrate this work in one place, it is generally appropriate to appoint someone relatively senior in the IT community as an "architecture manager" or some such title. This individual will take a longer-term view of the evolution of IT facilities within the organization, relieving many other groups from the burden of doing so and possibly introducing an element of neutrality that had previously been lacking. This person guides the progress towards data quality management and acts as custodian for the corporate metadata.

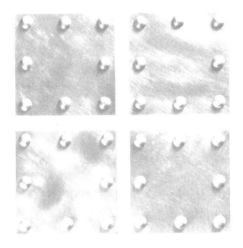

5

The Role of Metadata in Application Development and Support

5.1 Introduction

Arguably, the great challenge facing commercial IT practitioners at present is not the technical feasibility of using computing science to solve today's problems but managing the legacy left by the use of technology to solve yesterday's problems. In the past, computer applications were designed to meet the needs of specific users, within specific spheres of activity. Most companies employed significant numbers of systems analysts and programmers whose job it was to ensure that the company's activities were automated effectively.

In practice, execution of this brief left these practitioners in a state of perpetual conflict between analytical precision and expediency. In physical engineering disciplines, the rules by which projects are undertaken, and the constraints under which people within those projects work are defined and understood universally.

Applications development does not have constraints imposed upon it by the laws of physics, however. Computer systems can be made to behave in any way which the programmer desires, given sufficient time and intellectual prowess. Quite rightly, this flexibility has been portrayed as a great strength of the computer as a tool. It is also, however, one of its great weaknesses.

There are very few people who have been involved in formulation of computing strategy in commercial organizations who will not have spent considerable time bemoaning the amount of "reinventing of wheels" that has gone on in the past. This freedom, caused by the inherent flexibility of the tools available, has led to the following problems:

- The duplication of many commonplace situations;

- Wasted time spent on developing systems and subsystems that have already been developed;

- People being trained and retrained to use systems that are inherently very similar in principle but annoyingly diverse in practice.

The problem of wastefulness, particularly the lack of reusable work, pervades IT from top to bottom. In particular, the lack of a cohesive approach to metadata is as apparent at the strategic level (enterprise business process reengineering and corporate data management) as it is at the tactical level (design and implementation of computer applications).

5.2   Metadata and the management of consistency

Up to this point, we have concentrated on explaining, in detail, what metadata represent and suggesting means by which they should be managed and how they should evolve within a typical organization. We have built a case for effective control of metadata at both strategic and tactical levels of IT management. Before going further into the strategic importance of metadata control, it is worth considering some specific ways in which understanding of metadata and incorporation of techniques focused on metadata management can benefit the IT function tactically.

In particular, we should consider the way in which the use of predefined metadata components can drive efficiency and robustness in application development. Readers who are experienced data analysts, who have used CASE tools, or who have long careers in systems analysis under their belts will be clear as to the importance of this level of conceptual understanding. At a tactical level, such people will be happy with the idea that the metadata within an organization should be actively managed if the IT infrastructure is to remain under control. What may not be clear, however, is the way that metadata control can be brought to bear to achieve degrees of consistency and reusability of application components, in much the same way as object-oriented techniques achieve these benefits but without presupposing the deployment of the supporting object-oriented technology.

Practical issues have been addressed that enable the reader to see the benefits to be brought to those who manage the strategic and tactical direction of a medium- to large-sized IT function by a clear understanding and active stewardship of the appropriate metadata constructs. The key factor in achieving these efficiencies is the achievement of a high degree of reusability between situations that are conceptually similar.

This can apply on several levels, as with "real-world" engineering. For the sake of this discussion, we will examine three such levels of consistency management that we shall term local component reuse, component library management, and classified concept reuse.

5.2.1 Local component reuse

All systems are made up of identifiable components that are designed to fulfill a particular purpose or set of purposes. In the case of computer systems, these components can include data types, pieces of logic, and hardware components, among others. We will limit our discussions to these "soft" components, since the "hard" components (physical devices) are governed more by the "classical" engineering constraints.

If no consideration at all is given to the consistency of components, a system can still be built to fulfill the requirements of the users. However, the cost of building such a system, where a component is redesigned and built from scratch each time it is needed, is far greater than if some degree of management is exerted over the choice of components and consistency is actively managed (even arbitrarily).

If this approach were adopted for a car manufacturing company, then individual employees would work each requirement to join two pieces of metal together from first principles. They would not automatically repeat the approach that they used on the previous vehicle they built, nor would they ask colleagues how they solved the problem. Instead, they would act as if the problem were inherently new—that no two pieces of metal had ever previously been joined together in the context of car manufacture. After due consideration of the problem, they might well invent a process similar to spot-welding, using nuts and bolts or riveting, or they might invent some new process that did the job equally well but that was not conceptually similar. If they were in no way interested in consistency, then they would feel at liberty to forget this method and would start again from scratch when they faced their next requirement for fixing metal on the same vehicle.

Clearly, in the context of car manufacture, this situation is ludicrous. The cost of manufacturing each single car would be vast, and the resulting machine, even if it fulfilled specifications, would only be maintainable by a team of technicians dedicated to that one vehicle. The only context in which this type of engineering is viable is where there is a one-time construction to be made of extremely high value and for a purpose that is utterly new, such as the construction of a spacecraft. Even then only certain aspects would be justifiably managed in this fashion.

However ludicrous this may sound, it is often the way that naive or amateur programmers or systems designers approach their tasks: Each piece of logical complexity is considered on its own merits and is solved as an isolated problem. This does not affect the basic quality of the system produced, but it does mean that it will be costly in the extreme, both to produce and to maintain.

5.2.2 Local library management

A refinement on this situation is the adoption of an approach that enables the system developer to reuse parts of a system that was developed previously, possibly for an unrelated purpose. For software developers, this approach marks an increased level of sophistication, encompassing the use and management of "library routines," "copy files," and the like.

Under this approach, our car manufacturer would maintain a "memory" of the way things were done for other vehicles of the same type or for problems of the same type encountered on the current vehicle. Workers whose vehicles were in need of a spot-weld would remember that the vehicle they were working on had already experienced several repairs of this type and would make use of the same tools and techniques to perform their current task.

In the systems development process, this is akin to a project that, when well managed, will maintain libraries of common logic, to be used by all programmers within the project when they encounter a problem that will benefit from that approach. This represents the level that is attained by many in-house development environments, where the needs and economics of a project drive the evolution toward more efficient methods.

5.2.3   Global library management

A refinement of the local library approach, and one that brings further benefits in terms of efficiency of development, efficiency of maintenance, and robustness, is where the components have a life greater that the scope of existing activities. Whereas a local library involves the reuse of instances of logic, etc., a global library involves tailoring a generic approach to meet specific needs. An independently maintained library of subroutines, or data structures, or whatever, that is in a form that can be reused by different projects, possibly a long way in the future, even further magnifies the benefits mentioned above.

For the car manufacturer, this is akin to using common components on different types of vehicles—different models, built in different places that have been designed maybe decades apart. The reuse of such components further enhances the production process and provides the benefits of bulk ordering and economies of scale to boot. The "project" mentality, where the needs of a particular production line are paramount, has been subsumed in the greater needs of the enterprise—in this case to produce a wide variety of vehicles as cheaply and as reliably as possible.

This represents the level generally achieved in car manufacture and elsewhere in "real-world" engineering concerns. Standard-sized nuts and bolts are used. The spot-welding robots are conceptually similar whether being used to build a Ford Escort or an Opel Kadett, or even a washing machine! No one would dream of reinventing the basic relationship between the gearbox, transmission, and engine for a single car model, let alone a single car. Such changes do, of course, occur, but they are evolutionary changes to the process or tool, rather than special components built for one car type only.

Back in the systems development environment, the global library management approach implies that components of systems must be managed independently of the actual systems in which they are used. Without such independence, we cannot guarantee that such use will be consistent or, more importantly, that people will even know where to look to find the appropriate tools.

This level of consistency management is rare in commercial IT activities. A major reason for this apparent oversight is the emphasis on a "project-based" mentality around the application infrastructure in most organizations.

The development and stewardship of a global component library does not come free of charge. Most application development activities are individually financed projects that must meet deadlines and budgets of their own and that have self-contained and clearly defined (if not clearly understood!) deliverables. Such an approach is clearly not conducive to the development of a global approach. If components are developed by one project, how will the management of that project feel the benefit of their reuse? Such considerations lead to the introduction of artificial commercial constraints, back-charging between projects—some of which have already been finished—and all sorts of utterly meaningless complexity.

If it is to be managed globally in such an environment, then the application infrastructure must be managed as a project itself. The problem with this is that such a project will not have a self-contained product, nor be demonstrably self-financing, and will hence require a leap of faith on the part of the management holding the purse strings to be fully accepted.

5.2.4   Reuse of classified components

Because of such difficulties, we can imagine that there is little chance of achieving an effective, practical level of component management within most real business organizations. However, if we further refine our approach to the point at which all components are managed at the level most appropriate to their nature and that conceptual similarities are only enforced where relevant, then a clear case can be built for global management. The basis on which such a method will be built needs further explanation, during which the role played by a clear understanding of metadata will become apparent.

Imagine, once again, our car manufacturer. If it has the time to reflect on the abstract nature of the components used in all its cars, the company will recognize certain recurrent concepts. Cog wheels will be used for a variety of purposes within the cars. They will form components of the gearbox, transmission, steering, and other subassemblies in a modified form. The car maker has a very good understanding of what each of these things does individually and of the laws of nature that govern the behavior of intermeshed toothed discs rotating on axes through their centers. In this way, they can manage the actual instances of cog wheels such that they are similar enough to fit the conceptual model and hence to behave in a predictable fashion, at the same time as being different enough each for their own distinct purpose.

We can begin to see that, in analyzing its components in this way, the car manufacturer is building up a classification hierarchy that can be used in turn to formalize the essential similarities and important differences between each pair of components.

What is rarely done in real-world engineering, possibly because the costs would generally outweigh the benefits, is to ensure that this "model" is optimized. By this, I mean that there may be more differences between a cog wheel and a clutch plate than strictly necessary to fulfill their purposes. A tradeoff is made where it is determined whether it is better to optimize the individual component at a low level or a high level in the hierarchy. If this level is set too high, then conceptual purity may have been gained at the expense of introducing cumbersome and unnecessary constraints on the behavior of individual components. If the level is too low, then there is little benefit to be had from the analysis at all. In general, for car components, this consistency is managed at a "medium" level to ensure that the components are common to the point where companies can benefit from bulk prices from their suppliers, without it profoundly affecting the individuality of their different models of car.

For software development, the case for optimizing this classification of similarities and differences is much stronger. The "buying in volume" argument exists more strongly, since once a piece of generically applicable logic is developed, there is little marginal cost each time it is used for a different but appropriate purpose. Also, unlike engineering, where there is a vast real difference between the specification and implementation of a component (a spark plug and a blueprint of a spark plug are two radically different things, conceptually), there is little such distinction in the world of application development. Formal representations of logic, where sufficiently complete and robust, are capable of being interpreted directly by the computer and therefore essentially become the logic. A program written in a third or fourth generation language can be considered both as a representation or "picture" of the logic and the logic itself. The gap between specification and implementation can be said to have disappeared.

5.3   Developing a component-driven approach

The world of IT (as opposed to IM) is gradually working toward a situation where reusability of system components is being taken seriously. The emergence of middleware standards such as common object request broker architecture (CORBA) and distributed component object model (DCOM) is ensuring that the deployment of IT systems is at last beginning to look like a mature, predictable, and (most importantly) effective discipline.

These so-called middleware facilities provide a common means of exchanging complex data objects between diverse systems. The means by which they achieve this is perhaps best typified by CORBA, which is being developed by the Object Management Group (OMG). This standard provides a framework for separate platforms to exchange "objects" in a predictable and standardized manner. Each participating platform makes use of a so-called object request broker (ORB) process that manages the communication and exchange of objects with peer ORBs on other systems. This general concept underpins a great deal of the advances made in the area of middleware and simplifies the interfacing of complex system components.

Perhaps most significant from a business point of view is the way in which effective ORB technology underpins so-called process-ware technology. An example of process-ware is CrossWorlds, a middleware product enabling different packaged business software modules from the likes of SAP, Baan, and PeopleSoft. This type of product provides cross-application business process functionality, utilizing a "hub-and-spoke" approach to the communication between the individual ERP tools. For instance, a company may decide that the sales and distribution functionality offered by SAP's R/3 package matches its needs best but that the human resources capabilities of PeopleSoft are more appropriate.

Most significantly, the process-ware approach allows modules from the individual tools to be implemented on a "mix-and-match" basis, while still allowing effective integration to be achieved. This is done at the business process level, rather than the technical level adopted by more traditional generic interfacing products. This allows a degree of transparency and flexibility not previously possible, improving intersystem operability and reducing overall development costs where a "best of breed" approach is adopted to choosing individual functional modules. The closer such middleware products come to being agents for business object types (as opposed to technical object types) the more important a thorough understanding of the underlying metadata becomes for their successful deployment.

To understand the objects that are manipulated by such tools, the business concepts that each object is representing must be understood both at the generic and specific levels. In order to control the correspondence between the differing levels of abstraction, it is most convenient to see the objects in the form of a hierarchy. We might start by considering the generic object BUSINESS PARTNER and specify a subclass CUSTOMER, a sub-subclass CASH CUSTOMER, and so on.

For this hierarchy of logical components to be useful to the enterprise, and most particularly useful to those charged with the construction of systems within it, it must fulfill certain criteria. As with any other "instrument of policy," it must be widely accessible, it must be timely and accurate, and it must be well-understood, both by those who steward it and those who use it as a reference source. The role of metadata analysis in such a scheme lies primarily in ensuring that a sufficiently broad understanding can be achieved to make such a component model generally useful and hence to bring the benefits of ultimate reusability.

To understand further the way in which a library of metamodel objects will be used, consider the following scenario. A developer within an application replacement project has a need to develop a system controlling a certain aspect of a manufacturing process. As part of this development activity, the developer will have to specify and implement a piece of logic that maintains the instructions used by the operators of the manufacturing plant concerned when they make a new batch of product.

The organization for which they all work is concerned with the manufacture of certain chemical compounds that are made by mixing certain basic compounds together in large vats, under a specific set of physical circumstances. The system being specified will enable the plant operators to reference the methods that they need to use to produce these chemicals, to log any differences that occur from the standard procedure, and thus to provide a quality-enhancing facility within the production process.

The analyst begins by trying to understand some of the basic concepts involved in the process of mixing a new batch of the chemical product. After a period of reflection and consultation with users, the analyst develops the following list of issues that are important to this activity:

1. What are the basic raw materials used?

2. In what proportions are they used?

3. How much of the end product is required?

4. Is the production process split into stages?

5. What are the physical constraints under which mixing takes place? At what temperature? At what pressure?

6. Do these factors differ by stage?

7. Is the order of stages critical?

The analyst, being perceptive, recognizes that these concerns are similar to those faced by a cook in the process of preparing a meal and decides to talk to a colleague who has been busy with a system for the recording of recipes onto a database, for use in the plant kitchens. Working with this colleague, the analyst develops a database structure for the new application, using those parts of the kitchen system that are relevant to the chemical plant and adapting those parts that are not. This analyst is exhibiting the sort of behavior we might expect from someone who has a thorough understanding of the metamodel and the inherent similarities between these apparently diverse applications.

Getting away from this slightly improbable scenario, we can see how useful a mechanism is one that allows people to reuse not only those things that are rigidly defined as identical but that are somewhat similar. It cuts down on the development time for the new production system and makes it possible to avoid a lot of the mistakes that were found and corrected during the construction of the kitchen system. Furthermore, it means that there will be the possibility, in the future, for people with experience in maintaining the kitchen system to also work on the IT side of the plant system, with only minimal retraining appropriate to the real differences between the systems. In an extreme case, it might also mean that, when the employers are looking for a new plant operator, a sous-chef with a yearning for a change in career might be a good candidate, since the conceptual basis for the two sets of work is so similar!

The metamodel library will be extended to include a reference to the new meta-object "chemical recipe," which will have structural and behavioral similarities with the original meta-object "food recipe." They will both be signaled as subclassifications of a more generic concept "recipe," which will define the extent of their similarities. The more precise concepts will be used to define the minimal extent of their uniqueness and hence their necessary differences.

5.4   The price of reusability

Trying to assess the financial impact that the introduction of reusable components will have is a difficult process. Clearly, in the long term, we must anticipate that reuse of logic and data structures will be advantageous. However, when this discipline is first being introduced into a commercial environment, the costs associated with adapting existing working practices within the IT development teams, possibly reengineering the legacy systems to improve their reusability, can seem quite significant, compared to the eventual advantage gained.

There is no magic answer to the problem of selling the culture change required for reusability to take hold. However, a few tactics have proved successful in the past in helping to get over this hurdle. They include an emphasis on the independence between data design and process design. Once users and developers get used to the idea that applications and databases do not necessarily "belong" to each other but form part of a corporate pool of data and logic that can be made use of in different contexts, the concept of generic reusability will begin to take hold.

Clearly, a lot will depend on the approach adopted by developers. The importance of metadata (in terms of a catalog of data and logic that is already available) should be sold heavily into the IT community. Once they recognize that this is an issue that is not going away, the use of the metadata catalog to avoid reinvention of the wheel should follow naturally.

For the business community, presentation of analogies, such as the car manufacturer mentioned in Section 5.2.4, should let nontechnical personnel see the common sense of the reusability approach and the importance that metadata plays in it (although probably not mentioned by name).

Also aimed at the user community, it may sometimes be useful to present a quantitative case, based on previous experience in application and database development. To sell the idea of reusability and to highlight the fact that it will bring hard-dollar benefits, it may be worth determining the cost effect that reusability would have had on projects conducted in the past. To do this with any credibility will require involvement of someone with a very solid knowledge of the existing business application portfolio, but it will provide a strong argument if business is arguing that the introduction of metadata-driven reusability is a nebulous, academic concept.

In the early stages, it is vitally important that the data is truly designed to be reusable. Getting off to a false start will lead very quickly to complete failure of credibility within the business, and possibly IT, community.

5.5   The metamodel library

Having defined a common basic metamodel, we can use it to begin to build up a series of definitions for generic situations that are common-place in the building of systems. Because the common basic metamodel provides a standard not only for the behavior of data, but of events as well, these definitions can be used to form the basis for libraries of process structures and data structures.

Indeed, one of the great strengths of the metamodel approach is that it allows us to treat data and processes as homogeneous where it is appropriate and convenient to do so. In the ultimate case, we can envisage being able to generate both logic and database structures using the same mechanism, thus avoiding much of the complexity inherent in a software engineering approach and bypassing the problems caused by data/application dependence in one fell swoop!

Consider the following examples, one that defines a generic approach to a type of process, the other a generic approach to a data structure. Both can be used in a variety of situations without changes to their fundamental structure. The great strength of this particular approach is that, once a given situation is recognized as belonging to a category of problem, the solution is predefined. For instance, a designer or programmer who has dealt with control loops within an electronic model should feel equally at home with the analogous concept in an accounting context!

The main questions to be faced if we adopt this approach will no longer be concerned with "how" we implement a solution to a given problem but "what" type of problem it is. Thus, once an extensive library of such metamodel components has been built up, a larger and larger proportion of the problems faced will be identifiable as of a type that has been solved previously. By reusing individual solutions, or recognizing that a new problem is a compound of several presolved issues, considerable savings can be made in terms of development cost, and the robustness of the overall system is much more likely to be preserved as it develops.

Most fundamentally, this shift of emphasis also implies that the focus of skills within a typical IT department will have to shift from being centered on the solution of specific problems to the recognition of generic solutions to whole groups of related problem types. For the analyst and the IT manager alike this will require, at least, some refocusing or retraining to improve their awareness at a different level of abstraction. At worst, it will result in some individuals being intellectually unsuitable to a progressive role in the IT department at all. The ability to think in conceptual terms and to relate strongly to the business needs for data are by no means widespread; neither are such skills closely akin to the more traditional need within IT for analytical purity and precision of thought.

Sections 5.6–5.8 present three case studies detailing a series of meta-models applicable to various parts of an enterprise's activity. What characterizes these models is the way in which a single concept can be applied to diverse parts of the business. This highlights the value of maintaining a conceptual overview, enabled by a thorough understanding of metadata, and the way in which this overview can be applied in a concrete and cost-effective fashion.

5.6 Case study 1: Matrices

5.6.1 Background

A common construct that appears in a wide variety of business situations is the matrix. By developing a general model for the matrix metastructure, we can, as before, ensure that the basic rules that apply to the handling of such constructs are applied in every relevant circumstance and that time is not wasted on reinventing the processing required to control them.

Let us start by trying to understand the general structure of a two-dimensional matrix. Then we will extend the metamodel to include the n-dimensional case.

A two-dimensional matrix comprises a grid within which the cells contain values, the significance of each being denoted by its position vertically and horizontally within that grid. The basic values connected with this construct are, therefore, the following:

1. The variable determining the significance of a particular position on the x-axis;

2. The variable determining the significance of a particular position on the y-axis;

3. The value taken by the x-axis variable for each row;

4. The value taken by the y-axis variable for each column;

5. The value contained in the cell itself at the intersection of each row/column pair;

6. The significance of the matrix as a whole.

5.6.2 Entities

More formally, the entities that are expressed in this metamodel are listed as follows:

- MATRIX;

- ROW;

- COLUMN;

- CELL.

The MATRIX entity defines the context of the matrix, its meaning, and structure. This entity will contain the following attributes:

1. An identifier for the matrix, being the primary key of this entity;

2. A descriptive text indicating the purpose of this matrix;

3. An indicator determining the originator of the matrix design;

4. An INDIVIDUAL who maintains business ownership for the matrix, as a metastructure, if appropriate.

It is important to note that the cardinality of the matrix (i.e., the number of dimensions that it has) and the actual content of each cell within it are determined dynamically. The first is determined by the number of instances of the AXIS SLICE entity (see Section 5.6.3) associated with it, the second by the number of CELL ATTRIBUTE instances associated with the matrix.

The ROW entity (a specific case of the AXIS entity for a two-dimensional matrix) defines the nature of the notionally "vertical" discriminator on a two-dimensional grid (i.e., what makes one column of the matrix distinct and important as regards the other columns?). The ROW entity will have attributes as follows:

1. An identifier for the matrix concerned, forming a part of the primary key for the ROW entity, and a foreign key reference to the MATRIX entity;

2. An identifier for the row of the matrix that it represents, forming the remainder of the primary key for the ROW entity;

3. An optional value associated with the ROW (for instance, the year number, if the rows represent an annual time series);

4. An optional descriptive attribute, defining the significance of the ROW.

The ROW entity is, in fact, a special case of the AXIS SLICE entity, which is discussed in more detail in Section 5.6.3 below. The COLUMN entity is identical in structure to the ROW entity and represents a further subtype of AXIS SLICE. The CELL entity is a "header" for each instance of the entries within a MATRIX. As such it is identified by a combination of the MATRIX identifier (a foreign key reference) and foreign key references to each of the AXIS SLICEs that intersect at its location in the matrix (in the two-dimensional case, ROW and COLUMN).

5.6.3   The generic matrix model

The discussion in Section 5.6.2 assumes that the matrix is inherently two-dimensional and that the CELL possesses an atomic value that is stored within the CELL entity itself.

If we extend this concept to allow for the n-dimensional case, then a new entity AXIS is introduced to explain the significance of each axis. Another new entity, which we shall call AXIS SLICE, is introduced to represent the individual "slices" of the matrix determined by a specific value being taken on a particular AXIS. In the two-dimensional case,

ROW and COLUMN form subtypes of the AXIS SLICE and are thus eliminated from the generic model.

A further refinement can be introduced to allow a CELL to be non-atomic in nature. This means that each cell, instead of having a simple, interpretable value, can in fact be a structured, complex entity in its own right. To allow for this, an entity called CELL ATTRIBUTE, which represents all those atomic data that can be associated with an individual cell, is created in the model. The list of allowable CELL ATTRIBUTEs is defined at MATRIX level, which assumes that all CELLs within a given matrix have the same attributes. (If this is not the case, then a further refinement is necessary.)

The actual values that are the "essence" of the matrix are stored within the intersection between CELLs and the CELL ATTRIBUTEs, which we shall call CELL ATTRIBUTE VALUE. The relationships that are included in our final version of the metamodel are discussed in Section 5.6.4.

5.6.4 Relationships

The relationships included in this final model are the following:

1. A MATRIX has its cardinality determined by the existence of one or many AXES.

2. An AXIS reflects one dimension of one, and only one, MATRIX.

3. A MATRIX has the atomic values taken by its cells represented by one or many CELL ATTRIBUTEs.

4. A CELL ATTRIBUTE represents one atomic datum that is of relevance to each cell of one, and only one, MATRIX.

5. An AXIS has its scope determined by one or many AXIS SLICEs.

6. An AXIS SLICE represents that subset of a matrix determined by a fixed point on one and only one AXIS.

7. A CELL is identified by one or many AXIS SLICEs.

8. An AXIS SLICE is composed of one or many CELLs.

9. A CELL ATTRIBUTE VALUE represents the value of an atomic datum relevant to one CELL.

10. A CELL has the value of its atomic data represented by one or many CELL ATTRIBUTE VALUEs.

11. A CELL ATTRIBUTE VALUE defines the value, in a cell, of one, and only one, CELL ATTRIBUTE.

12. A CELL ATTRIBUTE has its cell-dependent value defined by zero, one, or many CELL ATTRIBUTE VALUEs.

For concrete examples of a matrix structure being built, the instances of AXIS SLICE will generally be represented by explicit entity types, as will the cell. This, in turn, provides a generic approach to resolution of certain many-to-many relationships (themselves indicative of matrix-style relationships).

Note that it is possible to construct more elaborate models, based on the MATRIX concept, to represent other related ideas. For instance, by extending the way in which a cell behaves to include the ability to take referenced values, or formulae, we can begin to build a model for a simple spreadsheet.

5.7 Case study 2: Work planning

5.7.1 Background

In many areas of an enterprise's activity, there is a need to keep a record of facts such as the following:

- The work that has to be done;

- The amount of time that has been planned to do it;

- The people whose responsibility it is to do the work and to supervise it;

- How close it is to meeting the original plan.

Once again, there is a generic model that can be defined for this type of activity and used as the basis for work monitoring applications in many varying contexts.

5.7.2　Entities

The initial list of entities that are within the scope of such a metamodel are listed as follows:

- UNITs OF WORK, which can be recursively decomposed. It should be possible to denote which of the units are at the "bottom" of the hierarchy, since this will be the level at which details about the progress of the work will be managed. A variety of pseudonyms can be used for this type of concept, some of which are general; others refer to a specific "level" of the hierarchy, by convention (e.g., TASK, PROJECT, JOB, or PROJECT PHASE).

- RESOURCES, in general, to perform the work. Subtypes of this entity may include the following:

  - PEOPLE;

  - MACHINES;

  - SPACE;

  - RAW MATERIAL.

- Each of these will be administered as separate entities but can be treated in the whole as a superclass from the point of view of their dependencies within a planning framework.

5.8　Case study 3: Control loops

The concept of a control loop is characterized by the ways in which an action is performed, a test is made on the success or otherwise of that action, and, possibly after some corrective measures are taken, the action is repeated, followed by the test, and so on. This pattern is applied to "safety measures" in many apparently unrelated areas.

5.8.1　Examples of control loops

In manufacturing, a serial process might be controlled by such means, ensuring that if a product reaches a certain stage and appears unsatisfactory, then it must be returned for some corrective measures, followed by a retest. Similar processes apply in the management of financial records, in scientific experimentation, and even in judging certain sporting activities. As with many of the case studies in metadata analysis that follow, the aim is to enable the reader to understand the commonality of such activities in a way that will enable the processing relevant to that commonality to be reused across apparently unrelated applications.

Let us start by considering the basic concepts involved in the implementation of such a control loop—the points that bind the diverse uses of this mechanism together—described as follows:

- The control takes the form of a test, or series of tests, and the action to be taken in the event of success or failure (possibly several different types of failure) must be expressed.

- The circumstances under which the test takes place and what event triggers it must be defined.

- The agent that executes the test is defined, together with the person responsible for determining its success or failure (if different).

- There may be a limit on the number of times a test may be repeated before the process is terminated (for instance, by the batch of product being permanently rejected).

5.9 Further examples of reusable constructs

There is an almost infinite variety of other reusable contraints that can be applied to common business problems. The degree to which a generic understanding of this type is necessary will vary from one business or industry to another.

5.9.1 The hierarchy

One of the most common types of metastructures found in business is the hierarchy, where an instance of an ENTITY is related in a predefined way to many other instances of the same ENTITY. This structure has several uses, of which probably the most common and well-understood are the "decomposition" and the organizational hierarchy.

In the first case, the relationship between the "parent" instance of the entity and the "child" instance is that the child forms a distinct part of the parent. Examples of this might include the process decomposition, breaking down a set of activities into simpler and simpler subactivities or an organizational structure that defined work groups as part of departments and departments as part of divisions, etc. Note that, in this latter case, although the various levels are referred to by different names, they are conceptually similar and can hence be thought of as instances of the same entity.

The organizational hierarchy relates the parent and child instances together with a tie of "responsibility." This is characteristic of a rigid organizational structure, such as may be found in military organizations, where a person is wholly responsible for a group of others, some of whom in turn will have supervisory responsibilities of their own. In modern commercial organizations, the reporting relationships are often more akin to a matrix, where individual A reports to individual B for one part of his or her activities and to individual C for some others.

5.9.2 The bill of material

The bill of material concept seeks to express the precise nature of the components needed to create an instance of some more complex entity and the manner in which they should be combined.

This concept is a generalization of the hierarchy discussed in the previous section, since each component can form a part of many different hierarchies, and there may be variable numbers involved. This can be extended to a general "construction" model where there is an ordered series of actions and possibly multiple components under varying conditions.

5.9.3 Logical tests

There are many examples of a formalization of program logic already available. Indeed, most programming languages are elaborate versions of the need to define a basic syntax to describe actions that are taken under particular circumstances. The languages themselves are defined and described by so-called metalanguages, such as Backus-Naur form, which enable a precise description of their syntax to be made. The purpose of including this area in a general study of metadata is to address the need for a means to express with some precision the tests and decisions that form a vital part of so many other aspects of the metamodel.

It is, of course, possible to simply describe the conditions under which a control loop, for instance, operates in textual form. More formally, one can include as an attribute the reference to a piece of program logic that performs the test. Both of these methods at least recognize the need to control the consistency of certain tests, but they do not necessarily make it any easier to do so.

5.9.4 Program logic

If we extend the requirement to record the nature of certain tests to a more general one to be able to analyze large and complex sequences of logical instructions, then there are clearly more appropriate means to achieve this. These include the use of high-level languages themselves, or at least pseudocode representations.

5.9.5 Journeys and movements

The movement of goods or people from one geographical location to another is yet another common concept for most organizations. Although there are obvious differences between the way in which rail passengers are treated and the management of containerized freight on bulk carriers, there are a surprisingly large number of similarities as well!

In each case, the organization concerns itself with the items to be moved, their source, their destination, the means of transport, and the timing of the journey. They are also interested in the costs of the journey and who is meeting those costs, the possibility for splitting it into subjourneys, the existence of the necessary paperwork, and the condition of the items at each stage.

5.10 Application development

Many of the concepts that are embodied in a well-considered metamodel are used to assist in the business of managing the IT infrastructure within an enterprise. The metamodel provides a record not just of what the systems present in an organization are doing, but what they were intended to do and what they would do ideally, given the right circumstances.

The entities that we have studied, especially within the DATA MANAGEMENT metamodel, form the basic concepts of interest to systems analysts, when they are defining the context and operation of a new system. They model ENTITYs and their ATTRIBUTEs; they define the business rules that will constrain the new system, in the form of RELATIONSHIPs between the ENTITYs, and they use process DECOMPOSITION as a means of describing the modularity of the application being constructed.

In the past, this analysis was done longhand. For the last few years, so-called computer-aided systems engineering (CASE) tools have been available to assist in this process, by providing a friendly, graphical input mechanism that doubles as a drawing tool and by fulfilling certain "book-keeping" functions for the analyst.

There are several problems commonly faced by organizations that have adopted CASE tools as a basis for their systems development. These problems have often led to a certain lack of enthusiasm for the tools in particular and for an analytically robust approach to systems development in general among their staff.

The early CASE tools provided several facilities intended to automate, or at least facilitate, the process of system construction. These key components usually include a graphical front end, fulfilling two distinct (and not necessarily complementary) purposes. First, it enabled the analyst to draw diagrams of various sorts (process decomposition, data-flow, entity-relationship, etc.) that were already in place as part of many "standard" systems analysis methodologies. These diagrams were interpreted and the metadata derived from them stored in a database (or knowledge-base as they were sometimes known). This emphasis on diagramming enabled analysts to manipulate their metadata in graphical form, rather than reconstructing laborious pseudotextual analyses. Second, and most distinctly, diagrams were produced from the metadata-base that represented the analysis done. A fundamental problem with the use of CASE tools lies in the confusion that exists in many people's minds between the diagram input and the diagram output, as we shall term them.

The diagram input is, as we have said, a means by which the analytical information can be captured using predominantly graphical rather than textual means. A relationship is recorded by drawing a line between two entity boxes on a screen and defining a title, cardinality, etc. for the relationship so created. This is clearly a simpler method than recording in some formal data-description language the rules binding the two entities together. However, it is debatable whether it has any virtues at all over the creation of a simple metadata record, by selection from lists of predefined entities, in a modern GUI environment, without recourse to any diagrammatic representation at all. Indeed, in some cases, the physical and aesthetic constraints imposed by the need to understand the finished diagram cause a considerable waste of effort on fine-tuning. The input diagram is interpreted and validated by the tool and is stored in a structured form in a database as metadata, in fact.

The output diagram is not, in general, a copy of the input diagram but is an interpretation of the formal structure recorded in the metadatabase. While this might seem a rather academic point, it is important for (at least) two reasons. First, by removing any implication that the input diagram and the output diagram are closely codependent, or even identical, we can consider each on its merits. One is used to store metadata, which as we have said can probably be done more efficiently and effectively by other means. The other is used to provide a visual representation of the metadata to simplify communication of ideas. We can envisage a CASE-style tool, therefore, with structured nondiagrammatic input and diagrammatic output without becoming concerned that we are somehow breaking the rules.

Second, it provides the key to why an understanding of metadata is so important in the proper analysis of systems, both manual and automated. Metadata lies at the heart of all CASE systems, and many other types of system development aid. Much of the dissatisfaction with these facilities is caused by the expectation that they will simplify and improve control of software development projects. The important aspect here is not the CASE tool itself but the metadata. By understanding the way in which metadata works, the tools that are bought to manipulate and control metadata can be understood and thus used properly.

It also means that, by constructing a simple metadata-base in-house, it is possible, in the right circumstances, to achieve the real results expected of CASE (admittedly without diagrammatic output), without the need to invest in (usually very expensive) proprietary software.

5.11   Business process development and reengineering

One of the main messages of this book is the need to consider data as key to the operation of any business. The way the data behaves and is used throughout the enterprise is key to the ongoing efficiency and ultimately the success of that organization.

Much is talked about the way in which, by considering and radically redesigning the business processes, the performance of an organization can be radically improved. What must not be forgotten is the way in which data and metadata play a role in the success of such endeavors.

Business process reengineering requires that a thorough understanding of the existing operation of a business be built up to implement controlled and beneficial change. Before such levels of understanding can be reached, the data itself must first be understood and the way in which data is used by the existing processes analyzed and documented.

Without proper definitions of the major business entities, it would be impossible to reengineer the business processes to ensure that unnecessary "handoffs" are limited. These handoffs, or transfers of responsibility, occur when the flow of a process passes from one part of an organization to another. A good business process reengineering activity will seek to ensure that such transfers are limited to those that are strictly necessary (e.g., for formal control) and that the organization is restructured to simplify the flows where possible. For instance, if a piece of work is passed back and forth between two separate departments on multiple occasions, then a strong case exists for combining the work into a single new department, with closer working ties and simpler lines of communication.

Good metadata management underpins good business process reengineering, since process management relies on a common understanding of the information being processed (that is, common business rules and data definitions or metadata). Without effective metadata control, it would be impossible to state with any authority that what is handed over by one organization is, at a conceptual level, what the receiving organization thinks that it is getting!

Successful implementation of business change requires common understanding not only horizontally (between people fulfilling different functions, for instance) but vertically (between those in strategic levels of management, tactical management, and operational personnel). A strategic decision to reshape the business in a particular manner must be translated into practical steps to be taken at the operational level. Without a framework to refer to, the likelihood for misunderstanding is high, and the chances that such misunderstandings will be effectively resolved are limited. A well-structured and well-understood metadata-base will provide such a framework that can be referred to and refined as the cascade from strategic to tactical change is deployed.

5.12 Legacy systems and the mapping problem

We have established that one of the major challenges facing businesses across the spectrum is the effective management of change. In most cases, it is very unlikely that change will take place on a global level. Rather, aspects of the "new order" are phased in to work alongside the "old order." Before long, just what is in each section is forgotten, as the change process itself evolves in some other direction in response to business circumstances.

As this scenario progresses, it becomes increasingly important to manage the differences between the various "generations" of tools, processes, and computer systems that are, at any one time, supporting the organization. An understanding of metadata concepts is once again key to the effective management of such chaotic situations, since it allows the individuals within an organization to determine the static points (representing some "universal" or "static" truths about the business) and hence to manage the volatility elsewhere.

Proper metadata management is key to providing a bridge between the old and the new in the area of legacy system control. If subject area views are built, not only for new systems and activities but for those that have been preserved from previous eras, then the way in which the old and new interact can be better documented, better understood, and inevitably better managed.

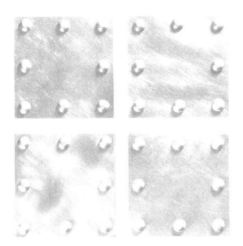

6

Metadata in Data Warehousing and Business Intelligence

I N MOST LARGE ORGANIZATIONS, the deployment of IT systems over the past 20 or 30 years has taken place to service the needs of individual departments or functional groups. Typically, the systems that have been bought or built to meet these needs have been designed or evaluated in a local context, relevant to the scope laid down by the clients for the system, and highly focused on their business concerns. In many cases, this degree of focus has been critically important for ensuring that IT projects concerned with application development and deployment remain under control and that the resulting systems are well-suited to the needs of their clients.

Two significant trends have led, over recent years, to a breakdown in this insular view of data management within IT deployment activities. Increased integration between applications has gained favor in many large organizations. This integration can take the form of closer coordination of function and data content between previously distinct business applications (e.g., production control systems and general ledgers) or of automation of the information supply chain from data capture through transaction processing to provision of management information, within a data warehouse, for example. These two forms may be referred to as *horizontal* and *vertical* integration, respectively.

In the first case, the use of highly integrated, packaged applications—ERP systems such as SAP R/3, Baan, and PeopleSoft—has focused attention on the way that data, as well as processes, can be integrated or made to conform to a common set of rules. These systems aim to offer a wide view of the business activities and combine data from diverse sources in a cohesive and reusable way. The spread of ERP systems as a practical alternative to self-built "islands of functionality" has been instrumental in forcing the IT and user community to think more carefully about the ways in which one part of their organization may interact with others.

A second factor that, although rather different in its intended purpose, has had a very similar effect, is the popularity of data warehousing. Once again, data warehouses aim to offer the user an integrated view of the organization, coupled with the ability to manipulate and analyze data from diverse sources. Clearly, to be capable of this, the data warehouse concept must be underpinned by a cohesive set of rules governing the way in which the data content behaves. This chapter explores in detail the way in which an effective understanding of metadata is a key factor in the success of data warehousing projects.

6.1   The data warehouse paradigm

The concept of data warehousing has been developed to define a model for the provision of information within typically large and complex organizations. The phrase was coined by Bill Inmon, in his seminal work on the subject [1], to describe a situation where data is brought into a central point, controlled and improved in quality, and dispersed (also in a controlled fashion) to a variety of users.

This model may not seem to differ that radically from the more traditional approach to decision support systems. For many years, separate databases have been built downstream of major transaction processing applications, reflecting the information of those systems, but separate from them for reasons related to performance or control. To understand the real distinction between data warehousing and basic decision support, a clear understanding of the concepts is required. In fact, the phrase *data warehouse* is used to convey not just the model itself but the hardware and software technology that has made the manipulation of very large databases possible in recent years.

The basic problem that data warehousing was defined to address is that of a more sophisticated user, who may need to draw data from a variety of sources and perform complex operations on this data. These operations typically center on statistical (refining patterns from the bulk of past data) or predictive (extending these patterns to model future possibilities) analysis. In the base case, where the operational computer application had been developed separately and had its own standards for both data and metadata, such analysis has always been problematic.

Unless data can be drawn together and made to conform to a common pattern of behavior, there will be difficulties. Data must be made accessible to all users whilst preserving both the consistency (ensuring that one entity in the real world can be identified as such) and the integrity (ensuring that the business rules constraining the data are obeyed, even across multiple source systems) of the data as a whole. Without such control, anyone requiring a broader view of the corporate information base would need to build in his or her own consistency checks (effectively relying on what we might call self-built metadata).

This do-it-yourself approach will bring the benefits of enforced consistency to a broad view but will not impose any control over the consistency between views. The problem of seeing enterprise-wide data as a single cohesive picture still remains, but the possible inconsistencies are now more visible to a higher echelon of people within the organization.

Effectively, this is taking the familiar "islands of automation" problem and making the same mistake in the context of metadata. This is, of course, inherently wasteful, since the effort of imposing these rules would be duplicated across many users. It would also be error-prone and inherently incomplete, since few users, even the more sophisticated, would have sufficient knowledge or self-discipline to impose truly "neutral" business rules on the data. Nearly everyone, when faced with this problem, falls back on their biases, built up over the course of their careers. A marketer would see a customer as someone to sell to; an accountant would see a customer as someone to bill. While not wrong or mutually incompatible, these views of the entity CUSTOMER are inherently incomplete and biased, which will inevitably lead to problems when large-scale, enterprise-wide reporting is attempted.

The analogy that Inmon chose to describe the new model for information provision was a warehouse or distribution center. In a real-world warehouse, goods are received from a supplier at a goods-in bay. At this point, they are checked to ensure that the quantity and description match the purchase order and that they have been delivered undamaged. If the quality is acceptable, they are taken into the warehouse and stored. The location and description of each batch of goods is recorded to ensure that they can be accessed and retrieved easily.

At a future point, the goods are removed from the warehouse and shipped to a customer or a smaller, satellite distribution point to meet a local need. Once again, checking and control are necessary to ensure that the correct quantity and specification of goods are dispatched. As we can see from Figure 6.1, a data warehouse environment, as envisaged by Inmon, bears a strong resemblance to this model of "real" warehousing logistics.

Data is gathered from a variety of source applications and databases (the suppliers) and taken into a staging area (the goods-in bay) where the quality is checked. Once we are assured of the data's timeliness, completeness, accuracy, and conformance with the standards laid down, they are accepted into the data warehouse proper and stored for future use. This journey from the source database into the warehouse is often described as an extract, transform, load (ETL) flow, and the availability and use of metadata are critical to the successful execution of these data flows. The data flows themselves can be triggered by a "push" from the source system (effectively, the source application gathers the data and signals to the ETL tool when it is ready) or a "pull" from the staging area environment (control of the overall transfer process is exerted from the data warehouse). As a general rule, the pull approach suits complex environments better, since it supports metadata control from a central point on the architecture. This leads to a simpler and more robust design and improved control of the transfer process. In some cases, ETL tools that

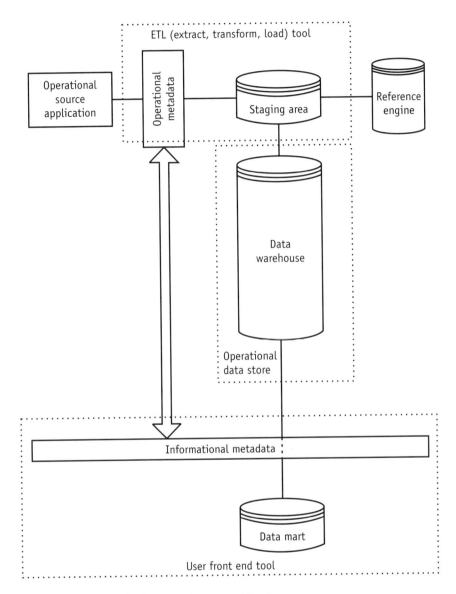

Figure 6.1 A generic data warehouse architecture.

interrogate the source system metadata directly are available. This is applicable to specific source database management system (DBMS) technologies (e.g., the ETL tool may be able to make use of Oracle system tables) and will thus not be true in the general case. It is worth noting that, although there are not as yet any universal standards for metadata sharing, some ETL tools provide a wide variety of protocols for sharing metadata with specific source DBMS technologies.

Eventually, the data is moved out from the warehouse environment, either to a smaller, localized store (a so-called data mart, analogous to a local distribution center), or directly to the user who requires the data for analysis and reporting (the customer). Once again, if the end user is to have a clear, complete, and universally applicable view of what the data means and how they have been constructed, then metadata have a key part to play.

These two distinct types of metadata will require separate facilities to ensure their control and propagation. The first type, known as operational metadata, will be predominantly of interest to IT personnel charged with the design and control of ETL facilities. The second will require more delicate handling, as they relate to the perspective that end users will have on the information within the data warehouse. This second type is known as informational metadata.

Informational metadata also has an important part to play in the control of data marts. The key point of data warehousing is the ability to bring the whole scope of the enterprise (at least as far as information is concerned) under a common set of controls. By doing so, consistency can be achieved at both data and metadata levels.

Consistency of data, in this context, implies that the contents of the data warehouse are free from redundant data (e.g., two different records representing the same customer), code duplication (e.g., the same customer identifier being given to two different customers—very common if the data are sourced from multiple systems), and erroneous data.

Metadata consistency extends this to ensure that the data content obeys a common, consistent set of business rules. For example, it defines the meaning of the term "customer group" and ensures that it is applied consistently wherever it is used in the data warehouse. It also defines the rules for referential integrity and ensures their consistent application. If, for instance, an account must have an associated currency that is one of an approved set, then this rule is checked and enforced before the data are allowed within the warehouse environment.

The data within the data warehouse environment is quality-assured, usually within the staging area that acts as the entry point for data. The same cannot be said, however, for data marts, since the refragmentation of data is inherent to the whole idea of marts. If the marts are designed as nonupdating environments (as is usually the case) then there should be no issue with the integrity of data breaking down, even though there are multiple copies in existence. Care must be taken, however, to ensure that the metadata are propagated into the mart environments at design time in a controlled and complete fashion.

The technique of data marting, or drawing off limited subsets from the main data warehouse and using the information they contain for focused business needs, is quite common in the context of business information provision. Data marts prove very useful where the following conditions exist:

1. The data must be segregated to improve the performance of the system from the user perspective. This is nearly always a significant issue with data warehousing. By limiting the scope of the database (and hence its size), significant advantages are achieved.

2. The data must be secured from unauthorized access by the simple expedient of maintaining a physically separate copy within a data mart and restricting the use to which data is put. This does, of course, imply that direct access to the data within the main warehouse itself will be forbidden (in the so-called mart-exclusive data warehouse architecture).

3. It is important, on occasions, to strengthen the concept of ownership within the database. Some part of the organization should feel overall responsibility for the content and structure of each mart, effectively taking ownership of it on behalf of the enterprise as a whole. The provision of a physically distinct, bounded environment can help significantly in such a case.

This reversion to the situation where databases are kept physically distinct from each other can clearly bring benefits, but there is a price to pay in the reintroduction of possible inconsistency, which can negate the whole basis for installing a data warehouse environment. By allowing physical separation of data into compartments, to be used by different groups within the business community, the ability of the organization to control data consistency from the center is diminished.

The first step that can be taken to address this problem is to ensure that the data mart environments remain read-only. By depriving users of the ability to change data, the contents of the data marts should remain as they were at the point of exit from the data warehouse. In this way, data consistency can be preserved.

The preservation of metadata consistency is more problematic. If the business rules are to be applied consistently across all data marts, then the design, construction, feeding, and use of all marts must be subject to common, central control. If the builder of such a feed decides to ignore a particular rule, the impact should be small since the rule will have been checked at the point of entry into the data warehouse. However, rules may be adapted to specific purposes. New rules may be introduced that contradict the rules within the data warehouse. Interpretations of the rules that may be misinterpreted by users (e.g., renaming customer types as customer groups, because the users like the name, even though the customer group concept has been globally defined as something different). In such cases, metadata consistency will undoubtedly suffer.

Experience shows that the data mart approach is very widespread within data warehouse installations. Many organizations recognize the particular benefits that such an approach brings, without considering the impact of uncoordinated mart development.

Marts are (quite rightly) seen as a quick and relatively inexpensive delivery mechanism for fulfilling business information needs. If these advantages are not to be outweighed by the reintroduction of inconsistent data and metadata, then steps should be taken to avoid uncontrolled deployment.

A coordinated, architected approach to data marts, bound together with a practical application of data and metadata control techniques, can yield the required benefits without endangering this consistency. The core problem that has to be faced is how to ensure this metadata consistency and what tools are available to help in this area.

6.2   Approaches to data mart deployment

The data mart has been described above as a subset of the data contained within a warehouse, extracted into a separate environment. Although it helps us to understand the basic problem that the possible fragmentation of metadata will bring, this top-down approach is by no means the only method used to deploy data marts, or even the most common.

In many cases, the data marts are designed in the absence of a full-blown data warehouse from which to source data. Indeed, the deployment of data marts can be seen as the primary activity, an end in itself. It is easy to see how such an approach can be defended. After all, the marts are fundamentally user-focused and as such deliver the basic benefits of a data warehouse environment in manageable chunks. This splitting up of the problem also has the significant advantage of enabling each part of the development effort to be economically justified. In most commercial environments, the possibility of building a full-scale data warehouse environment is limited less by technical constraints than by the perceived cost of implementation. If this cost can be spread across a number of efforts, each with a tangible, identified, and quantified benefit, then the chances of success are significantly increased. By maintaining a tight focus on particular business problems and working toward a new architecture in evolutionary stages, the costs involved are distinctly easier to justify, than by seeking financial support for grandiose schemes.

In this context, the data warehouse becomes a clearinghouse for data on its way to the marts, effectively fulfilling little more than the purpose of a universal staging area. This in itself is by no means a fundamental flaw, provided that effective metadata control is in place at the entry and exit points to this area (operational and informational metadata control, respectively). The practical difficulties of achieving this control without a physical, persistent data warehouse to impose and preserve the integrity of the overall database should not be overlooked.

It is important to point out that there is not, at present, a wealth of tools to assist in the process of metadata control and that many of the tools that do exist are either embedded within, or dependent on, the database or ETL tools themselves. This lack of openness will cause further problems in complex, diverse environments, even where metadata control tools can be identified.

Therefore, both the top-down and the bottom-up approaches to data mart deployment have significant disadvantages. The adoption of an approach predicated on a pre-existing data warehouse would undoubtedly be more expensive to implement and more complex to design and deploy and would raise significant financial and political difficulties along the way.

The mart-driven, bottom-up approach appears more pragmatic, but the dangers of reverting to uncontrolled, independent systems presenting isolated, mutually inconsistent versions of the "truth" should not be understated. Also, it must be remembered that the boundaries between these marts are liable to vary over time. Without a central, coordinated data warehouse, and the metadata to control its contents, it is unlikely that such flexibility will be achievable. In addition, the requirement to deploy independent data marts quickly can lead to a focus on sourcing from individual operational systems, rather than taking an enterprise-wide view. This will further diminish the value of the resulting system as a generic, universally applicable tool.

A third, hybrid approach, known as the *federated warehouse,* seeks to combine the advantages of both the bottom-up and top-down deployment techniques, while limiting the dangers. In this model, the concept of autonomous data marts, controlled by a common core of metadata, may coexist with an enterprise data warehouse (EDW) dependent on the same metadata. The possibility for building further independent marts or for extending the EDW and drawing further, dependent marts from it, can both be supported. This approach is more complex that the other two but has the virtue of incorporating the advantages of both.

However, because of its inherent complexity, it is also the most thoroughly dependent on metadata control for its successful, continued evolution. Metadata will be used to ensure that a common picture of the data is defined in all the destination data marts, whether they are dependent on or independent of the EDW.

Generally speaking, metadata fulfill three major functions at each stage of the data life cycle within a federated data warehouse environment. In the first place, they provide a common language for defining the behavior of data. The formal metadata syntax allows robust definition of the business rules and meanings associated with the data that is being transferred from the source operational systems to the EDW and eventually to dependent or independent marts. This is closer to the traditional view of metadata, describing how, for instance, sales orders and customers are related to each other, ensuring that the term customer group has a consistent, universal definition and that the set of values to be used for currency codes are all defined.

Second, metadata control the data flows themselves. The operational metadata will contain not only definitions of the data but formal descriptions of the flows which occur, the rules governing data transformations, dependencies between transformations, and timing factors affecting the execution of the data transfers. The fact that the customer masterfile within the EDW is loaded from the sales order processing system on a daily basis and that it must follow the daily load of general ledger data and be followed in turn by the load of sales orders together with details of how any possible duplicate customers are removed from the flow in the process are all described in the metadata.

Third, metadata will communicate the nature of the data within the warehouse environment to users and IT developers with a need to understand the business basis for warehouse data. In one sense, this is merely the ability to access the definition and control data described above, but it is vital that the proliferation of metadata throughout the technical and nontechnical communities is managed in an effective and understandable fashion. Figure 6.2 expands the generic architechture (shown in Figure 6.1) to describe a federated data warehouse in operation and to indicate the points at which metadata is critical to the success of the system.

The EDW can fulfill a number of distinct roles in this type of architecture. In the first instance, it can simply be the superset of all data required by the dependent marts that are extracted from it. This provides a very safe, thorough mechanism by which the quality of data can be put under consistent control, within the marts, but evidently represents a significant level of data redundancy.

Each data item included in the EDW will, in such a case, occur also within at least one of the mart structures. While it must be remembered that a significant amount of data redundancy is to be expected in a data warehousing environment, it may represent an unnecessary overhead in this case.

In such a case, the EDW will start with a narrow scope of data, sufficient to ensure that the first mart to be implemented has the contents it requires and that these contents will obey the metadata constraints that

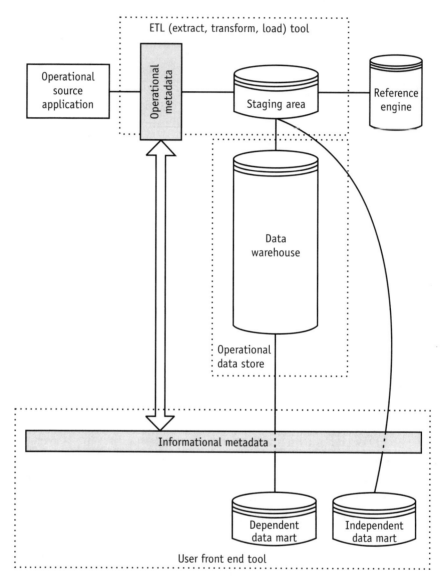

Figure 6.2 The federated data warehouse.

will be imposed by future extensions of the ETL boundary. Figure 6.3 diagrams the way in which this type of EDW is built up.

In Figure 6.3, the *x* (horizontal) axis represents the business scope of applications, or marts, within the scope of the data warehouse. The

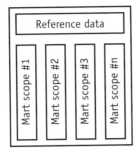

Figure 6.3 Mart data scope.

y (vertical) axis represents the amount of detail that is stored within the data warehouse environment for each part of the scope. Each vertical slice represents the data associated with a mart, and the total scope of detailed information provided by these marts evolves incrementally over time. The horizontal block, *basic reference data,* at the top of Figure 6.3 is a small portion of common data that effectively future-proofs the first mart deployments without implementing a full-scale warehouse in the first instance. As more marts come on stream, the vertical blocks within the EDW fill up and complete the true enterprise-level scope for the data content.

Alternatively, the EDW can form an enterprise-level data mart, providing a broad but shallow view of the data. It will help to understand this concept if we consider the basis on which a large proportion of data warehouse access is based.

In many cases, data warehouse applications are built to enable users to navigate their way through various levels of the database, seeing different tiers or levels of detail. A user may wish to drill up and down between a national-, regional-, or city-based view of its business, or between annual, monthly, and daily sales totals.

By defining the EDW as a "broad but shallow" mart, the implication is that it will cover a large swathe of the enterprises business but be limited to the higher levels of detail. The marts drawn from it will be restricted in the same way but will be more focused on specific functional areas or business activities. These marts contrast with the independent marts, which will allow significantly greater "drilling up and down" through the various data hierarchies. In either case, it must be emphasized that the compatibility of these marts with each other, and with the EDW, is dependent on the quality and extent of metadata used at each stage in the data warehouse process.

All business rules implied by the EDW, or by the operational metadata applied within the staging area, will be inherited by the lower-level marts, in an ideal case. Thus, the possibility for putting a different, conflicting interpretation on the data in the marts from that implied by the operational metadata is minimized.

In summary, the operational metadata define and control the global business rules that are enforced on the data as it enters the data warehouse environment. Once within this environment, the interpretation that is put upon the data by users is governed by informational metadata, which also ensures that the behavior of data in the separate data marts is mutually consistent.

In practice, this implies that metadata must be explicitly managed at a number of levels, described as follows:

- The rules contained within the operational metadata must be controlled to ensure that they are correct, that no necessary rules are omitted, and that no rules that are included as universal are, in fact, partial.

- The rules within the informational metadata must be presented in a form that is easily understood by the end user of the data—the prime purpose of this metadata is to ensure that the user can access and manipulate the data efficiently and correctly. This will not happen unless informational metadata is robust and simply presented in business terms.

- In addition, a control mechanism should be in place to ensure that the operational and informational levels of metadata are consistent *with each other!* If this is not the case, then the metadata is acting to degrade data quality rather than improve it.

6.3   Operational metadata

Operational metadata exerts an influence at the incoming boundary to the data warehouse environment. It determines the acceptability or otherwise of data that is sent to the warehouse and controls the process by which such transmissions are made. Significantly, it also offers the means by which systems developers, seeking to extend the data warehouse, can understand the developments that have gone before.

It is fundamental to the nature of a data warehouse environment that the scope of the system will be in a state of constant flux. Changes in business circumstances, new front-end reporting and analysis tools offering new opportunities for examination of the data, and the realization that the consistency and completeness offered by a data warehouse can significantly benefit many parts of the enterprise will all contribute to this need for constant evolution.

This being so, it is vitally important that these changes, which are so fundamental to the nature of a data warehouse can be made efficiently—using techniques that have been developed for other purposes—and safely—remaining consistent with the business rules defined for previous "slices."

Systems developers (and, to a lesser extent, users) will rely on the pool of metadata developed for previous slices during the building process. Operational metadata to support this constant extension of the data warehouse should include the following entities (at minimum):

- APPLICATION ENTITY, defining the tables that exist within the source application and that are accessed to find the data to be transferred into the warehouse;

- APPLICATION ATTRIBUTE, recording the individual fields that are used as source data from the APPLICATION ENTITY;

- TARGET (WAREHOUSE) ENTITY, providing a neutral, enterprise definition of each entity within the data warehouse environment;

- TARGET (WAREHOUSE) ATTRIBUTE, providing a neutral, field-level definition of each data item;

- TRANSFER DATAFLOW, defining the end-to-end flow relating to an independent segment of work within the data warehouse load activity;

- TRANSFER JOB STEP, a subdivision of the TRANSFER DATAFLOW, enabling the developer to understand how the transfer will work, in what order the steps are taken, and under what circumstances they are considered successful;

- APPLICATION, defining any computer system acting as a data source;

- TRANSFORMATION, an activity, generally at the TRANSFER JOB STEP level, that changes the structure or content of some portion of the data being transferred;

- PHYSICAL DATA STORE, recording the actual source, intermediate, and destination files used within the transfer;

- RULE, (at its simplest) describing the constraints that are placed on each item of data (generally at the attribute level) as it passes into the data warehouse environment, possibly including validity checks, range checks, complex dependencies with other attributes, date and time dependencies, or other external effects;

- DEPENDENCY—specifically dependencies between TRANSFER JOB STEPs—adding further sophistication to the work flow concept, enabling the developer to define the order in which job steps take place (also records the need to finish one work step before another is started or, conversely, the possibility for performing the work in parallel, where appropriate). Clearly, a more sophisticated implementation of this feature would be possible within project management software, such as Microsoft Project™. It is also worth considering the extent to which the ETL tools will enable the recording and control of these work flow models.

These metadata elements are all basically static (in other words, they will not change unless there is some change made to the data load process itself). As such, they are not affected by the content or size of the source and target databases, nor by other external influences.

Several companies offer tools that can significantly enhance the capability to manage this operational metadata. In some cases, the tools (such as those offered by Prism, ETI, and Acta) combine the operational metadata management with sophisticated ETL capabilities, effectively subsuming the staging area within their scope.

These types of tools rely heavily on the capture and management of metadata. They are sold as efficient mechanisms for developing and controlling the ETL sequences but are in fact significant advances in the area of automated metadata management. In some cases, the basic metadata model has been extended to include dynamic features that provide information on such factors as data volumes, volatility, load run times, and flags set in the source systems in readiness for data transfer.

Whether static or dynamic, the metadata that controls the extraction, transformation, and loading of data is captured via a graphical interface, enabling the developer to see the data loads in diagrammatic form, building interdependent jobs and identifying and choosing source and target data fields from menus, etc. Without a robust, underlying metadata model, however, it would not be able to control the loads effectively, no matter how sophisticated the front end of the ETL tool may appear.

6.4 Informational metadata

By contrast, there are very few tools that are aimed at controlling and presenting the informational metadata. The information required by end users to make a balanced judgment about how to use the contents of a data warehouse to service their business needs is far more nebulous than the specification and control of dataflows.

Essentially, informational metadata is provided to ensure that each user has a consistent, well-understood picture of the contents of the data warehouse environment and that they can use this to formulate an appropriate method for meeting their business information needs. In a particular case, a business analyst may have a requirement for reporting sales volume and revenue figures over time, for a variety of customers and products.

Data warehousing software will provide analysts with the means of constructing such analyses and manipulating them in a variety of sophisticated ways. This will only be inherently useful to the analysts, however, if the assumptions that they are making about the data are correct and well-understood. The informational metadata must therefore incorporate answers to questions such as the following:

- Does the official sales volume figure net out returns of faulty goods?
- Does the revenue figure include or exclude sales taxes?

- Are the figures for a particular time period based on the calendar, or on financial closings?

- Do customer groups refer to holding companies (i.e., real owners) or to some generic similarity between customers?

- When someone in another department talks about product types, to what is he or she referring?

Clearly, even for such a relatively simple report, the potential for misunderstanding and misanalysis is great if the answers to these questions are unknown and unobtainable. It is the job of the informational metadata to control and proliferate answers to these questions, thus ensuring that the users of the data warehouse and data mart environments are working according to a consistent set of rules.

In practice, there are few tools on the market that handle the informational metadata-base in a generic manner. Most offerings in this area are deeply embedded within the tools that provide the decision support facilities to the end user.

Recently, however, a new type of metadata management tool has been introduced to the market. These tools, typified by the MetaExchange™ system from Pine Cone Systems, aim at the large-scale data warehouse market and seek to respond to a need for companies to control metadata along the entire chain of BI systems.

MetaExchange™ endeavors to integrate the metadata from a variety of systems, taking different perspectives into account. The source systems for data, the data warehouse, and the marts spawned from it will all have autonomous data models that are managed as a single library. In addition, the technical, operational, and informational metadata are managed in a cohesive fashion to ensure that the rules that are embedded within them remain compatible.

The physical sharing of metadata is achieved by means of middleware interactions with a so-called metadata hub. Standard protocols, such as CORBA and DCOM, are used to enforce object-level consistency, and emerging standards for metadata definition, including XML, are supported. The purpose of this hub is to control sharing of metadata (via these mechanisms) and business data (by supporting a common neutral business data model). The control of business data is reinforced by the concept of identified *systems of record* for each part of the overall business database.

6.5 Decision support and OLAP

Once the data have arrived within the data warehouse environment, there is clearly a need to extract them in a form that can be easily and powerfully manipulated by end users, the consumers of information. These information consumers come in a variety of types, broadly defined as follows:

1. Basic users, requiring standardized reports from the warehouse environment on a regular basis to highlight fixed types of information.

2. Exploratory users, who need to be able to view the data at a variety of levels of detail, manipulating them to determine the patterns of behavior within the business. This user typically makes heavy use of the "drill-up" and "drill-down" facilities within an online analytical processing (OLAP) tool. The work performed is used to make or contribute to tactical level decisions within the organization.

3. Analytical users, who need to be able to perform sophisticated statistical analyses on the data, determining the correlation between different business factors and making or contributing to strategic level decisions as a result.

These different types of users form a BI continuum, effectively defining a spectrum of needs, ranging from the basic to the sophisticated. The manager of a data warehousing project has the responsibility for identifying which of these groups of data consumers exist within the organization and what tools can service their needs.

This brings us back to the inherent problem with informational metadata, which is that each BI tool will generally have an embedded mechanism for controlling the metadata that fulfills a focused purpose but does little to guarantee consistency across the enterprise. Bearing in mind the likelihood that the data consumers will be spread widely across the BI continuum and will thus require different tools, this can present a major problem.

6.6 BI tool type 1: Multidimensional OLAP

The first category of tool that should be considered is the so-called multidimensional OLAP (MOLAP) facility. These tools utilize a multidimensional model of the data and allow navigation from one level of detail to another online, in real time. As an example, these tools would offer the ability to see sales figures broken down by sales area by year. The user would be allowed to change the level of detail dynamically, by drilling down into a given year to see monthly figures and into months to see daily figures. Similarly, the user could break down the sales areas into districts and individual customers. The point of OLAP tools is that this flexibility is provided in real time, *regardless of the amount of recalculation needed.* Bearing in mind that data warehouses typically contain vast amounts of data, the ability to be able to present summaries at different levels, while maintaining acceptable response times, is clearly a nontrivial problem.

Imagine a data consumer who would like to view a worldwide sales matrix, giving volumes by country, by product line, and by time, along three axes, or dimensions. This user has a further requirement to be able to "drill down" from a country into a regional level and from there into a city level, having the sales figures along the other two dimensions dynamically updated in real time. This user may further require the facility to drill down on more than one dimension simultaneously, jumping from a national product line view to a regional, individual product view of the same base data, once again in real time. Bearing in mind the number of records involved in making these calculations for a large company (assuming the ability to drill all the way down to individual sales order lines), there is a considerable problem in delivering the necessary speed to the end user.

For this reason, some vendors have abandoned the traditional relational database technology and have implemented OLAP tools based on a multidimensional model. The database engines for these arrays or "cubes" of data are generally proprietary, close architectures. It is not possible to access the data using SQL, since the structures employed within the multidimensional databases are not relational. In most cases, the vendors have implemented proprietary mechanisms within the DBMS to ensure that the online response times can be minimized. As a consequence, neither the data nor the metadata (in the form of systems tables) are directly accessible via industry-standard relational access tools based around SQL. Table 6.1 shows a typical multidimensional model.

Each dimension listed in Table 6.1 represents a characteristic type by which the user may wish to analyze the data. The tiers are the levels of detail to which the user may navigate, and the measures are numeric data that may be aggregated across any or all of the dimensions.

Because of the closed nature of such tools, and because of the targeting of these tools toward particular groups of analytical users, facilities to manage metadata on an enterprise-wide basis are rarely incorporated.

6.7   BI tool type 2: Relational OLAP

A further category of decision support system (DSS) tools have evolved to service the needs of data consumers typically at the lower end of the BI continuum; these tools draw directly from a data warehouse or mart environment. These relational OLAP (ROLAP) tools have the advantage over MOLAP tools in that they do not require massive extra storage, since the data is not physically copied from the mart environment. From our perspective, this means that the metadata within the mart level can be accessed and are directly relevant to the eventual use made of it.

Table 6.1
Multidimensional Model

Dimension	Time	Product	Customer
Tier 0	All time	All products	All customers
Tier 1	Year	Product group	Customer type
Tier 2	Quarter	Product category	Customer
Tier 3	Month	Product	
Measures	Sales revenue, sales volume, number of items returned		

ROLAP tools do, however, have significant performance disadvantages over MOLAP, which is often a critical factor for large data warehouse implementations.

ROLAP tools, such as Business Objects™, have limited metadata access as part of their report design and construction facilities. Since they rely on direct access to their source relational database for their reporting abilities, they must in turn have some degree of access to the native metadata within the source DBMS itself. In the case of Business Objects, this metadata is accessed to build so-called universes, or views of the data from which formal or ad-hoc reports can be produced. The universes can in themselves provide a means for formalizing and recording metadata, at the risk of introducing yet another version of the "truth" embedded within it.

6.8   Informational metadata summary

If the relational approach is adopted, the possibility for "self-built" metadata control and proliferation should be considered, since the metadata themselves is both relatively simple and easily accessible within the data dictionary of most industrial strength relational database management systems (RDBMS). The following entities will need to be controlled and proliferated around the enterprise to ensure that users have a clear view of the informational metadata:

- Entity within application;
- Aliases—alternative names for entities and attributes—ensuring that there is common understanding of the business rules, despite the use of different jargon within the enterprise;
- System of record (the single system that represents the authoritative source for each item of data);
- Attribute within application;
- Global entity;
- Global attribute;
- Domains;

- Volumes;
- Cardinality;
- Volatility;
- Dimensions;
- Tiers;
- Measures;
- Nonmeasure attributes.

6.9 Metadata management and proliferation within a data warehouse

Most current implementations of data warehousing solutions include separate metadata repositories within the application from which the data is sourced, within the ETL tool, and embedded within the OLAP or DSS front end.

Often, certain parts of this metadata-base are shared across tools (for instance, the source data dictionary may be accessed directly by the ETL tool to define source attributes), while others are independent and isolated.

In theory, there are several approaches that can be adopted to ensure metadata consistency:

1. Adopt a universal metadata control tool that will maintain active consistency between the various repositories—unfortunately no such tools exist at the time of writing.

2. Rely on the bilateral sharing of metadata between the various components along the information supply chain—this will provide a partial solution but is likely to exclude some of the more "user-facing" elements of metadata control.

3. Build automated tools that check on the consistency of the various repositories and produce control reports for the data architect to examine and use to take action. This may well prove effective but will require companies to build a profound knowledge of

the internals of all the individual metadata repositories along the information supply chain.

4. Define a combination of manual procedures, documentation standards, and automated facilities that will enable effective consistency to be managed. For many companies, this will be the most practical approach in the medium term.

If we adopt the "hybrid" approach (4), the whole process will be driven by the documentation and interlinking of metadata entities. This can be achieved in a number of ways:

- *On paper:* The simplest to implement but the least controllable and updatable mechanism—likely to be significant drawbacks;

- *Using a work flow tool (e.g., Lotus Notes) to record the various metadata entities as separate document types and to utilize the built-in look-up features within the tool to maintain some sort of integrity:* Will also ensure that the metadata is accessible to developers and users alike;

- *Doing the same sort of thing as an intranet implementation—once again, a good method of sharing metadata—by setting up linked pages, or possibly a simple intranet-accessible database, containing metadata for the enterprise:* Open access that is simple and quick to set up and reasonably easy to use (if well-designed);

- *CASE tools (likely restricted to the "technical" end of the metadata spectrum):* Contain extensive metadata but tend to be tailored for use by systems analysts and people with a solid understanding of data modeling, rather than the general user population, which can severely restrict their use for proliferation of informational metadata;

- *Building a dedicated metadata management utility from scratch:* Probably overkill, and it requires a very peculiar combination of skill to design and build such a tool!

6.10   Conclusions

In the longer term, the management of metadata across a data warehouse environment will always present a significant problem, certainly with the existing technology. The basic issue is how to ensure that the behavior of the data—which arrives within the warehouse environment and is transformed and loaded into separate data marts, restructured by OLAP and DSS tools, and then separately interpreted by users—remains consistent.

At each stage, the possibility exists for reinterpretation of the business rules that govern this behavior, introducing inconsistencies. These inconsistencies will be carried forward into the reports, leading to errors of judgment, misreporting of statistics, and time wasted in trying to reconcile apparent conflicts in the figures.

All of the above are included in the list of problems that data warehousing has set out to solve! We therefore need to ensure that the metadata, which defines and controls the behavior of data at each stage, is under control and consistent.

Reference

[1]   Inmon, W. H., *Building the Data Warehouse,* Wiley-QED [Technical Publishing Group] New York, 1993.

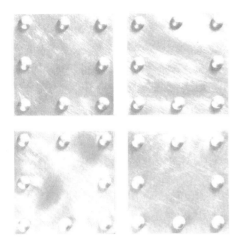

7

The Role of Metadata on the Internet

7.1 Information storage on the Internet

No one can deny the profound impact that the Internet has had on the world of information over the last few years. The ability to access data on a variety of subjects has clearly been improved by the resources of the World Wide Web to the extent that it is in danger of becoming a victim of its own success. As more data becomes available, the process of finding specific information becomes more complex—the sheer amount of data available to the Internet user is seen as both the greatest strength and the greatest weakness of the medium. The fact that anyone can search through a vast number of pages using standard search-engine software and obtain listings of relevant sources of information is the single feature that has transformed the Web from a technological curiosity to a common, universal medium for information exchange.

Once new Web users get over the wonder of being able to search through such vast swathes of information, they are likely to begin experiencing mild irritation at the manner in which the searching is performed. Many searches on the Web are beset by the same set of characteristic problems:

- The search results returned are incomplete, owing to the inability of the search software to interpret the match criteria in a context sensitive fashion.

- Too much information is returned by the search engine.

- Lack of intelligence exists in the search engine, or possibly in operators (or users) in constructing their criteria for selection.

There are, at present, no common standards for the way in which information is defined within the context of Internet pages. Up to now, the whole emphasis within page construction has been on the appearance and document level structure of each page and the way in which navigation between pages has been achieved, rather than any inherent concern for what the pages actually contain by way of information. The structure and basic content of the page is defined by the constructs embedded in hypertext mark-up language (HTML) and its later derivatives and extensions.

With the arrival of Java as a major means of defining program logic within an Internet context, possibilities have opened up for more intelligent handling of data. It should be recognized, however, that Java only provides the same level of robust data control through metadata as third-generation languages (such as COBOL) have for traditional transaction processing systems (sparsely, and at the programmer's discretion).

The content of the pages, in any meaningful sense, is not defined or controlled in this area, with the exceptions of a few standard HTML constructs defining:

- The familiar hypertext link itself, typically indicated by blue, highlighted characters;

- Substructures within the page, such as titles and dates;

■ The ability to explicitly recognize e-mail addresses.

This lack of inherent structural control, which we now see as a lack of underlying metadata models, contributes significantly to the relatively constrained way in which search engines currently operate. Imagine these constructs being extended to cover (unique) tagging of the following entities:

■ People;

■ Countries and other geographical entities;

■ Companies;

■ Public bodies;

■ Academic institutions.

Clearly, some benefit would be felt from the ability to categorically recognize instances of these metadata entities. The lack of such tagging leads to much Web searching being inherently error prone. Someone with an inquiry on these types of entities uses a search engine, expecting an exact match with the text string input as the search criterion. Some of the more sophisticated search engines might take into account small mis-spellings, phonetic similarities, etc. If however, the person, institution, or company has changed names, it is very likely that the chain of historic information will be lost, unless it is picked up explicitly by the user (e.g., "I know that company B used to be called company A.") or the provider ("I'll insert a link to the old company Web site before the take-over.") of the data. If an authoritative, permanent, and neutral reference to these types of entity were provided, it would significantly improve the completeness of a typical trawl through the Web for information.

7.2   Setting standards for data

In principle, of course, no one would disagree with the basic notion of maintaining this common reference system for Web-based metadata. In practice, however, the issue of how to develop and control such a set is beset by problems.

Within an organization, however large, it is nearly always possible to establish a formal procedure by which data should be controlled. Very often, however, this process is far more difficult to implement and maintain over time than was originally envisaged.

If, instead of considering a single enterprise, the scope of this problem is expanded to encompass the full scope of public domain data, the complexity becomes vast. Not only have we lost the capability for the internal control (by use of what we might loosely term corporate discipline) upon which we can rely within large organizations, but the problem itself has become significantly larger in scope and more complex.

By the scope of the problem, we are including the overall set of activities that need to be considered to maintain the coherent set of interrelated data items needed to run the business. One major problem that arises as we expand the scope of data control is the need to consider other related data types within a classification hierarchy. For instance, if we begin by wanting to control subscribers to a service, we have to recognize that these people may also be employees, providers of service content, etc. Instead of controlling the metadata (in particular the coding sets and business rules) for subscribers, we end up having to control the much broader (and more nebulous) concept of "people." At each stage, the developer of a coding set to identify data has to face the choice between the cost and complexity of a generic approach (e.g., coding for all people—a problem that many national governments have failed to address!) and the likely reworking of codes when the full breadth of the problem becomes apparent.

Similarly, the World Wide Web requires a deeper consideration of metadata to encompass a truly global set of data. If someone is to define the formal rules for identification of companies, for instance, he or she must be sure that it is universally applicable, not merely an American or European standard that is grafted onto the rest of the world.

There are three fundamental questions that need to be answered to make this paradigm shift toward content-based rather than structure-based Web page management:

1. What formal mechanism is to be used to enable definition and formalization of metadata elements within Web pages?

2. How will the standards for these new mechanisms be defined and policed?

3. How will the next generation of search engines be able to make use of these constructs?

7.3   Extensible mark-up language (XML)—the beginnings of metalanguage

The first hints that the Internet environment is maturing to the point of having a structured approach to metadata control is with the definition of emerging standards for the so-called extensible mark-up language (XML).

Like HTML, XML is concerned with the definition and structure of Web pages. The key differences between the two syntaxes lies in the focus that XML has on the meaning, or context of elements within the page itself, rather than HTML, which is concerned predominantly with the layout and cosmetic appearance of Web pages.

As a point of reference, it should be noted that the XML syntax is, in fact, a subset of standard generalized mark-up language (SGML-ISO 8879). SGML is designed as a completely universal mark-up language, enabling the definition of document standards for anything and everything that may be recorded and shared between organizations. XML has been defined as a simplified subset of SGML, avoiding the complexity of total generalization, while presenting a much richer and more flexible environment than HTML.

Put another way, SGML is generic language for defining document structure in all its guises. Many SGML *applications* exist, defining specific dialects of XML for types of documents in particular circumstances. One such SGML application, defining simple, hierarchical document structures with hypertext links between them, is HTML. XML is a defined and limited subset of SGML, enabling practical application of the generic protocol without undue complexity. It remains compatible with SGML at all levels (and as such is, inherently SGML itself) although without the full capabilities of the parent language.

An analogy might be to consider SGML as a natural language—French, for instance. XML is a student-level French dictionary, enabling a wide and flexible range of communication in that language but not, inherently, defining the French language in full. HTML might be considered analogous to the French legal system, which makes use of the French language to define a set of rules (the legal framework within France and some other countries), as such being a broad application of the French language rather than the language itself.

The already familiar HTML defines the structure of a page using "tags" to separate out the elements of the document and define their purpose within certain, predefined limits. Certain of these tags take the form of metadata, controlling the subset of page elements relating to other pages, e-mail addresses, etc.

XML generalizes on this idea by opening the tag concept to the definition, in principle, of any metadata elements within the page. The number of possible tag types within the XML protocol is, in theory, infinite. The proliferation of tag types will, of course, require control, per se, but this will be at the metadata level, rather than the data level, an inherently less complex and costly activity.

To summarize, XML expands and extends the context of basic page mark-up, as offered by HTML, because of two important factors:

1. Focus on page content rather than cosmetic appearance. Whereas the HTML tags are concerned with distinguishing between page header and the body of text, XML may be used to define parts of the page as company names, chemical formulae, trademarks, people, etc. It is this emphasis on content that enables us to see XML as a true metadata tool, since it provides a structural basis for the behavior of information content rather than merely its appearance.

2. Extensibility of the language set. Clearly, if XML is to be used as a universal metadata definition tool, it needs to encompass formal definitions of all types of data that appear on the Internet! Doing this *explicitly* within the language definition will obviously be impossible, due to the almost infinite business scope of the problem. To get around this, XML takes a higher level of abstraction, defining and formalizing the mechanisms by which metadata will

be defined for specific areas, rather than defining the metadata itself. In other words, XML states that, if an application requires types of fruit, or makes of automobile, or building materials to be identified explicitly within a Web-page context, this is the framework that must be adopted to define these things. What XML is patently not doing is setting the data standards themselves. Rather, it sets metadata standards that are used by appropriate expert bodies (whether internal to a corporation or external—trade organizations, national governments, or global standard setters such as ISO) to define their own data standards, which can then be applied consistently and used by future search engines, etc.

Another key factor inherent to XML is the way in which it enables the same information to be presented to different types of users in different ways, once again by using a metadata-driven foundation. This is achieved by separation of content and structure. Content will be included in the Web page itself, written up in a relevant dialect of XML, and the structure to be applied to this content is held separately in a *style sheet,* which is defined in extensible style-sheet language (XSL), itself a dialect of XML. This two-tier arrangement ensures not only that the XML protocol can be almost infinitely extensible to incorporate different content types, but that "artificial" differences of interpretation can be avoided by allowing different views on the same content, where appropriate.

7.4   Current XML metalanguages

There are already several XML-based protocols in use within the Internet environment. These early takers have tended to have a technical focus. Mark-up syntaxes already in use, based on the XML metalanguage, include the following:

- Research definition format (RDF): Providing general-purpose Web site content definition and rating facilities, as a facilitation mechanism for research-based activities. These rating facilities provide a generic mechanism for scoring the relevance of content to a particular search query.

- CASE data interchange format: For inter-CASE tool communication, enabling metadata to be shared between different CASE tools—perhaps the most obvious use of metalanguage, at least for the data analyst.

- Signed document mark-up language: Provides a common standard for definition of Web-based documents requiring identifiable authorization by specific parties (analogous to signature of a paper-based document).

- Extensible forms description language (XFDL): Provides a syntax for definition of business forms, extending into work flow and document management tools.

If we extend the concept of XML as a metalanguage, to include the generic commercial model, we can see how the whole concept of content control on the Internet can be changed for the better.

7.5   The problem of data standards

One of the most visible and clearly recognizable problems associated with data quality in large organizations is the control of coding standards. At its simplest, this issue revolves around how to identify major business entities, such as customers, products, and suppliers. In principle, each real customer of an enterprise should be identified uniquely and consistently across the organization. Any analysis of the customer base in an enterprise relies on this inherent ability to identify single instances of data within the customer database and to associate them with single, real-world customers.

If the data and the reality do not correspond—for instance, if duplicate records exist for the same customer—then problems will occur. At best, every analysis of the customer will require that the multiple records are recognized as being the same real customer, causing extra effort. At worst, the problem will be ignored and incorrect conclusions drawn from the results of the analysis. The same problems can and do occur in just about every area of commercial activity.

The Internet, being inherently a public-domain environment, will need public setting of metadata standards (in terms of recognizing that certain bodies have responsibility in certain areas) and in maintaining the content of data within the Internet environment as a whole. For example, if we consider the concept of a "company," the questions that might be raised concerning formal definition and control in the public domain include the following:

- What body has responsibility for defining the identification of each company? Should it be central government or some governmental organization or other body? Should it be the company itself?

- What identifiers are used for companies? Should existing codes be used (e.g., VAT numbers or company registration numbers)? Are these universal? If not, how will exceptions be handled?

- What basic information should be recorded for each instance of the entity? Should we have a centrally maintained page for each company, detailing its registered address, appointed officers, public financial data, etc.? Who should be responsible for defining this and recording the information on a timely basis (e.g., the company itself or a public body)? Where should this information be stored?

- Are there subsets of information that should be treated as optional or that could be extended to meet specific needs (e.g., extra fields for publicly quoted companies)?

This list of questions can be extended almost ad infinitum. A clear message that arises from this is the need for someone to take control of the entire issue of metadata within the context of the World Wide Web and to manage it on behalf of the world in general. As this will undoubtedly involve a significant amount of effort and coordinating ability, it begs the question of what the motivation of such a body would be and how it would be funded. The immediate response would be to assign these responsibilities to some existing public body with a similar remit—for instance, the appropriate committees within the ISO organization, which currently set standards for such things as country and currency codes, or the World Wide Web Consortium (W3C).

Alternatively, a multitier approach could be defined, where basic overall metadata (that is, the tag types and their associated syntax for the highest levels of the XML hierarchy) would be defined centrally, and all other definitions would be delegated to appropriate bodies.

This second approach has, for the time being, been adopted as the basic model and is reflected in the standard-setting work currently being done by W3C. The infinite extensibility of the XML medium means that, at least in principle, anyone can be assigned appropriate responsibility for defining the structure of substructures within the metadata model, the tag types required, and the *domains* needed to support them. These domains define the set of values applicable to a particular usage of data and may be bounded (e.g., definition of the set of allowed values of currency code) or unbounded (e.g., structural definition of a telephone number).

For this to work effectively there will be some necessity to maintain object-style "inheritance" rules. In other words, once again taking companies as an example, the control hierarchy might be defined as follows:

- All companies in the world will be recognized by a certain tag, of the form <company>CompanyName</company>.

- The CompanyName should be the formally defined name, as registered with the authorities in the country within which the company is domiciled. A full identifier will be defined by the authorities in this country and will take the form COUNTRY_ID + COMPANY_ID where COUNTRY_ID is the ISO alphabetic-3 country code, and the COMPANY_ID is a unique code within each country, assigned by that country's authorities.

The responsibility within each country can be further delegated and split (for instance, between limited liability companies and publicly quoted companies and partnerships). As long as the boundaries between these levels of responsibility are unique and do not overlap, and the properties of the coding structures are consistent with the higher levels, conflicts can be avoided, and the overall coding scheme can remain under control.

In much the same way as naming conventions for Web pages are currently defined uniquely worldwide, it would be useful if a basic fact sheet were maintained, on a page that is identified using the COMPANY_ID, embedded into a Web address (e.g., WWW.CO.COMPANY_ID.MET). The structure of this fact sheet would be fixed by an appropriate standard setting body and would record the basic company information and links to other, free-format pages (including, presumably, the home page of the company in question). The content of these fact-sheet pages could thus be specified as including the head office address in a particular format, the names of officers of the company, financial extracts, etc. in a predictable, standard form.

The advantages of such a standard, over the present chaotic situation, should be clear. The Internet will be evolving into a true public domain database rather than merely a collection of data, as at present.

7.6 The future of the search engine?

The profound impact this additional robustness will have on the operation of the Internet can be seen when we consider just how the operation of Web searches will be simplified. At present, a major source of frustration for anyone who uses the Internet in any but the most superficial way is the relatively primitive manner in which search engines operate.

In essence, mainstream search engines still work as little more than text-search mechanisms. At their most basic, the user may specify a word or words, and the search engine will return a set of page references that contain them. In some cases, the pages are ordered by relevance, according to some algorithm that may incorporate such factors as the following:

- Whether the search criteria appears in the header of the page;

- The number of instances of the word within the page;

- How early in the page the word is first mentioned;

- How many linked pages also mention the word.

This relevance ranking can help the user to identify the more appropriate pages. There is no attempt, however, in most cases, to place the word or words being used as the basis for searching in a semantic context.

For instance, the user may specify the string "JAGUAR" as the input to a search. The results of this will be a list of page references, some of which will refer to carnivorous animals, some to automobiles, and some to other topics unrelated to both. This is because the test that the search engine performs is simply "does the page contain the text 'JAGUAR'?"

For a moment, imagine an improved situation, where the search engine has the capability to recognize that some pages are referring to cars, others to big cats. The search engine, depending on its degree of sophistication, may do the following:

- Return separate lists of references to cars and animals;

- Perform the search, then ask a secondary question of searchers, to determine which category they are interested in, before displaying the results;

- Access some publicly available metadata-base or classification system, where it can determine that the phrase "JAGUAR" is a subclass of cars and a distinct subclass of animals. The search engine then asks a subsidiary question—are you interested in "cars" or "animals" or "general searching"—BEFORE searching the Web for results.

We can clearly see from this just how search-engine technology could evolve in the near future to become far more user-friendly and effective. The third option above is clearly the most sophisticated, requiring the existence of a metadata dictionary that would be constantly maintained to provide these generic classification trees. It is worth noting, however, that all three of these options require the sort of generic, versatile tagging provided by XML and inherently not provided by HTML. To state the problem at its most basic, for next-generation search engines to perform as described above, the Web-page definition syntax needs to allow for something akin to <car>Jaguar</car> and <animal>Jaguar</animal> (although probably not in that precise form!). HTML, by contrast, really only allows the search engines to imply that "Jaguar" is a *word* without any reference to its meaning or documentary context.

The next logical step we can take in our exploration of metadata within the context of the Internet is to see just how we can make use of the *context* that we are giving to these words contained within Web pages. Clearly, once this context is established and its integrity is assured by whatever means, then the content of the World Wide Web becomes data, rather than merely documents. The potential for a metadata-driven convergence between Web content and what has traditionally been database technology can lead us into an exciting new medium for data control and exchange.

It may well be observed that a considerable amount of information is already controlled and exchanged via the Internet. Up to a point, this is true, but the integrity (that is, the underlying quality) of the data relies on *explicit*, rather than *implicit* control and, as such (the Internet being what it is), is not consistently applied.

To explain further, an example of an implicit control is that enforced by a well-designed relational database. The rules that govern the data, ensuring that a sales order must have a valid customer, that the customer must have a credit limit, etc., are defined within the data structure itself (via metadata stored in system tables, data dictionary, repository managers, etc.). Any changes made to the database are forced to conform to these rules, and the database integrity is thus assured.

Explicit control covers rules that have to be deliberately checked each time a change is made to the data. This applies to most so-called information within the Internet at present. Even the most basic of integrity rules governing HTML-based tagging are not applied actively. The most obvious example of this is the use of link tags. The page referred to could have been deleted; its address could have changed; or its contents could have altered, making them irrelevant. In fact, the inclusion of a link tag reference does not imply that the linked page need ever actually have existed at all!

It is important to recognize that these problems cannot be solved by improvements to the query mechanism alone. Without massive improvements in the metadata infrastructure of the World Wide Web, users of query and search tools are left in a position analogous to using SQL to query flat files, when the mechanism was defined for efficient access to relational databases. This situation is very wasteful of resources and, at times, extremely frustrating. Without significant improvements in the overall quality and integrity of Web-data content, this waste will continue—a source of concern to all serious users of the Internet.

It should also be appreciated that this extra control will not come "free" but will require a degree of formal, explicit control not currently in line with the overall philosophy of the Internet. Explicit structure and configuration control will cost money to apply. Most likely, this will come from groups of corporate users with a vested interest in sharing data. The challenge will be to ensure that the issue of standard setting is not jeopardized by the introduction of unnecessary diversity by rival commercial interests.

7.7 One step further—DBMS Web integration

With a metadata infrastructure underlying the content of the Web, a much more robust approach to internal integrity can be assumed. A document that is structured using an XML dialect must conform to the rules of that dialect. We can thus be assured that the rules implied by the original definition are adhered to, that an engineering specification in the appropriate dialect will be interpretable by any individual or software designed for the generic purpose, and that where appropriate, the content will be matched against appropriate coding standards.

The next logical step from this is to make use of this inherent structure to allow queries against the content of XML documents. Standards are currently being proposed for a generic query solution. These currently include XML-QL, defined by Bell Labs, and a Microsoft-led proposal known as XQL.

Both of these will allow structured queries of XML-based documents, effectively extending the basic search capabilities currently available to include compound, algorithmic tests and comparisons, in much the same way as SQL operates on a relational DBMS.

A parallel approach to this RDBMS/Web integration is exemplified by the Oracle Corporation and its introduction of XML support within releases of their mainstream relational DBMS product. Oracle 8i incorporates sophisticated references to XML components, allowing basic transparency between traditional RDBMS and XML structured data.

Both of these developments seek to highlight the importance now being placed on enriching the structural capabilities of the Internet, such that the information contained within it can be shared and interpreted in a full business context, rather than being treated as purely a textual (and multimedia) resource.

On the subject of multimedia, another metadata-related aspect that is being worked on in the context of the Internet is the ability to define and record content-specific attributes of audio, video, and other such objects in an intelligent, predictable, and interpretable fashion. Having a library of video news clips available for public access is one thing, but enabling users to query this resource by such criteria as "find clips containing footage of Jaguar cars" or "find clips containing President Clinton speaking on economic topics" would clearly add massively to their usefulness. A multimedia content-based XML dialect would clearly enable such references to be made. It is worth heeding the warning, at this point, however, that such ease of use depends on controlling both the structure and content of pages at the metadata level. A common construct such as SGML or XML is clearly necessary for this but will not be sufficient without discipline on the part of those constructing pages or metadata libraries. More specifically, either all references to a particular person have to be in precisely the same form (e.g., <person>Bill Clinton</person>), or a metadata library of synonyms and homonyms must be maintained by someone. Only with this extra resource will it be automatically possible to ensure that all references to the following, for example, are treated as identical:

- <person>Bill Clinton</person>;

- <person>President Clinton</person>.

7.8 Summary—toward second-generation e-commerce

In summary, the advent of XML-based dialects that define the metadata for an infinite variety of information types will enable the Internet to finally deliver on its original promises. Full and effective use of the new mechanisms, coupled with an appreciation of the underlying metadata, will help to bring this about, provided that the people stetting the standards and deploying the Web pages address the key issues. These include the following:

- Control of Web-page contents: Some "formal" Web pages need to be standardized and recorded for each company, each product, or each service (in the form of a technical specification—not an advertisement!), with products, applications, and price lists.

- Control of layout to enable simple recognition of key data within the page and to allow automated analysis of content by the searching party. Imagine a Web user being able to frame a query as: "Find me companies that manufacture a machine component that I may be able to use as a subassembly for my product (specified as follows) and give me a list of the top five by price and/or market share." This highlights the gap between the Internet as a data collection and its potential as a true global database.

- Recognition that effective and efficient searching is key to gaining competitive advantage through Web presence. Companies should determine what types of query on their Web sites by potential customers will enable them to gain competitive advantage and work with the standard setters in their industry and with their internal Web-site developers to ensure that it will be possible.

- Ensuring that each object has supporting metadata enabling recognition of its type, domain, and content (this last being especially useful for searching out and identifying multimedia objects—natural language queries on graphic, audio, or video content).

Because the information contained within Web pages will be richly and formally structured, convergence between Internet and database technologies will occur, and because publicly accessible, agreed standards for a wide variety of document types will become available, many aspects of electronic commerce will be facilitated. Examples include the following.

- Electronic data interchange (EDI) via the Web will become a simple reality. Once common standards for major business document types such as purchase orders and invoices are defined as XML applications, together with appropriate control mechanisms, the old style, point-to-point EDI protocols will become an irrelevance, and e-commerce will take on a more realistic, pure market feel.

■ Archives of public-domain data will be inherently more useful, since the effective indexing mechanisms will be able to operate in an infinite number of dimensions, rather than utilizing the old "library-book" classification model based on hierarchies. This will open up significant new markets for information providers, where the data capture has been relatively simple in the past, but data usage has been hampered by the complexity of performing value-added analysis from multiple sources, for instance.

■ Comparison of products from different sources will also "oil the wheels" of the electronic marketplace. If technical specifications, price lists, and discount schemes are all held in standard format, then spotting the right product at the right price becomes a highly automated process.

In short, if the opportunities afforded by the adoption of metadata-driven Web-content definition are taken up fully, the changes that will occur to the activities requiring sharing of information, on a philanthropic, collaborative, or commercial basis are truly revolutionary. Active and full cooperation between general and industry-specific standard setters, developers of search technology, and developers and users of corporate Web sites will lead to the realization of massive efficiencies in information sharing as a facilitator for e-commerce.

The Basics of Metamodeling

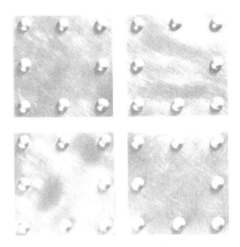

8

Design and Management of Metadata-bases

8.1 Introduction to the metamodels

To gain a thorough appreciation of the ways in which the capture and control of metadata can bring significant efficiencies across a wide range of commercial activity, it is necessary to understand the way in which data structures should be designed and deployed to control sections of this activity. Each data structure, or metamodel, represents a part of the overall IT activity within an organization.

Part III will detail the structure and working of the "core" metadata, covering these main threads of activity within the IT department of an enterprise. The threads (representing management of machines, data, processes, and people) are naturally distinct, enabling autonomous control to be exerted on them at a tactical level. However, when long-term strategic views are required, or direction-setting decisions are made, understanding the interactions between the activities, and the overlaps between the metamodels that formalize them, will form a crucial part of the decision-making process.

The complexity of these interactions and the lack of understanding in this area on the part of those making the decisions have led directly to many of the perceived weaknesses of IT within large, diverse organizations. Later in Part III, a common basis for avoiding such overlap issues will be described to reinforce the importance of metadata management to the overall process of IT deployment and control.

Part III, together with the appendixes describing the formal data structures within each metamodel, provides an encyclopedic view of the enterprise metadata. For convenience, it is split into the four submodels that correspond to the areas of activity most commonly associated with the IM subject area within a commercial concern. The four, interdependent submodels are considered distinctly, with a view to describing their interactions. These four models are listed as follows:

1. The data management metamodel;

2. The application management metamodel;

3. The activity management metamodel;

4. The infrastructure management metamodel.

The models are described separately within Appendixes B–E. Each section should therefore form a complete, localized view of the business activities associated with each of these subject areas and the data structures underlying them.

Each entity of the metamodel is treated separately and discussed in the following manner:

- *Entity design and usage implications:* Explains just how the various "rules" as defined by these relationships and attributes, affect the behavior of the entity, giving examples, where appropriate, of potential problems.

- *Ongoing management principles:* Gives a framework for the stewardship of each entity type, in such a way as to preserve its inherent quality and consistency.

In addition, formal definitions of the entities and the relationships that bind them together and constrain their behavior is given in the appendices, structured as follows:

- *Definition:* Gives both a formal and informal definition to the entity, and explains its role within the metamodel.

- *Data context diagram:* Explains, in broad terms, the way in which this entity relates to other parts of the metamodel and the behavior it exhibits as it passes through its life cycle.

- *Basic relationships:* Gives a formal statement of the underlying business rule behind each relationship with another entity and a looser, textual explanation of the significance to be placed on each such relationship.

- *Basic attributes:* Lists and explains a minimal subset of attributes associated with each entity, their purpose, and examples of their usage.

The purpose to which this section will be put depends on the perspective and role of the reader and on the type of organization to which he or she belongs. For the business reader, the aim is to give a thorough yet understandable introduction to the nature of data itself, by achieving a practical understanding of the constructs that make up a generic metadata-base.

The IT professional can be formally defined as someone whose primary area of activity lies within one of the four "architectures" that provide contexts for the individual submodels. For these people, the intention in providing them with a cohesive metamodel is to allow them to take a step back from their day-to-day problems, and to see the patterns that exist in their work. A grasp of the concepts covered will also enable the members of each group to develop a more profound understanding of the concerns of their colleagues in other "architectural" groups.

For the IT manager, whose view extends across these architectures, the aim is to give a blueprint for a "holistic" approach to the management of an IT function within a complex organization. IT managers should analyze the ways in which the subarchitectures overlap and the sort of conflicts that can arise in their own situation when they do not interact in a consistent and predictable fashion. In the process, the metadata models will allow IT managers to manage more effectively and to provide greater and more visible value to the organization that they support.

In summary, Part III is not meant to define a complete metamodel, nor is it intended to be a prescription for successful implementation of a metadata control mechanism. It is intended rather as a guide for a catalyst for change. The issues that are raised in each organization by consideration of these models should enable an appropriate response to the problems that exist within that organization. The actual parts of this metamodel that are implemented and the amount of effort that will have to be exerted to bring the metadata under control will vary from enterprise to enterprise. These discussions should enable those responsible for planning such an exercise to see the full picture and to be aware of the issues that will arise.

The structure used for splitting the metadata into separate sections is also nonprescriptive. The author has found that this type of split enables both IT and business personnel to see the task ahead more clearly, but it is by no means the only right answer. The entities are discussed in some detail but without reference to a formal metamodel. For those who have reached the stage of implementing a physical metadata-base, the structures are formally defined in appendixes to this work.

8.2   Basic data structure metadata

This portion of the metadata model defines the basic building blocks of metadata, namely the means by which business data can be structured, in the general sense. The entities described are recognizable as the type of data that might be found within the internal structures of a CASE tool or as constructs within the data dictionary of a database management system.

8.2.1   The ENTITY entity

The ENTITY entity forms the backbone of the enterprise data model. The inherent accuracy, quality, and completeness of this data set are vital to the effectiveness of any metadata-driven management approach.

Management of entities

It is therefore important that one master file of the ENTITYs within this enterprise model should be maintained for the entire corporation and that, if at all possible, a single individual should be assigned custody of this entity. It is suggested that this role of custodian for the ENTITY entity should be one of the key roles of the metadata manager, whose overall job specification is described in more detail in Chapter 4.

The ENTITY entity represents the basic definition of any type of thing that may be considered as relevant to the activities of the enterprise. It provides a common basis for all DATA MODEL ENTITYs that are used to describe the behavior of data types in a specific business context, or by a particular APPLICATION. As for the ATTRIBUTE entity, the ENTITY entity acts as a library, from which data types may be chosen for use on any new project. Once again, the rules that are defined for the behavior of an ENTITY within the enterprise model are implicitly carried over to any data model for which they are selected. This enforces a high degree of consistency between areas of the infrastructure that may not interact in any controllable way.

In addition, it will be the responsibility of the project data analysts to ensure that any new circumstances surrounding an ENTITY that might be considered generally applicable are included in the ENTITY entity (and its context), and thus be available as "library" items for use elsewhere.

Evolution of the entity metadata

The ENTITY entity will evolve in a controlled manner as its use is extended over time in application projects. The data analysts and the metadata manager will reflect this evolution on the metamodel as the result of coordinated analysis and discussion. The inclusion of any ENTITY within a new data model view implies acceptance of the following, for data usage by the new project:

- The ENTITY will be used in a manner consistent with its existing definition in the metamodel, and any additional constraints on the behavior of the ENTITY that are applicable only to the new project will be included in the DATA MODEL ENTITY entity definition.

- Any additional constraints on the behavior of the ENTITY that are generally applicable must be included in the ENTITY definition and must be checked against the usage of this ENTITY by all other relevant data models.

Identification of entities

The primary identifier of the ENTITY will be as specified and controlled in the metamodel, subject to any technical constraints that might arise. In some instances, such constraints (e.g., the use of software developed by a third party) prevent the use of a common identification mechanism. In such cases, it should be considered an integral part of the development project to ensure that a robust and comprehensive automated process is developed. This, in turn, will ensure that the different systems remain consistent over time.

Any new ENTITY that is identified as being of general applicability should be included in the ENTITY entity, after appropriate checking to ensure that no such ENTITY already exists within an existing data model.

All of the above will ensure that the enterprise metamodel remains complete and accurate, while the data model views (represented by the DATA MODEL ENTITY entity) will be complete, relevant, and mutually consistent. This will, in turn, significantly reduce the likelihood of confusion arising in the business over inconsistent language and greatly simplify all dealings with data that are derived from more than one system.

8.2.2 The ATTRIBUTE entity

The ATTRIBUTE entity represents the universe of characteristics that may be taken by each particular entity. It provides a common basis for all DATA MODEL ATTRIBUTEs that are used to describe the behavior of ATTRIBUTEs in a specific business context. In this sense, the ATTRIBUTE entity acts as a library, from which attributes may be chosen for use on any new project that makes use of the ENTITY to which the ATTRIBUTEs belong. In making the choice from this menu, a data analyst involved in building a data model for a new project is acknowledging the rules that have been recorded in the ATTRIBUTE entity and agreeing to abide by them.

Control of attribute values

The format and set of possible values for an ATTRIBUTE does not depend on the ATTRIBUTE itself; rather it depends on the DOMAIN to which it belongs. Thus, any management activity centered on the consistency or quality of data values should be performed at the domain level, rather than individual ATTRIBUTEs.

As a general rule, an ATTRIBUTE only exists within the context of one specific ENTITY. Any given ATTRIBUTE may or may not exist within the context of a particular DATA MODEL. In general, it is advisable to include primary identifying ATTRIBUTEs in all DATA MODELs that contain the ENTITY to which they refer.

In addition, it will be the responsibility of the project data analysts to ensure that any new circumstances surrounding an ATTRIBUTE that might be considered generally applicable should be included in the ATTRIBUTE entity (and its context) and thus be available as library items for use elsewhere.

Evolution of attribute metadata

The ATTRIBUTE entity itself, being part of the enterprise data model, falls under the custody of the metadata manager. (See also Section 4.3.) It is up to the metadata manager to ensure that any evolution of the IT infrastructure takes account of the metamodel and that consistency across the universe of data usage is therefore preserved.

As an example, consider a new project that has been set up to develop a plant control system for a manufacturing company. The data analyst for this new project has access to the existing metamodel and reviews the current contents with the metadata manager.

Depending on the scope of the new project, he or she will decide which ENTITYs are of relevance and which ATTRIBUTEs will be taken as part of the DATA MODEL VIEW for the new application. The inclusion of the ATTRIBUTEs in this view implies acceptance of the following for data usage by the new project:

1. The ATTRIBUTE will be used in a manner consistent with its existing definition in the metamodel. If there is an existing ATTRIBUTE associated with the PRODUCT entity called "package net weight" then any ATTRIBUTE that is thus named within

the new application should be totally consistent with the universal definition in the ATTRIBUTE entity.

2. Any additional constraints on the behavior of the ATTRIBUTE that are applicable only to the new project will be included in the DATA MODEL ATTRIBUTE entity definition. If it is found that a new ATTRIBUTE, "production batch flag," is needed for the plant control system and is not used elsewhere in the business for any purpose, then it should be included on the data model for the new application. The default assumption will be that new constraints will be generally applicable. The case for making them applicable to one system only will have to be made and agreed with the metadata manager.

3. Any additional constraints on the behavior of the ATTRIBUTE that are generally applicable must be included in the ATTRIBUTE definition and must be checked against the usage of this ATTRIBUTE by all other relevant data models. The project may make use of an ATTRIBUTE for "density" that must be constrained to a value between zero and one, whereas this is not implied by the general definition. In this case, either the definition has to be changed to match the new circumstances, or a separate ATTRIBUTE (named manufacturing standard density, for instance) must be defined for the purpose. In the former case, great care must be taken that the new constraint is consistent with the use being made of this ATTRIBUTE by other applications, even though it was not explicitly stated beforehand.

4. The format and domain of the ATTRIBUTE will be as specified in the metamodel. The analyst does not have the right to decide that the product number ATTRIBUTE will be differently coded or structured for this application than from those that already exist.

5. Any new ATTRIBUTEs of the ENTITY that are identified for specific use of the project must be included in the DATA MODEL ATTRIBUTE set. Note that the default assumption should be that new ATTRIBUTEs would have general applicability. It should

remain to be proven that their scope is local enough not to be included in the enterprise view (i.e., the ATTRIBUTE entity).

6. Any new ATTRIBUTEs of the ENTITY that are identified as being of general applicability should be included in the ATTRIBUTE entity, after appropriate checking to ensure that no such ATTRIBUTE already exists within an existing data model.

All of the above will ensure that the enterprise metamodel, represented by the ATTRIBUTE entity, will remain complete and accurate, while the data models (represented by the DATA MODEL ATTRIBUTE entity) will be complete, relevant, and mutually consistent. This will, in turn, significantly reduce the likelihood of confusion arising within the business over inconsistent language and greatly simplify all dealings with data that is derived from more than one system.

For a more detailed discussion of the importance of data consistency in all its aspects, see also [1].

8.2.3 The RELATIONSHIP entity

RELATIONSHIPs can only exist between pairs of ENTITYs and may be taken by any instance of each end of the "pairing." In itself, this does not imply that all RELATIONSHIPs are mandatory. It does nevertheless lead us to the conclusion that if it is not possible for a definable subset of a particular ENTITY to take part in the RELATIONSHIPs defined for the ENTITY as a whole, then further restructuring of the data model must take place. This restructuring should take the form of explicit recognition of the subtype in question, and the reassignment of the RELATIONSHIP to the complement of the new subtype.

Entity relationship (ER) diagrams

The temptation to look upon the construction of entity relationship (ER) diagrams as merely the means of achieving a satisfactory database structure in an application should be strenuously avoided. The management of RELATIONSHIPs is the key activity if a thorough and correct understanding of the operation of the business, from a data perspective, is to be maintained and communicated.

Compromise and conflict in the setting of business rules

Each RELATIONSHIP represents a business rule—a circumstance that constrains the way that the business is conducted in some manner. By understanding these constraints and applying them in a systematic manner to the construction and use of computer applications and manual procedures, a great deal of the problems associated with poorly designed systems can be avoided.

If, on the other hand, a constraint (or business rule) is omitted from one application or procedure, then errors are very likely to be introduced, resulting in complexity and inefficiency in the operation of the business.

For example, imagine that a RELATIONSHIP between the DELIVERY entity and the CONSIGNMENT LOCATION entity exists in an enterprise. This RELATIONSHIP is formulated as:

"A DELIVERY is delivered to one and only one CONSIGNMENT LOCATION."

All procedures and applications within the enterprise that observe this rule should therefore do one of the following:

1. Enforce the rule by ensuring that only one CONSIGNMENT LOCATION is referred to in each DELIVERY record;

2. Ignore the rule by implying no relationship between the DELIVERY and CONSIGNMENT LOCATION entities within their scope;

3. Consider the rule irrelevant, since one or both of the entities concerned are excluded from their scope.

If the rule is contradicted, however, it will become impossible to reconcile DELIVERY records in applications or procedures that allow more than one "drop" per delivery with those that do not. The definition of what a DELIVERY is will have been altered for one application, and inconsistency and error will result.

The only way around this would be to amend the rule, allowing it to become more general—effectively stating that a delivery can be decomposed into multiple drops. This would imply that the drop location can no longer be an attribute of the DELIVERY but must become dependent on the component DROP entities.

The overall ownership of the RELATIONSHIPs, and hence of the corporate ER model, will lie with the metadata manager. (See also Section 4.3.) It is the metadata manager's responsibility to ensure that all business rules included in this "model" are correct in the context of the business and that the model itself is as complete as possible.

When applications or procedures are added or amended, the metadata manager, in conjunction with the project data analyst, should ensure that the model implied by the new operation is consistent with the enterprise model. This consistency is implied by the lack of conflict defined above (i.e., nothing can happen under the constraints of a new model that explicitly contradicts the rules within the enterprise model). It does not matter whether new rules are introduced, or old rules are ignored, provided the basic noncontradictory nature is established.

Provided robust analysis of the business rules is done at each stage, this consistency can be preserved as the application infrastructure evolves. However, there may be times when a new development has highlighted a case where the operation should be fundamentally different from that already implied by the enterprise model. The reality behind such a problem may be one of the following:

1. The enterprise model is "right" and the new model is "wrong."

2. The enterprise model is "wrong" and the new model is "right," but there is no contradictory implementation of the rule.

3. The enterprise model is "wrong" and systems exist that have implemented and enforced the contradictory rule.

In each case, the differences between the models must be reconciled. The responsibility for this reconciliation lies with the metadata manager and the project data analyst, who may have to involve further business and project management and personnel to arrive at a satisfactory conclusion.

Case 1 is inherently the simplest with which to deal, since it involves adjustments to elements of the infrastructure that are "new." The resolution of this situation will be a matter for the new project, acting under pressure from the rest of the business to fall into line.

Case 2 will arise where the existing version of the enterprise model has assumed a greater level of constraint than is actually the case. This might happen where a one-to-one RELATIONSHIP has been enforced in the past, but it turns out that one-to-many is an accurate reflection of the business. In such an example, it is possible for the applications and procedures that have been created to comply with the old version to coexist with those that comply with the new.

All applications that make use of both the ENTITYs involved in the RELATIONSHIP should be checked (by examination of the DATA MODEL ENTITY entity) to ensure that their implementation is, in fact, noncontradictory. Once this has been established, the enterprise model should be changed by having the cardinality of the necessary RELATION-SHIPs adjusted, together with any definitions that are not in line with the new structure. It should be noted, however, that no changes are required to existing applications in this case.

Case 3 is by far the most serious, since it implies that existing applications are operating in flat contradiction to the realities of the business. Fortunately it is also the least common case, since, were such a circumstance to arise, it is likely to have been corrected as a "stand-alone" problem already. Once again, it is the responsibility of the metadata manager and the project representative to ensure that the problem is brought to light and that adequate steps are taken to ensure its resolution.

Management of relationship metadata

In general, the RELATIONSHIP entity will be managed by the metadata manager and will evolve in a series of steps, depending on the areas of activity within the application infrastructure. When a new project is initiated to develop a new process or application, a person within that project should be identified as having data analysis responsibility.

This person, in conjunction with the metadata manager, will be responsible for developing a logical data model for the scope of his or her activity. This process will be structured as follows:

1. Selection of existing entities from the enterprise model (ENTITY entity) that are relevant;

2. Selection of business rules involving those entities (RELATION-SHIP entity) that are relevant;

3. Augmentation of the entity list with new instances that have been considered for the first time and construction of the application model view (DATA MODEL ENTITY entity);

4. Inclusion of new business rules and reconciliation with the enterprise model (ENTITY and RELATIONSHIP entities).

Depending on the complexity and political sensitivity of the project, there will be considerable analysis, "selling," and refinement behind each of these steps, but the structure of this activity holds good for the general case.

8.2.4 The KEY ATTRIBUTE entity

Identifier control is critical for proper data management on two levels: domain control, making the possible set of values that the identifier of an entity can take the same, regardless of which system we are talking about, and business identifier control, which is needed to make sure that an identifier used in two different systems is referring to the same "real-life" instance of the entity and that, where a real-life entity occurs on two systems, it is identified in the same way!

8.2.5 The SUBTYPING entity

An ENTITY set can be split into many subsets. Each of these subsets form a potential subtype entity, although not all will be relevant to the business and will hence remain implicit. The subtypes defined can be distinct from each other or overlap, even within the scope of the same categorization.

The concept of classification

Classifications based on different categorizing attributes (known as orthogonal categorizations) can, of course, overlap to any extent. Subtypes of an ENTITY are, of course, ENTITYs in their own right and are thus capable of partaking in the metamodel in exactly the same way as other ENTITYs (i.e., forming RELATIONSHIPs, being further subtyped, taking distinct ATTRIBUTEs, etc.)

As with RELATIONSHIPs, there is no entity within the metamodel such as DATA MODEL SUBTYPING. This implies that, if a subclassification exists, it is applicable (although not necessarily explicitly applied) to all DATA MODELs that contain both relevant entities (i.e., instances of the DATA MODEL ENTITY entity). This is particularly significant, since it emphasizes the potentially global nature of all business rules, including classifications, and thus the elimination of business rules that are explicitly contradictory from one part of the business to another. There is no sense in assuming that one entity can be a subtype of another for one part of the business only. It must be the case globally, if at all.

Management of classification metadata

The management of the way in which ENTITYs are classified is closely akin to the construction of ER models. Each subtyping activity represents the imposition of a constraint on the way a business operates and defines the behavior of certain data ENTITYs within the context of that operation.

Therefore, the control of the SUBTYPE entity within the metamodel should be handled in much the same way as the RELATIONSHIP entity; namely, the following should be true:

1. The metadata manager should have overall ownership of the SUBTYPE entity.

2. The metadata manager and the data analyst from a development project should have joint responsibility for evolving the SUBTYPE structure to match new developments.

3. The resolution of problems resulting from attempts to reconcile the subtype structure for new projects with the existing enterprise model should be coordinated by the metadata manager.

8.2.6   The DATA MODEL entity

As a general rule, a data model should reflect the way in which people view data. Therefore, each use of data is only relevant in the context of the definition of that data within one and only one model.

This further implies that the enterprise data model is not used directly but instead places a common framework on all other models, enabling them to be used in a mutually compatible manner, while retaining their own richness and complexity.

Local and global views of metadata

The overall definition of the DATA MODEL relating to a particular project, business activity, or application should be the responsibility of a data analyst assigned for the purpose. Data analysts should report to a relevant business process owner who will retain overall responsibility for the quality of the business data model and all that it may imply.

The enterprise view (as defined within instances of the ENTITY entity and the ATTRIBUTE entity) and the views of particular groups of users (as defined in the DATA MODEL ENTITY entity and the DATA MODEL ATTRIBUTE entity) will frequently diverge.

Reconciliation of conflicting views

Difficulties are often encountered during the process of trying to reconcile these views. In practice, there should be a tendency to keep the enterprise view as simple as possible, while taking care not to omit business rules that are universally applicable and important. The scope of the enterprise model should, of course, be considered "universal" or "neutral" at all times.

By contrast, effort should be made to capture all relevant business rules within the data models, enabling a rich and robust picture of the operation to be defined, while maintaining consistency with the enterprise model to be maintained within a precise, relatively narrow scope in each case.

8.2.7 The DATA MODEL ENTITY entity

A given ENTITY may or may not be relevant to the function of a part of the business and hence may or may not be included in that part's data model. However, if an ENTITY is included in a particular view, then its behavior is determined by that view. This implies that the view must be consistent with, but not necessarily identical to, the enterprise view. (See also Appendix A.)

Data model control

The key issue, once again, is ensuring that the DATA MODEL ENTITY entity is actively controlled over time. This will ensure that its use remains accurate and complete from a business perspective, while being mutually consistent with other, overlapping DATA MODELs.

As with the DATA MODEL ATTRIBUTE, an ongoing metamodel support role should be defined, reporting to the relevant business process owner. This person should be made responsible for ensuring that the DATA MODEL for his or her application remains consistent with everything else. In particular, this person should take action when he or she does the following:

- Detects evolutionary changes to the data model that will affect existing components of the enterprise model (instances of the ENTITY, ATTRIBUTE, or RELATIONSHIP entities, inter alia).

- Detects evolutionary changes to the data model that introduce new DATA MODEL ENTITY instances. These should be checked for correspondence with DATA MODEL ENTITY instances in other models, or with ENTITY instances in the enterprise model.

- Becomes aware of changes to other models that could affect his or her own data model, through peers in other areas or through the metadata manager.

8.2.8   The DATA MODEL ATTRIBUTE entity

Local views of attributes

Not all attributes of an ENTITY are relevant to a given data model. However, all DATA MODEL ATTRIBUTEs must be recorded as ATTRIBUTEs and hence form part of the enterprise view of data. This enables the maximum appropriate level of consistency to be drawn between one data model and the next, since it facilitates the reuse of data items across different parts of the business.

A general discussion of the way in which DATA MODEL ATTRIBUTE and ATTRIBUTE entities should be managed is given under the ATTRIBUTE entry in Section 8.2.2. Particular care should be taken at the time that a data model is created to ensure that it not only meets the needs of the application or business area for which it is being constructed but is consistent with the "rest of the world" (as represented by the enterprise view and other overlapping DATA MODELs).

Data model control

Explicit analysis and careful cross-checking of the way that ENTITYs, ATTRIBUTEs, and RELATIONSHIPs are used for a particular context is strongly recommended. This will ensure that a picture is built that preserves this mutual consistency and thus avoids much of the confusion arising from multisystem infrastructures in complex business environments.

An important facet of metadata management that is frequently overlooked is the need to evolve an applications view of the world over time. In more enlightened organizations, some effort will be devoted to ensuring that a good data model is built for a new system. Very rarely, however, does this responsibility get translated into ongoing stewardship of the business rules that are operated by an application, once it has become a live and stable part of the infrastructure.

It is imperative to identify someone who will ensure that the application data model remains consistent with the rest of the world. Such a responsibility should be explicitly built into the job role of someone more generally charged with the support of the live application. He or she will be responsible for ensuring that any significant changes to the operation of the application are translated into appropriate changes on the meta-model. This person will also coordinate with the metadata manager to ensure that changes made within his or her own or other overlapping applications do not result in inconsistency.

8.2.9   The DATA MODEL RELATIONSHIP entity

This entity will be used to indicate those relationships between ENTITYs that are carried over into a particular DATA MODEL. The precise nature of the RELATIONSHIPs will be determined on a case-by-case basis but will determine the business rules that apply to the subject area in question.

The simplest way in which RELATIONSHIPs can be mapped onto DATA MODEL RELATIONSHIPs is to consider the ENTITYs that are chosen from the enterprise data model to form the subject area data model. All the RELATIONSHIPs that exist between pairs of these ENTITYs are candidates for inclusion in the list of DATA MODEL RELATIONSHIPs.

Some may be left out (for instance, if the attributes that are forcing a "foreign key" relationship are not present on the subject area model). Others may be added where there are specific business rules that apply to one subject area only (provided they represent a constrained version of the enterprise model and remain compatible with it). See also Appendix A.

8.2.10   The DATA MODEL SUBTYPING entity

As with other aspects of the DATA MODEL concept, the DATA MODEL SUBTYPING entity is intended to indicate which SUB-TYPINGs are relevant to a particular subject area model. It is unlikely that there will be subtype relationships existing between two entities in a particular subject area and nowhere else. Most differences between the DATA MODEL SUBTYPING set and the SUBTYPING records that are relevant to the DATA MODEL ENTITY records chosen will therefore be in the form of eliminating unnecessary or irrelevant structures. ·

In the first case, simplification will take place where the enterprise model has, for instance, a hierarchy of subtypes of the form A is a subtype of B, B is a subtype of C, C is a subtype of D. On a particular DATA MODEL, it may only be necessary to record the DATA MODEL SUBTYPE for "A is a subtype of D" since the ENTITYs B and C may not be included, or for some other reason.

The second, and possibly more obvious, case is the exclusion of a subtype because it is, by its nature, irrelevant to the subject area for which the DATA MODEL is being developed.

8.3   Metadata and data value control

Once the basic structure for the data is defined, further constraints can be placed on its behavior by restricting the population of values that particular parts of the database can take. It is very common practice indeed to enforce such rules as the following:

- "The customer's name must be twenty characters, alphabetic."

- "Each currency code must correspond to an entry in the currency table."

- "All order dates must be later than January 1, 1998."

- "Credit risk rating must be 'H,' 'M,' or 'L.'"

The metadata defined in this section will also be found within CASE tools and data dictionary structures and will also be found embedded (in a nonobvious form) within program logic for applications.

8.3.1   The ATTRIBUTE TYPE entity

It is vitally important to recognize that, even when the need for a particular ATTRIBUTE TYPE is identified, it will not be a trivial matter to get all interested parties to agree to its definition. Wherever possible, external standards should be considered (e.g., ISO and CCITT). The standard data types used within common programming languages can also provide a useful library of basic types in this context.

Generalizing on attribute behavior

The ATTRIBUTE TYPE entity will by its nature be very stable and constrained in the values it should take. Nominally, ownership of this entity should fall within the responsibilities of the metadata manager. It will be part of his or her responsibility to ensure that the allocation of ATTRIBUTE TYPEs and DOMAINs to individual ATTRIBUTEs, both within the enterprise model and within each data model, is optimized.

This will be done by periodically reviewing such usage to ensure that where patterns of repeated data types occur standard ATTRIBUTE TYPEs exist to cover their definition. For instance, the metamodel may be set up in the first instance with basic ATTRIBUTE TYPEs for integer, text, flag, real number, etc. Periodic reviews may indicate that additional standard types are needed for postal code, vehicle registration number, national insurance number, product code, etc.

Managing attribute types

It will be the responsibility of the metadata manager to ensure that entries are made in the ATTRIBUTE TYPE entity, thus enabling an appropriate degree of consistency to be used across the whole organization when dealing with data of these specific types. This in turn will relieve individual project teams and developers of the decision on the basic validation logic to be used for many ATTRIBUTEs captured by their applications.

8.3.2 The DOMAIN entity

The maintenance of proper control over the data on a day-to-day basis depends to a large extent on the control of domains. A large proportion of the data within an enterprise is constrained by one domain or another. The currency codes that are allowed, the account numbers within the chart of accounts, and the units of measure applicable to particular purposes will all be defined as sets of values, often stored in a reference table within a particular database. Unless the dependencies between the diverse occurrences of these codes and the domains that control their value are understood by the business users and implemented by the developers of application systems, then the integrity of the overall database will degrade over time.

Overlapping and interdependent domains

DOMAINs have a potentially complex nature, since each DOMAIN represents a set of values that may be applied to other data items (ATTRIBUTEs) within the organization. As such, they are subject to the normal mathematical properties of sets, which will to a greater or lesser extent be relevant to the way they are managed by the business.

Some DOMAINs will be subsets of others. (The set of working days will be a subset of the days of the week, and the DOMAINs will behave accordingly.)

Some pairs or groups of DOMAINs will be complementary. (Within the superdomain of VEHICLE REGISTRATION NUMBERs, SHIP REGISTRATION NUMBERs and AIRCRAFT REGISTRATION NUMBERs will be mutually exclusive siblings.)

Some DOMAINs will have other DOMAINs embedded in them. (The DOMAIN for full postal code in the United Kingdom contains an embedded reference to a postal town.)

For practical, organizational purposes, some DOMAINs will be split to enable effective management of the set as a whole. (An arbitrary split between one set of products and another may be made, based on some embedded meaning, and the two parts of the DOMAIN administered separately.) This separation of responsibility may simplify the process of administering each individual part, but extra levels of control will be needed to ensure that the split is "clean" (i.e., that there are no overlaps or gaps between one set of responsibilities and another).

Control of domains within large organizations

For each entry in the DOMAIN entity, there should be a process by which that DOMAIN will be controlled and individuals identified to exercise that control. Because of its nature as a corporate repository of data control information, only one master copy of the DOMAIN entity must be maintained.

As for the ATTRIBUTE TYPE entity, the overall responsibility for this entity should rest with the metadata manager. To preserve a consistent picture for the value control over similar data spread over diverse and physically dispersed systems throughout the organization, the key aspects to consider when stewarding this entity are the following:

- Definition of standard DOMAINs covering as large a proportion of the ATTRIBUTE base as possible, without introducing unnecessary and irrelevant constraints (it is possible to go too far with this, recording formal, enterprise-wide definitions of domain that are only of interest to one small part of the company);

- Ensuring that new projects/applications make use of all appropriate domain constraints and are implementing data validation consistently;

- Ensuring that the communication with those supporting legacy applications (already in place before a regime of metadata control was introduced) are actively managed to ensure domain consistency;

- Determining and preserving the integrity of the domain infrastructure (e.g., recording the relationship between one domain and another—domains can be subdomains or complements of others);

- Ensuring that owners of each of the actual DOMAINs are identified and properly briefed and are executing their responsibilities in a way consistent with the overall good of the enterprise—in addition to knowing that the CURRENCY codes to be used are in a particular set, knowing who "owns" this set, who is responsible for adding new codes when necessary, what is the process for getting a new code set up, etc.;

- Ensuring that processes are defined and properly executed for the dispersal of the DOMAIN across the enterprise. Each individual DOMAIN will be managed by an individual who will be responsible for its population. What mechanisms must be in place to ensure that copies of the DOMAIN are available to other individuals and/or applications that need them?

8.3.3 The IDENTIFIER entity

The basic requirement in this area is to understand what each type of data is doing in the organization (the ENTITY entity) and how it behaves in relation to others (the RELATIONSHIP entity). Following from this, one of the major practical issues is to ensure that the means of uniquely identifying one instance of an ENTITY is defined and used consistently across as much of the organization as possible.

Identification of business data—keys and coding

The practical effect of this is the need for central custody of the IDENTIFIER and KEY ATTRIBUTE entities. Once again, the role of the metadata manager is key to ensuring that any new application being proposed conforms to the standard identification mechanisms defined for the enterprise or, at the very least, that appropriate mapping mechanisms are built to ensure a "bridge" to the standard.

Common coding problems

As should be obvious, having two or more systems within an organization that capture basically the same data but identify it in different ways seriously reduces the usefulness of both systems and impairs the efficiency and effectiveness of any part of the business that has dealings with both.

For instance, if the way in which a sales system identifies product is inconsistent with the means of identification used by a production system, then it will be very difficult to do the following:

- Transfer relevant data in an automated fashion from one to another;

- Use the data from one in discussions with people who are only used to dealing with another;

- Use the data from both in a consolidated manner to produce an informational overview (e.g., for senior management).

If, on the other hand, the IDENTIFIER entity is put under control at the time an application is created and is actively managed over time, then the following are true:

- The opportunity for automated data sharing is increased;

- The ability to communicate between departments/functions is improved;

- Reconciliation of data across systems becomes simpler and less error-prone.

There are a couple of general rules that should be followed when defining the manner in which an ENTITY should be identified:

1. Avoid the use of independent embedded meanings. The important thing to remember here is the word "independent." Many people get very dogmatic about the use of zoned fields in keys, since they have been told that such usage implies embedded meaning and that embedded meaning is inherently evil! It must be remembered that the real problem with such usage is where a possibility exists for a component of the key to change, without inherently changing the instance into something different. If you use a concatenation of a product code and a package identifier to identify the entity PACKED PRODUCT, this is not a problem,

even though the component parts of the key are inherently "meaningful." We may safely assume that if the package code changes to something else, then we are talking about a different PACKED PRODUCT. If, however, we had used a code for the color of the wrapping as part of the primary key, an independent embedded meaning would exist since, in most businesses, the color of the wrap will not affect the nature of the product itself.

2. Do not make use of meaningful identifiers at all, unless absolutely unavoidable. In fact, the issue of meaning in keys or parts of keys is best avoided altogether. Even where we use "safe" keys without any dependent embedded meaning, there is always a risk that the business will change inherently and so invalidate the use of the original code or confuse people into wrong assumptions.

For the general approach to managing the IDENTIFIER entity, see also KEY ATTRIBUTE entity (Section 8.2.4).

8.3.4 The FOREIGN IDENTIFIER entity

The FOREIGN IDENTIFIER entity and the RELATIONSHIP entity are very closely related. The FOREIGN IDENTIFIER provides the means by which the RELATIONSHIP is enforced, and by which the explicit correspondence of an instance of one entity to an instance of another is denoted.

Establishing links between entities

In general, therefore, for an instance of the RELATIONSHIP entity to exist there must be an instance of the FOREIGN IDENTIFIER entity. At a lower level of abstraction, the values attributed to a FOREIGN IDENTIFIER within an instance of an ENTITY imply the existence of an instance of a particular RELATIONSHIP.

Since it is a fundamental part of the metamodel structure, custody of the FOREIGN IDENTIFIER entity falls within the remit of the metadata manager. Their prime purpose is to ensure a proper correspondence between instances of the FOREIGN IDENTIFIER entity and the RELATIONSHIP entity, at the metamodel level, and (in conjunction with the project data analysts) to enforce the implementation of appropriate rules for referential integrity. This will involve ensuring that the rules implied by a relationship are adhered to, no matter what changes are made to the content of the database.

The correspondence between the foreign identifiers and the relationships that they are enforcing should be preserved automatically if possible, manually if not, for the overall integrity of the metadata-base to be preserved.

8.3.5   The ENTITY OCCURRENCE entity

In general, the entity ENTITY OCCURRENCE will not be managed explicitly by the enterprise. This data is the superset of all "real" records in the scope of the organization. Any such real entity will, of course, be represented explicitly, leaving the superset entity empty at all times. There is value, however, in including it in the metamodel, since it facilitates the explanation of behavior common to all entities.

8.4   Application deployment and configuration control metadata

We now progress to consideration of the metadata that will help us keep control of the computer applications themselves. This section will include metadata describing the computer systems, their history of releases, indications of whether they were acquired from third parties, and other data relevant to change and configuration control.

8.4.1   The APPLICATION entity

The APPLICATION entity as a whole will be owned by the IT management for the enterprise as a whole. This may be the IT group director, or a specially appointed application architect depending on the complexity and size of the organization.

Each instance of the APPLICATION entity should have an "owner" identified, who will have overall responsibility as described above, and be the source of all information to be "filled in" on the APPLICATION record itself.

8.4.2 The APPLICATION MODULE entity

In general, there is no fixed hierarchical decomposition for an APPLICATION. An APPLICATION can be split down in many different ways, depending on the purpose of the decomposition.

8.4.3 The APPLICATION INSTALLATION entity

It will be possible to implement more than one physical copy of an APPLICATION across an enterprise. For instance, a general ledger system may be developed centrally and deployed in each affiliate office within a large multinational. It will be possible (although not necessarily advisable!) for different modifications to be made to each copy of the original application. It will certainly be possible for new releases of the application to be installed at each site at slightly different times. For this reason, there is a need to track the individual instances of APPLICATION that are deployed. The APPLICATION INSTALLATION entity may be used for this purpose. The actual release level of a particular APPLICATION INSTALLATION is independent of that of other instances of the same entity.

Multiple deployment of applications

The management of APPLICATION INSTALLATIONs will vary according to the organizational structure and the complexity of the IT function within an enterprise. Broadly speaking, there are three areas of activity that will affect the management of this entity:

- *Application deployment:* When an APPLICATION is new, the way in which it is deployed to various parts of the organization will usually be managed as a integral part of the development project. During this phase, the ownership of the APPLICATION INSTALLATION entity will be assigned to the APPLICATION owner, once he or she is determined. The "custody" of the entity implies responsibility for ensuring that the data concerning each APPLICATION INSTALLATION is accurate and reflects the broader needs of the business. This further implies that such data will remain under the management of the "development" project.

■ *Application evolution:* Once an APPLICATION is installed and in use, there will be a series of evolutionary steps, usually in the form of APPLICATION RELEASEs that are deployed across the APPLICATION INSTALLATIONs. An organization (usually within the IT function) will be responsible for the support of each live APPLICATION and hence will take over the custody of the APPLICATION INSTALLATION entity once the original project team is disbanded. If there are many separate installations of the application that are supported from a "center of expertise" or some such organization, then the custody of this entity clearly rests with them. If there is dispersed management of the application (to be discouraged), then the custody is merged with the responsibility for installation management. (See installation management entry.)

■ *Installation management:* Another organization will be responsible for the machines and what runs on them. They will see the APPLICATION INSTALLATION less as an issue of "on which machines are my APPLICATIONs being run" than of "what APPLICATIONs are running on my machine?" A more detailed picture of the management of APPLICATION INSTALLATIONs from this perspective is given under the infrastructure management metamodel. Although not forced by the data model, the tendency should be to keep releases broadly in line. Separate owners may be identified for each of the decompositions, depending on context, but overall consistency between them is achieved by responsibility of the application owner.

8.4.4 The SOFTWARE SUPPLIER entity

The SOFTWARE SUPPLIER is a subclass of the SUPPLIER entity that is very likely to occur elsewhere in a mainstream business context. Whether there is any distinction of purpose between these two activities depends on the actual purchasing management responsibility within the organization. If there is distinct purchasing activity and organizational responsibility attached to the buying of computer software, then this entity may be managed explicitly as part of the IT metadata-base. If the purchasing of such items is handled centrally, along with paper clips, company cars, and new desks, then the only major problem is to ensure that attributes specific to this IT subclass are defined and monitored in the appropriate way. The concept of purchasing in a large organization relies on different people or groups having delegated authority for specifying and authorizing the purchase of goods and services. They will do this with reference to different criteria, depending on the nature of the proposed purchase. Provided the flexibility exists to manage these criteria properly, as a means of managing the suppliers in turn, then no explicit SOFTWARE SUPPLIER facilities will be required.

In such cases, the SOFTWARE SUPPLIER is reduced to the role of a "hook" entity, at the periphery of the metadata model. The management of this entity is only relevant to the metamodel where APPLICATIONs are purchased from, and supported by a third party, and the control of this arrangement is an explicit function of the IT department.

8.4.5   The APPLICATION RELEASE entity

There is not an explicit design principle behind the APPLICATION RELEASE entity. Once again, the nature of this entity depends fundamentally on the operation of a release management policy within the enterprise. As such, what constitutes an APPLICATION RELEASE depends on how the atomic points (from the perspective of the intended end users) within the life cycle of an APPLICATION are positioned.

Application release management

The actual management of APPLICATION evolution will vary from system to system, from location to location, and from business context to business context. The provision of metadata structures to manage the relevant meta-entities (APPLICATION, APPLICATION MODULE, APPLICATION RELEASE, and APPLICATION MODULE RELEASE) gives maximum flexibility while maintaining a consistent backbone to the application development activities.

Where the APPLICATION is large or complex, its management will be performed at the APPLICATION DEVELOPMENT MODULE level; otherwise the principles discussed in relation to the APPLICATION MODULE and APPLICATION MODULE RELEASE entities will be applied at the higher level.

8.4.6 The APPLICATION DEVELOPMENT MODULE entity

The management of the APPLICATION DEVELOPMENT MODULE entity over time is a combined responsibility of the application module owner and the application module coordinator. The application module owner is an individual within the business who will be responsible for the functional evolution and use of the APPLICATION DEVELOPMENT MODULE across the full scope of its use. This individual should have the authority to make decisions, or at the very least to coordinate the decision-making process relating to its use in all other places and by all relevant departments. For small or simple APPLICATIONs, this responsibility will be combined for all modules into the APPLICATION OWNER role.

The application module coordinator is the person in the IT function who has technical responsibility for the way in which the module develops as an IT department product. Typically, he or she will be a team leader within the application support organization and will be responsible for this technical evolution for all installations of the APPLICATION DEVLOPMENT MODULE. Once again, for small or simple projects, this responsibility will be at the APPLICATION, rather than the APPLICATION MODULE, level.

8.4.7 The APPLICATION MODULE RELEASE entity

There is not an explicit design principle behind the APPLICATION MODULE RELEASE entity. Its nature depends fundamentally on the type of release management policy operated within the enterprise. The changes to an APPLICATION that appear invisible, or atomic, to the end user will not follow any universal pattern. What actually constitutes an APPLICATION MODULE RELEASE in each case depends on how these changes are managed within the life cycle of an APPLICATION DEVELOPMENT MODULE.

Application module coordinators are responsible for ensuring that the APPLICATION MODULE RELEASE records within their responsibility reflect the way in which systems are deployed across the enterprise in an accurate and timely manner. This implies that they should be aware of, and react to, changes in the status of each relevant APPLICATION MODULE and the relationship between APPLICATION MODULE RELEASEs and APPLICATION INSTALLATIONs.

8.4.8 The APPLICATION USER entity

The main implication of metadata control in the area of system security is that, although the practical basis upon which the allocation of access privileges to individuals will vary across APPLICATIONs for technical and historical reasons, the management infrastructure defined by the meta-model should remain the same in all cases. Inherently, the relationships that exist between INDIVIDUALs and the APPLICATIONs or parts of APPLICATIONs that they are entitled to make use of have a broadly similar pattern, regardless of the business context. The construction and maintenance of facilities to manage this metadata is the responsibility of the security architect.

Aspects of access permission and control

A great deal of detail is required to describe the management of a security configuration fully in all but the simplest of organizations. The key issues to be considered in this context are the following:

- Management of users:

    - Is the INDIVIDUAL still employed by the enterprise?

    - Is he or she still doing the same job?

    - Are the details recorded correct?

    - How can users be grouped logically for optimal management of systems user ids?

- Management of APPLICATIONs:

    - Where are the APPLICATIONs deployed?

    - How are they used?

    - What business transactions are they intended to automate?

- Management of APPLICATION MODULEs:

    - Where are the APPLICATION MODULEs deployed?

    - How are they used?

    - What business transactions are they intended to automate?

- Does the modularity reflect an optimal structure for management of the security system?

- Management of the organization:

  - Is the way in which the business transaction is being performed changing?

  - How does such change reflect upon the APPLICATIONs that have been designed to automate these business transactions?

  - Does the organizational structure conflict with the way in which the business processes and/or the APPLICATIONs are managed?

- Management of the security system:

  - Are all users permitted to use those facilities that they need to do their job?

  - Are any users allowed to use facilities that are not required to do their job, and which represent a potential risk to the enterprise?

  - How can we ensure that the security system has enough conceptual flexibility to accurately reflect changes in the organization or in the structure or use of APPLICATIONs?

8.4.9   The APPLICATION SECURITY MODULE entity

Once the security profiles have been established, the job of administering the APPLICATION SECURITY MODULE entity is passed to the security architect. The responsibilities involved include the following:

- Recognition of changing business circumstances and reflecting these on the modular structure of the security system;

- Monitoring of actual system usage and fine-tuning the security structure as appropriate;

- Ensuring that individual users are assigned to the correct security groups and continue to be so;

- Ensuring that the security system reflects the evolving function of the application.

8.5 Process modeling metadata

In many organizations, formal business process models exist. These models are definitions of the activities performed within the enterprise and are often intended to represent an authoritative structure within which these activities should take place. This part of the metadata allows this structure to be recorded and cross-referenced to the computer applications that are designed to automate parts of the processes. It also ensures that any business process reengineering activities that are performed are formally recorded and the resulting structures taken into account within the more technical parts of the IT infrastructure.

8.5.1 The BUSINESS PROCESS entity

The activities that make up an enterprise-wide process modeling exercise can be complex. They tend to be fraught with difficulties of both technical and political nature. Unfortunately, achieving agreement on the BUSINESS PROCESSes that make up the enterprise activity and their definitions, contexts, and triggering EVENTs is key to the understanding of the business as a whole. In many, if not most, of the approaches to realignment of the business to meet changing circumstances, the importance of a clear process-driven view of the business is emphasized. Without such an understanding, the enterprise is laying itself open to the risk that not only its computer systems but its whole way of operating will be unable to respond to such changes, with potentially dire consequences.

A BUSINESS PROCESS has only one triggering event. If, after initial analysis, this does not appear to be the case, then some realignment of the way in which either the BUSINESS PROCESSes or the EVENTs are structured, defined, and decomposed will be necessary.

Successful process modeling

The critical success factors in ensuring that a sound process model is built for the enterprise include the following:

- The ability to position the model in a universal context: A process model must be built, at the top level, encompassing the entire business, and it must be decomposed in a way that reflects the vision of the enterprise as a whole. This does not, of course, imply that a detailed decomposition should be built for the entire company in one go. This is unlikely to gain management support or to succeed due to the complexity of the analysis required. It must, however, be clear just where each part of the business will fit on the decomposition, once the appropriate analysis has been performed (possibly at some time in the far future!). At a typical point of its evolution, a process model will be built that comprises perhaps two levels of decomposition for nearly all of the business. This will include an agreed definition for all subprocesses and a much more detailed analysis for one or two "islands" of activity that have been selected for early attention.

- Management support for the analysis: It is extremely unlikely that an analysis of the entire company, which is likely to use considerable resources, will be successful without the support of senior IT and line management. A business case must be built emphasizing the link between the soundness of the process model and the likely success of new systems development and/or process reengineering.

- Management commitment to ongoing support: Not only will the process model require resources to build, but it will need to be adjusted to keep in line with the prevailing business conditions. This adjustment and the need to analyze its effect on the systems and procedures already in place in the business is a further significant exercise and will once again not be feasible without management support.

- Agreed on organizational and procedural structures for process management: Management must agree on the way in which the process definitions, decompositions, and triggers are developed and documented and the appropriate organizational elements put in place to ensure that they are executed. These organizational elements include the following:

  - Appointment of a corporate metadata manager;

  - Existence of project process analysts within major development activities;

- Use of process modeling as a fundamental part of business change activities, as well as systems development;

- Appointment of process owners with appropriate authority and knowledge who maintain active involvement in all process related activities.

- Formal integration with system and procedure development techniques: The way in which the personnel involved perform the tasks of creating, agreeing on, and stewarding the process model should be agreed on and formally incorporated in appropriate procedures for IT development and organizational analysis in general.

The role of the process owners, the metadata manager, and other individuals in managing the BUSINESS PROCESS entity was discussed in Chapter 4.

8.5.2　The BUSINESS PROCESS DECOMPOSITION entity

Many of those who have spent long periods of time designing process decompositions, only to have their work dismissed by others as incorrect, incomplete, or inaccurate will be aware of the sensitivities involved in this activity. Far from being a clear-cut, analytical technique, process decomposition is a highly subjective and often politically charged minefield for the unwary. Those who have only used this technique at a tactical level, as an aid to systems design, may be surprised by this conclusion. The reasons behind it might therefore bear further examination.

Modeling the building blocks of the business

The first factor to keep in mind is the need for a process model to reflect the whole business. The top level of such a process decomposition is clearly no problem, since it will be a single, almost self-defining, universal process.

The bottom, or "leaf-node" level of a universal process decomposition is also straightforward. While the identification and definition of all "atomic" processes is undoubtedly a time-consuming and technically taxing activity, it is nevertheless purely analytical in nature.

However, the intermediate levels of decomposition cause a great deal of complexity and political difficulty that arises during the construction of a corporate process model. The way in which the universal process is decomposed (or, if you prefer, in which the leaf-node processes are grouped) is key to the development of an efficient process-driven business and yet is also fraught with a great deal of difficulties.

Managing imprecision and sensitivity to change

Unless the process decomposition is an exact reflection of the existing organizational structure, in which case it is unlikely to form the basis for any radical change, there will be a great deal of sensitivity to its structure. People will see it (to a certain extent rightly) as a blueprint for the future organization. Responsibilities will be regrouped, sometimes to the apparent detriment of certain parts of the organization. In some cases, whole functions may be eliminated from the corporate model or reallocated as subfunctions of something else. The managers who are being asked to help develop and implement this model may see that their responsibilities are reduced, increased, outsourced, or placed under someone else's supervision. None of this is likely to make the task of agreeing on a process decomposition that reflects the new way of operating either easy or noncontentious. This only reinforces the need, as discussed under BUSINESS PROCESS in Section 8.5.1, for the prior establishment of management support. Those companies that are successful in the use of process modeling as a support to business process reengineering or a process-driven realignment of their computer systems architecture are those in which the need for such change has been sold and where active, ongoing support has been given at the most senior level.

Managing the process decomposition

It is to be expected that the business process decomposition for the enterprise will evolve over time. Initially, a skeleton structure will be put in place to ensure that the entire scope of the enterprise is covered. This will gradually be fleshed out, as a result of reengineering projects, or IT developments, over an extended period (possibly amounting to several years elapsed, in a large, complex organization).

The overall management of the decomposition is the responsibility of the metadata manager. He or she will coordinate the activities that are evolving the model and ensure that a single, authoritative copy of the entire decomposition is kept up-to-date. In doing so, metadata managers will coordinate to a large degree with the individual process or sub-process owners and the IT development teams as appropriate. They will also be called upon, from time to time, to act as arbitrators in case of particular sensitivities being encountered. Please note that the decomposition is a standard metastructure concept that is discussed in more detail in Chapter 5.

8.5.3 The BUSINESS EVENT entity

Generally speaking, BUSINESS EVENTs will act as the trigger either to one business process or to several business processes that fall within a closely related area of the enterprise's activity. The responsibility for recognizing and initial definition of the BUSINESS EVENT will therefore fall jointly on the relevant business process owner and the data analyst. Ongoing stewardship of the entity will rest with the business process owner, who will ensure that the definitions given reflect an accurate picture of the operation of the business.

Defining triggers for business processes

In cases where the BUSINESS EVENT triggers widely diverse processes, then the situation is more complex. This situation is unlikely to be recognized at the initial definition of the BUSINESS EVENT, since it will be focused on only one area of the business. In fact, it is likely to result from the recognition, during an analysis, that the trigger being proposed for a BUSINESS PROCESS already exists within the BUSINESS EVENT entity and acts as the trigger for another, currently unrelated process. The definition of the existing BUSINESS EVENT should be checked and agreed on by the metadata manager and the two process owners concerned to ensure that it does match the requirements of both cases, before the analysis progresses.

Management of business event metadata

The ownership of such instances is reallocated to the metadata manager, who will steward its ongoing use in both areas of activity.

8.6 Project and people management metadata

The metadata model can be further extended to include project manage-ment entities. The need for this, and whether value is added over and above use of standard project management software tools, should be considered.

8.6.1 The PROJECT entity

The PROJECT entity is defined by a single start and end date (planned and actual) and is the responsibility of a single manager. In the case of a more complex piece of work, where a PROJECT needs to be decom-posed into a set of subPROJECTs, then it is possible to use the standard hierarchical decomposition construct to achieve this. In more restricted cases, the PROJECT PHASE entity may be used (see below).

More generally, the detailed plan and breakdown would be managed separately from the metadata entity. As such, a simple reference is included as an attribute to store enough information for these details to be found, either on paper or in electronic form.

Management of project metadata

This metadata entity is not intended as a means of managing projects, per se. It does act as a "library card" record of the projects undertaken under a particular area of responsibility, and provides the necessary referential integrity check for ASSIGNMENTs (indirectly), JOB ROLEs, PROJECT PHASEs, etc. The ownership of this entity, implying the right and responsibility for determining which projects exist and how they should be described, lies with the IT management in a typical organization.

8.6.2 The PROJECT PHASE entity

This model is only relevant to a hierarchically structured project. For a more detailed discussion on hierarchies and matrices, as an organiza-tion/task model, see Chapter 5.

Where a project is split into phases within the metadata-base, the ownership of the phases is delegated by general IT management to the management of the PROJECT itself.

8.6.3   The PROJECT PLAN entity

In practice, there will be much more complexity to this, in terms of attributes and structure associated with a project plan. This entity has been included in the metamodel as a "placeholder," since this complexity will be far better handled using a separate tool. The existence of such plans should, however, be included in the metadata-base, as a "library" facility. (See also PROJECT, PROJECT PHASE in this chapter.)

8.6.4   The TASK entity

This entity will only be explicitly included in the scope of the metamodel if no more sophisticated activity monitoring is necessary and/or present. A more general case for the management of work being done within an IT department is that a project list will exist, with a few simple milestones (denoted by PROJECT PHASEs) that will be tracked by the SUPERVISOR concerned.

In addition, use will be found for the JOB ROLE entity since, more often than not, the work required in a particular function is redefined and restated each time a new employee is assigned. Having a library of such definitions can be valuable.

The breakdown of work effort to the point of TASKs is likely either to be performed within a full-scale planning tool or not at all. Once again, this entity has been included in the metamodel for the sake of structural completeness.

8.6.5   The IT EMPLOYEE entity

Once again, there is a general need for an entity that represents all individuals within the sphere of IT-related activities, but the level of detail required and the complexity of the related structures will depend on the context in which it is used. At the most basic, this entity will serve as an integrity check for all those occasions where an individual is identified in connection with IT activity. It will help to ensure that the identification of each person is consistent and unique across whatever scope is appropriate and thus to improve the overall usefulness of the metadata-base.

It should be noted that the allocation of attributes listed in Appendix D implies a strictly hierarchical organization (that is, each IT employee has strictly one supervisor with responsibility for several subordinates). The metamodel becomes more complex in cases where a different management model is in place—in the following situations, for example:

- Matrix management (where an individual effectively reports to a different manager according to the context, such as line management versus project management);
- Where an individual reports to a committee;
- Where supervision is at the task level.

The degree to which this entity is used as a distinct data type, rather than as a subset of the EMPLOYEE entity as a whole, and the level of detail required will depend on the context and the type of work falling within the remit of the IT department. In general, the overall ownership for this entity will be the responsibility of IT management, which will see fit to delegate portions of the entity scope to project or task managers within their sphere of influence.

8.6.6 The JOB ROLE entity

The JOB ROLE entity represents the level to which the work activities of the IT department (or the enterprise as a whole) are split, denoting work items that can be performed by one EMPLOYEE for one period of time. Together with the EMPLOYEE and ASSIGNMENT entities, it forms the basic metastructure by which the IT department work is defined and monitored.

The instances of the JOB ROLE entity are the direct responsibility of the person identified as supervisor and are used as the elements of a work plan for the INDIVIDUALs to whom they are assigned. See also EMPLOYEE and ASSIGNMENT in this chapter.

8.6.7 The ASSIGNMENT entity

The ASSIGNMENT entity represents an intersection between the INDIVIDUAL and the JOB ROLE. In other words, the information that is of interest to the enterprise concerning the performance of a particular JOB ROLE by a particular EMPLOYEE is contained in an instance of the ASSIGNMENT entity.

Because of the way in which the dates during which a person fulfilled the JOB ROLE in question have been included as attributes of this entity, the assumption is that each record can only represent one spell for a particular person in a particular role. It is possible within the organization for this role assignment to be repeated in a discontinuous manner. In such cases, either the JOB ROLE concept has to be redefined to reflect the time dependency of the activity, or the date has to be included in the identifier of the ASSIGNMENT entity to prevent possible duplication.

There are at least two ways in which this entity can be used. The first, which requires only a summary of the activity performed by the individual, with performance criteria if necessary, is the "personnel" perspective. This will be a relatively simple collection of data, associated with a particular employee and used to record a sequence of activities that go to make up his or her "career" within the enterprise.

The second, more detailed use is in connection with project and department management, where the entity will form part of a much more complex, separate planning database. A metadata structure example for such a facility is described in Appendix D.

The degree to which this entity is used and the level of detail required will depend on the context and the type of work falling within the remit of the IT department, as described above. In general, the overall ownership for this entity will be the responsibility of IT management, which will see fit to delegate portions of the entity scope to project or task managers within their sphere of influence.

8.6.8 The RESPONSIBILITY entity

A RESPONSIBILITY forms a subdivision of a JOB ROLE into a natural group of activities that may be performed by one EMPLOYEE under the supervision of another. In essence, if a formal job description is developed for a JOB ROLE, then the RESPONSIBILITY entity is filled with the "line items" within it.

For example, an analyst programmer JOB ROLE might consist of several RESPONSIBILITYs, as follows:

- Responsibility 1: Development of program specifications for the X system (reporting to the project manager for X);

- Responsibility 2: Support of the existing Y system (reporting to the application support manager);

- Responsibility 3: Scheduling of work and prioritization of task list for accounting application enhancement requests (reporting to the chief accountant).

The key facet of this entity to note is the way that RESPONSIBILITYs "belong" to a particular JOB ROLE but may nevertheless be performed independently of each other.

The metadata-base of RESPONSIBILITYs, if managed at all, will be the responsibility of the IT management. It should, of course, be noted that the constructs within the portion of the metamodel are by no means unique to the IT activities of the enterprise. People are given ASSIGN-MENTs; JOB ROLEs are defined; and PROJECTs are planned and managed in nonIT departments as well. As such, it may well be the case that this structure will be repeated many times across the enterprise. This serves to reinforce the usefulness of a common framework or metamodel that may be applied in all cases.

8.6.9 The SUPERVISOR entity

All SUPERVISORs must be recorded as INDIVIDUALs. As usual, with a subtyping relationship, a general requirement exists for an instance to be presenting the supertype before or at the time the corresponding instance is created in the subtype. Without this rule, the integrity of the subtyping relationship cannot be preserved.

Also, as is generally the case with subtypes, it is assumed that the attributes of the supertype implicitly belong to, and form an extension of, the subtype record. For this reason, only those attributes that are directly relevant to the role of a SUPERVISOR, rather than his or her existence as an INDIVIDUAL, will be included on this entity. At its simplest, this entity is maintained to ensure that all IT EMPLOYEEs with supervisory responsibilities are recorded and that the possibility for checking the referential integrity from other entities (PROJECT PHASE, PROJECT, TASK, RESPONSIBILITY) exists.

As with this entire metamodel, a far more complex structure can be envisaged that provides a complete work and personnel management tool for the IT function, if required. The nature of this entity will vary quite radically according to the structure, background, and underlying management philosophy of each organization. The intention here is to provide building blocks for a structure appropriate to all.

8.7 IT infrastructure management metadata

The final section of the metadata model that we shall consider concerns the nuts and bolts of the IT world—management of hardware and the network infrastructure. This will probably be managed internally, within the IT department, rather than being visible to the business community.

8.7.1 The COMPUTER entity

It may be imagined that most people working in the field of IT have a very clear idea of what a COMPUTER is. The main clarification that may be necessary in this case is the assumption, in our metamodel, that the COMPUTER is not the following:

- A virtual machine;

- A processor.

Hardware management and metadata

As you may well be aware, it is possible, and increasingly common, for a single computer to act very much as if it were several, independent machines, running different operating systems and having to communicate with each other "at arms length." For the purposes of our model, such machines are represented as one instance of the COMPUTER entity. Similarly, there are many multiple CPU machines that act as a single COMPUTER and that should be recorded as such, by our definition. The key principle underlying this definition is therefore the fact that it is impossible to divide the unit while preserving its inherent nature.

IT issues facilitated by effective metadata

In a typical enterprise, there will be a single manager or organizational unit that has responsibility for the COMPUTERs used. The key interacting issues faced by these people will be the following:

- Capacity planning (how much computer power is needed, by whom and when?);

- Planning and executing the deployment and configuration of COMPUTERs (when and where are the COMPUTERs to fulfill this need required?);

- Planning and coordinating the implementation of APPLICATIONs on COMPUTERs (what is going to be done with them?).

8.7.2 The NETWORK entity

The concept of NETWORK covers a wide variety of things in the real world. Any system that is designed to link together in a loose and independent manner separate NETWORK NODEs can be classified as a NETWORK.

The most readily appreciated form of NETWORK is the local area network (LAN). This is a mechanism that links several COMPUTERs in a limited geographical area, in such a way that they can pool the use of data, program logic and PERIPHERAL DEVICEs and intercommunicate in a dynamic, automated manner. The architecture or configuration of these LANs can vary, as can the need for a server, a machine dedicated to keeping the LAN running, rather than being a usable node in its own right.

Where there is a large and varied population of NETWORKs, it will be preferable to manage each subtype separately, since the attributes vary somewhat. For the purposes of studying a generic metamodel, this will not be necessary, if we assume that attributes relating to SERVER ID, etc. are optional.

8.7.3 The LOCATION entity

LOCATION is another example of an entity that has a definitive meaning outside the immediate context of the metamodel. The concept of a physical or geographical position is important to many aspects of the business. Being able to identify points in space in a precise and unambiguous fashion, whether they are internal to the organization or the addresses of third parties, is clearly a key concept overall.

In trying to come to a clearer understanding of the way in which this entity will be structured and managed, it is advisable to consider a set of subtypes that are different in their nature and usage. For instance, we may decide to split the set of LOCATIONs into the following subsets:

1. Geographical or descriptive LOCATIONs;

2. Postal LOCATIONs;

3. Specified or precise LOCATIONs.

The first case implies the use of the LOCATION as a means of communication. This will enable people to describe a LOCATION and distinguish it from others on the basis of some commonly accepted nomenclature. The degree of precision needed is only defined by the context of the communication. If a particular context requires that the London office should be distinguished from the Manchester office, then the city names alone may be sufficient to form unique and unambiguous identification.

The second case is driven by the need to identify a LOCATION in a precise enough manner that a third party (e.g., the postal services or a visitor to the organization's premises) will be able to deliver goods or people to that LOCATION with reference to data in the public domain (e.g., street maps and road signs). In other words, the "general public" will have the means at their disposal of arriving at the LOCATION, in the normal run of events.

The third case is more localized still, satisfying the need to identify parts of a building, complex, or plant that occupies a single postal location. The uses of this type of LOCATION are more often (although not exclusively) internal, examples of which include OFFICEs, ROOMs, and BUILDINGs.

This type of subtyping enables the metadata manager to design appropriately attributed structures for each case and to apply them to the business contexts in which they will be used. (See also ongoing management principles in Appendix E.)

Due to the disparate nature of its use, the management of the LOCATION entity will be widely spread. It would be normal for a "partition" to be introduced, whereby distinct subsets of the LOCATION set would be managed by different individuals within the enterprise.

For example, CUSTOMER LOCATIONs will be owned by the sales organizations and be managed on a day-to-day basis by the salesmen. SUPPLIER LOCATIONs will be owned and managed by the purchasing department. COMPUTER LOCATIONs will be owned by IT management and stewarded by the office services department. In general, each partition will only fall into one of the subtypes mentioned in Appendix E.

Depending on the organization, management of the NETWORKs will be the responsibility of the IT department, a subdepartment within the IT department, the "building the infrastructure" department, or in some cases will be contracted out entirely to a third-party organization. The level of detail, the management process, and the complexity of this part of the metamodel will vary considerably in each case.

8.7.4 The NETWORK NODE entity

The NETWORK NODE is predominantly a logical, rather a physical, concept. It represents a single identifiable point on a network. This will be, in many cases, a single COMPUTER that will appear only once in the NETWORK NODE list. However, it is, of course, possible for one COMPUTER to be connected to many networks or (in certain circumstances) for more than one logical partition of the same COMPUTER to appear on the same NETWORK.

In short, therefore, it is recognized that the NETWORK NODE entity has been designed to represent the intersection between the COMPUTER entity and the NETWORK entity. Within any organization of size, there will be a department or group responsible for planning, deploying, and monitoring the physical computing infrastructure. This group will therefore have control of the NETWORK NODE entity, the stewardship of which will form a major administrative component of its work.

8.7.5 The SERVER entity

In general, there will be subset of the NETWORK NODEs within an enterprise that performs the function of SERVER for particular networks. Because the way in which these NETWORK NODEs are managed will be inherently different from the general case, a separate entity will be used, containing appropriate attributes.

The management of the SERVER entity will be conducted as a subset of the physical infrastructure control and will, as such, be similar in form to the stewardship of the NETWORK NODE entity.

8.7.6 The PERIPHERAL DEVICE entity

In addition to the logical and physical representation of processing power, a large amount of capital is tied up in the provision of equipment that expedites effective use of the COMPUTERs themselves. A separate entity has been included in this part of the metamodel to facilitate the management of such capital equipment, which would include printers, monitors, scanners, and external storage media.

The PERIPHERAL DEVICE entity will fall under the ownership of IT management and be stewarded on a day-to-day basis by operational groups within the IT department that are made responsible for the deployment, servicing, etc. of such equipment.

Reference

[1] Tozer, Guy V., *Information Quality Management*, NCC-Blackwell, Oxford, 1994.

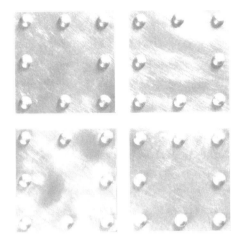

9

Interaction Between the Metamodels

9.1 Introduction

So far, this book has defined the nature of metadata, explained the importance of metadata in the context of a modern business environment, and developed a library of metamodel structures that offer an insight into the complexity of IT management.

To do the last of these, we have split the activities of a typical IT department into several distinct sections. Each represents a fairly natural partition of the entire model (in the sense that the concepts embodied in each submodel have a high degree of affinity with each other).

It should be clear from the way in which these partitions are made that there is a natural organization or management structure that will support these activities, in much the same way that it would for a "line" activity within the business. (Note that no assumption is made as to the completeness or correctness of this view for a particular organization. It should be taken as a typical case only, and refined for individual real-world cases.)

One of the key issues to recognize is that for IT, as for any other complex activity, it is not possible to optimize out the complexity. Even if an optimal model of the business can be found, it is extremely unlikely that it will be politically acceptable to implement it in the business itself. This optimal model will still require a high degree of interaction between groups of people fulfilling the functions described within the different partitions.

However well the "affinity analysis" is performed to develop the natural partitions in the business, it would be strange indeed if there were no interactions left between individuals in different partitions. It is with these residual cross-partition interactions that much of the complexity exists. Where you have two or more groups of people with different experience, expertise, goals, and priorities, then a degree of discussion must be included in any management of these "interactions." With this discussion comes an extension of the amount of effort involved, and inevitably a degree of compromise is introduced.

Chapter 8 details the manner in which the partitions can be built and modeled for an IT department. This chapter discusses the ways in which these partitions interact and the issues and problems thus caused.

9.2 Data/application metamodel interaction

Chapter 8 gives a great deal of attention to the data metamodel and the way in which the concepts it embodies enable analysts to define a "neutral" view of the data that is useful within an enterprise. An underlying implication of this, and one that is much discussed by IT strategists, is that the data within an organization exist in their own right. This is undoubtedly true, since there are instances of data that are recorded on many different applications, on pieces of paper, even in people's heads, while remaining consistent. These instances will still exist, from the business perspective, if any one of the applications is decommissioned, if the bits of paper are burnt, or if the people in whose heads the data reside change jobs.

However, when we come to examine the structure of data, and the relationships that exist between entities, it is clear that there is still very much an "application-dependent view" of such things. Data are, of course, very often shared between different applications, but this usually takes place in an application-dependent manner.

Explaining this further, we can see that the sharing can take a number of forms. The data can be read from a report produced by one application and typed onto the screen of another application. Data can be sent along an interface between the applications and interpreted and restructured accordingly. In a more sophisticated context, data can be dynamically shared between, for example, a spreadsheet and a word processing document on a PC, such that changes in one context can be reflected in another.

However, in all but the last case, there is always the notion of application ownership creeping in. Where data is copied, either manually or automatically from one system to another, there is still application ownership of data exerted on each copy individually. Even with the relative sophistication of object linking and embedding (OLE) such as would be used in the latter example, we will still encounter the notion that one application (the spreadsheet, for example) owns the data and that it is merely allowing the other application (the word processor) to use it.

The problem is that, for a neutral view of data such as that described in Chapter 8, we must assume that data exists in its own right and that all applications that have a legitimate interest in using that data have equal ownership over it. Even in the most advanced organization, this philosophical nicety is rarely observed.

To reconcile the need for a neutral view of data with the practicality of having application-specific structures and business rules that entirely represent the data's impact on the real world, the concept of a "view" of data must be introduced.

9.2.1 Views of data

A view of data is intended to represent the way in which certain entities, relationships, and attributes are perceived by a particular part of the enterprise. Most often, this takes the form of an application view of data, as seen by the users of a system when making use of the data in question.

This application view is, of course, heavily influenced by the physical structure and logic constraining the behavior of the data within the application system itself and, less strongly, by the use being made of the application within the business as a whole.

The shape of application data (as represented by the physical data model employed) and the business rules applied by the application (as represented by the relationships between the entities on this physical data model and other constraints applied in the program logic) will undoubtedly be different from the relevant subset of the neutral data model. The key concern here is not the differences themselves but the extent to which these differences imply that the application data model is "inconsistent" with the neutral view.

This concept of compatibility between the corporate data model (the neutral view) and the application view is key to keeping the application's use of data under control. Appendix A provides a formal definition of this concept. Briefly stated, the differences between two data models do not amount to incompatibility if and only if the data from one can be mapped, without external reference or breaking the business rules, onto the relevant part of the other.

For new systems under development, the neutral view forms a sound reference source for the development of the appropriate data structure. The development methodology used should be extended to ensure that this use of the neutral data model (as represented by the contents of the meta-entities ENTITY, ATTRIBUTE, and RELATIONSHIP, at the least) is explicitly included. In this way, the application data model (as represented by the meta-entities DATA MODEL ENTITY, DATA MODEL ATTRIBUTE, and DATA MODEL RELATIONSHIP, at the least) can be constructed in a manner that is compatible with the neutral model, in an efficient and systematic manner.

The three entities DATA MODEL ENTITY, DATA MODEL ATTRIBUTE, and DATA MODEL RELATIONSHIP are projections of, and behave in an analogous manner to, the three corresponding neutral entities (ENTITY, ATTRIBUTE, and RELATIONSHIP) but within the context of a specific data model. The interdependencies between these two metastructures, which will, at minimum, ensure that compatibility between the two models exists, can be defined as follows:

- Each DATA MODEL ENTITY must have a corresponding ENTITY instance. In this way, the ENTITY is recorded as an element of the overall neutral data model, and any future applications that impinge on this area must take account of the constraints placed upon the business by its nature.

- Each DATA MODEL ATTRIBUTE must be represented by either of the following:

  - A corresponding ATTRIBUTE instance with the same structure, domain, and usage;

  - An instance of ATTRIBUTE with a compatible structure, domain, and usage (e.g., the DOMAIN of the DATA MODEL ATTRIBUTE must represent a wholly contained subset of the DOMAIN of the neutral ATTRIBUTE instance or be proven to be purely local to the business area and hence to the application under analysis);

- Each DATA MODEL RELATIONSHIP must be represented by a corresponding RELATIONSHIP on the neutral view, or at least remain consistent with that view (i.e., the business rules implied by a DATA MODEL RELATIONSHIP should be "tighter," and not contradict, those that exist on the neutral view).

For existing or legacy systems (which may include new systems being implemented over which the enterprise has no control of the application data model, such as third-party packages), it is still useful to build a "view" of the subject area. However, there is, of course, far less chance that compatibility can be achieved.

Nevertheless, recognizing that there will be fundamental differences between these views and the neutral view can help to highlight problem areas in the old application and help to ensure that resources are diverted to solving the right problems. After all, incompatibility between the application view and the neutral view implies that the business as executed by the application is not in line with the rules that are necessary and applicable, in general. This clash of business rules can be directly represented as a specific inconsistency between the two data models. Because of this, what was only evident in a feeling of dissatisfaction with the operation of the application can be represented and eventually corrected in an analytical and objective manner. The ongoing task of managing these application views, whether for legacy or newly installed applications, should be arranged as a joint responsibility between the application support organization (which implies that the traditional role of application support as the refiner of program logic should be extended to encompass the welfare of the application data as well) and the metadata manager.

9.2.2   Interfaces

Another major implication of the compatibility of two data views is the possibility to transfer data in an automated fashion from one to the other. This transfer, or interface, has the benefit of ensuring that the contents of both databases are in line, at least at the time at which the transfer takes place, and that the contents of one database represent the same reality as the contents of the other.

Although this sort of controllability over copy-management does not imply application independent of data, it does bring many of the benefits that it accrues. More fundamental, however, is the way in which the compatibility of application views of data with the "neutral" view can affect the feasibility and simplicity of interfacing.

Let us suppose that an application wishes to send a piece of data, or "message" to another, and that this message is a restructured form of an entity, the context of which has been shown to be compatible with the neutral view on the part of both participating applications.

Although the fact that each of the applications is compatible with the neutral view will also make them compatible with each other, by definition, the developers should resist the temptation to build an interface directly from one to the other. Instead, if an approach is adopted whereby a two-phase interface is developed, the first phase of which translates from the source application format to the neutral format, the second phase from the neutral format to the destination application format, many benefits are achieved.

Despite being a two-stage translation, rather than one for a direct link, this approach has the virtue of introducing a form of "plug-compatibility" between the applications. If all links are built in this fashion, then the "stage one" can be used to send the message type from the source application not just to the application in question but to any other application requiring this data.

Similarly, the destination application can use the "stage two" to receive this type of data from anywhere, not just one particular source application. This, in fact, introduces a "telephone exchange" effect, where each message goes logically via an intermediate state that determines its form and ultimate destination. For very simple application architectures, this "two-for-one" approach may be uneconomical. For all but the smallest of enterprises the fact that new "nodes" on the application architecture will only increase the number of interfaces in a linear rather than an exponential fashion leads to a controlled infrastructure, especially where a highly decentralized data environment is envisaged.

9.2.3 Data consistency

In any environment where data that represents inherently the same thing in the real world is stored in more than one place, the issue of data consistency raises its ugly head. The way in which information consistency, in all its aspects, can be managed is a major subject in its own right that this book does not intend to cover [1]. It is worth considering, however, the way in which the management of "application" or "subject-area" views of the data can enhance the level of interapplication data consistency. Such consistency can imply some or all of the following:

1. Definition consistency: Implies that an entity A, when used in one application, represents the same concept as an entity A within a different application, at least insofar as those aspects of the nature of the said entity are relevant to the scope of both applications. Put simply, if something is called a CAT in one system, then it should be the same sort of thing as what is called a CAT on another system.

2. Format consistency: Implies that the way in which each instance of an entity is identified (the primary key) should be capable of transfer from one system to the other. If one application identifies CATs by a five-digit numeric code, and another identifies its CATs by an eight-letter alphabetic name, then there is clearly no

way of storing the identifier for one in the format provided by the other. Such consistency is particularly important where the ownership of an ENTITY might be split "vertically" between two systems (e.g., CUSTOMERs for one product line are owned by one system, whereas CUSTOMERs for another product line are owned by a different independent system) and where there might be transfers between the two (e.g., the CUSTOMER starts taking PRODUCTS from both product lines within the company).

3. Value consistency: Implies that we take format consistency one stage further and ensure that the identifier values used are the same in both systems, where the instances represent the same "real-world" thing. For example, if a CAT is known by the identifier "TIDDLES" on one system, it should also be known by that identifier elsewhere. This implies that data can be transferred between the system without the need to translate or "map" the codes used for the primary identifier.

4. Population consistency: The most stringent form of consistency is where it is expected that, for any instance of an entity on application A, there exists a corresponding consistent instance on application B and vice versa. This implies that the population of CATs on the first application is the same as on the second and that the same CATs are represented in the same manner.

If such views are complete and are compatible with the neutral model, then we are assured at least of basic definition consistency, reducing the amount of confusion that might arise in discussions between users of the different systems. (When they refer to a CAT, they no longer mean different things.) Users who use both applications can rely on the basic concept of a CAT being the same in both cases.

9.3 People/application metamodel interaction

Another area where complexity is caused by the intersection between two of the metamodels is the way in which the management of people affects the management of computer applications (and sometimes vice versa). Clearly, the major ways in which the two concepts impinge on each other are deeply embedded in the management of the typical IT department. The key interactions include the following:

- The specification of APPLICATIONs by INDIVIDUALs;

- The development and installation of APPLICATIONs by INDIVIDUALs;

- The use of APPLICATIONs by INDIVIDUALs;

- The support of APPLICATIONs by INDIVIDUALs.

The reason for the potential complexity is that neither the APPLICA-TIONs nor the INDIVIDUALs exist in vacuo. The INDIVIDUALs who specify the systems may also be users; they may also be system builders. This can have profound effects on the integrity of the security system and the robustness of the design. The APPLICATIONs can be the providers of data to other systems, for which expertise is required to interpret potential problem areas.

9.3.1 Security and access control

In general, applications are developed to complement the work of people, as a tool to record, process, and regenerate data. In all of this, it is usually important to recognize the group of people who are to use this tool and to be aware of just how they will be using it.

The simplest case is where an application may be used by anyone with the freedom to use whichever part of it they choose. In reality, however, it is far more likely that the application will be wholly off-limits to some people and only selectively available to others. The selectivity of this access may depend on the functionality of parts of the system or business-related factors such as user location or department or even the time of day.

A means must be put in place to ensure that the application is available to those who have a legitimate use for it and is denied to those who have no right to use it. For this, we must, as explained in Chapter 8, split the APPLICATION into appropriate subunits (called APPLICATION SECURITY MODULEs in our case), which are then allocated to the roles that are performed by people in the enterprise. These roles are then associated with INDIVIDUALs, who may only perform them under further restrictions (the aforementioned geographical, departmental, or time constraints, for example). It should be clear that the necessity for at least one intermediate concept is forced by the requirement for independence between the INDIVIDUALs and the parts of the APPLICATION they access.

Almost universally, they will be performing these accesses not because of who they are but because of a specific business role that they are fulfilling. In general, if someone else were to take over that role, he or she would be granted the same accesses, and the individual who was replaced would be given a new set, dependent on his or her new role.

The management of security is generally complex enough to be considered a distinct role from the application management. Indeed, the way in which people performing particular roles are allowed to use computer systems should be treated at a level high enough to ensure a consistent approach across applications. There is no point in denying someone access to certain powers on one system, if he or she is still allowed to perform the same task on another.

9.3.2 Expertise

Typically, an activity will be initiated in an enterprise to set up an application in the first place. This may take the form of a study to determine which third-party-supplied software is most appropriate to the enterprise's needs, followed by an implementation effort. It may, on the other hand, involve a full-scale development activity, from initially scoping the project, deciding on and specifying a solution, developing the necessary programs, and putting in place the facilities to support them, training the eventual users, etc.

Whatever form this development activity takes, it will be important to keep track of the individuals who have technical expertise related to the system. This will be of prime importance at the time the development is taking place, but it will remain important long afterward as a means of ensuring that the expertise gained is preserved and contributes to the long-term stability of the application.

9.4 Application/infrastructure metamodel interaction

The prime reason in most organizations for having computers at all is to provide the means by which applications (programs) may be run and hence to satisfy, directly or indirectly, the processing needs of the end users. The traditional structure of an IT department makes a split, at a very high level, between those personnel who provide hardware services and those who provide software services. This split has usually been made because the skills required in these two areas are distinct. Therefore, the ability to manage them effectively and to maintain a broad technical awareness of what is going on in each field has required a separation of function, both for operators and for supervisors.

9.4.1 Machine usage

This split has led to one of the chronic problems of IT management, namely the way in which a supply/demand balance for computing power can be measured and maintained. There is little, if any, common interest between the programmers and the hardware providers in many larger organizations. Without some form of common language, it is difficult for a good practice to develop covering the range of activities supporting the provision of machines to execute program logic.

When managed separately, the metamodels for application and infrastructure provide the tools for each of these IT subgroups. Where they overlap, an opportunity exists for building a structure that can ensure that the use of machine power in applications and the deployment of applications across physically distinct platforms can be managed effectively.

One of the more important facets of this overlap between hardware and software management is the degree to which an accurate picture of the costs incurred in running a particular piece of logic can be determined. Opinions vary as to the need to calculate the amount of money spent in performing particular automated tasks to a high degree of accuracy. In some organizations, a sophisticated and sometimes bureaucratic procedure for ensuring that all end-user departments are back-charged for their machine usage is in place. In others, it is assumed that the organization will support whatever costs are necessary, within reasonable bounds, and that such costs should be mutualized on a more or less arbitrary basis.

In some cases, accurate and supportable costs are available, linked not to particular departments but more to the execution of particular business processes (or at least to applications). A balanced view of this would be that in such cases the organization can control and monitor machine usage and balance the costs thus incurred with the benefits accrued, without the need for formal allocation of these costs. In this way, the user community can get a clear picture of where the money (whether real or nominal) is going, and the providers of IT infrastructure can get away from the feeling that they are viewed as an overhead by the rest of the organization.

For this to be done effectively, consistent data must be captured and shared on the subject areas of "application management" and "machine/infrastructure management." Surprisingly, despite the fact that both these functions invariably fall within the remit of the IT department (who should know better), this is rarely the case. In a metadata-aware organization, the possibility for getting this overlap under control and keeping it there is considerably higher than in other, less enlightened circumstances!

9.4.2 Machine optimization

There are other examples of the need to provide a consistent worldview between the "soft" and "hard" factions within a typical IT department. Once again, problems will arise where people regard the IT task as the provision and maintenance of processing power or as the provision and maintenance of program logic. As always, organizations or individuals that have to work closely together but that do not share common, or at least complementary or mutually supporting, goals will find it more difficult to discuss problems and achieve consensus on their solution.

At a more practical level, having a consistent view of where their subject areas overlap provides a channel of communication between different groups. As an example, consider the work of systems programmers, database administrators, and system operators. All of these people are charged with the responsibility of seeing that the various technical components do what they should do in an effective and efficient manner. Yet, for the most part, they are at the whim of the application programmers, application designers, and, in some cases, the end users themselves. When operators run batch jobs on a mainframe system, or when systems programmers make adjustments to these jobs, they do so for reasons relating to the behavior of the machines in their care. When application programmers construct a system, they do so with the objective of giving their customer (i.e., the end user) what they require from the system.

There is no inherent reason why the goals of these two groups should be contradictory, but they are often seen to be so. As with many other areas, a mutual understanding of the problems faced by each group and recognition of shared goals, where they exist, is a key to productive working.

In a normal organization, people cooperate to a reasonable degree to get their jobs done. Often, however, the most effective way of achieving shared goals is obstructed by vested interests, poor communication, or inconsistent language.

This sort of cooperative working can be facilitated (and hence made more likely to occur) if the factors that affect the work of each group are defined and communicated in a consistent and lucid way. In practice, this means aiming for a situation where each group within the organization has a clear picture of what the information they are providing to other groups is used for and what factors affect its usefulness. On the incoming side, it will also help for a group to understand the constraints and working pressures of other groups providing them with information.

As we have seen, there are very large areas of common interest between the hardware and software management groups. However, without a common structure and metadata-base, for which both feel responsible but over which neither have exclusive ownership, it is difficult for this common interest to remain clear in the face of expediency.

Reference

[1]   Tozer, Guy V., *Information Quality Management,* NCC-Blackwell, Oxford, 1994.

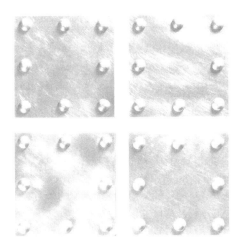

Appendix A:
Data Model Compatibility

ANY OF THE ACTIVITIES that involve the evolution of the meta-model have impacts on other parts of the model that may have been established for some considerable time. To determine the significance of these apparent discrepancies, it is necessary to have a clear idea of the concept of data model compatibility. Formally stated, two data models may be said to be compatible if the business rules that they embody do not contain mutual contradictions for the scope that they have in common.

The relationships and properties defined in one data model may be different to those defined elsewhere for a subject area that is common to both. Nevertheless, they may still be considered mutually compatible if it is possible to reconcile them without introducing constraints on one or the other model.

For example, a new rule that states that a department head has exactly eight subordinates does not contradict an existing rule that a department head may have one or many subordinates. The second rule merely restricts the behavior of the entities beyond that which is defined by the first. If, however, the first rule had stated that a department head has exactly seven subordinates, then there would clearly be a conflict.

The question of scope becomes more critical as we consider this problem more deeply. The scope of a business rule is meant to denote the set of circumstances under which the rule has to apply. This can be universal (in the case of an enterprise data model), or it can be restricted by department, subject area, geography, time, or any number of other criteria.

Thus, the scope of one model can exhibit various types of behavior in relation to the scope of other models:

- It can be a subset of another model (as all subject area models are subsets of the enterprise model or that process models relating to a decomposed superprocess are of that superprocess model).

- It can be a superset of another model.

- It can intersect with another model.

- They can have no scope logically in common.

The apparent contradictions between models are only "real" if the possibility exists for these contradictory rules to be applied across an intersection of the scopes of the two models. Thus, a subset model can contain rules that refine the rules within a superset but cannot flatly contradict any such rules. If such a contradiction does occur, then reconciliation between the two models should be undertaken, resulting in the adaptation of one or the other. In general, there should be a significant preference for changing the subset, since the likely impacts of this are less serious.

If the two models have an intersection, then care must be taken to define restrictions to the rules, such that there are no contradictions within that intersection. This can be done quite effectively, in most cases, by defining subtypes of the entities concerned and reassigning the relationships accordingly.

For example, if we have two models, and within one that is concerned with the Italian perspective on the business we have the rule:

"Each accounting document has one and only one reference number."

and within the second, which is the accounting perspective across all of Europe, it states that:

"Each invoice may have zero, one, or many reference numbers."

and the assumption is made that for both models, "invoice" is a subtype entity of "accounting document," then reconciliation can be made.

This can be achieved by defining a subtype of the invoice entity in the second model, called "Italian invoice," and associating the more constrained rule with this. In this way, any instances that are recorded under the scope of the second model will by definition be consistent with the first.

The beauty of this approach lies in the fact that this extension does not implicitly contradict anything in the previous version of either model but merely refines one such that it can cohabit peacefully with the other. The implications of such changes should therefore be limited to ensuring that all members of the new subtype already extant do in fact conform to the new rule. Assuming that the rule has always been in place, but was irrelevant until now for the second model, then this should not present a problem. Even where a "forced fit" is necessary, it will be by its nature a one-time exercise that will reinforce the consistency of the two models, once implemented. If, as in the fourth case, there is no intersection (for instance, if the two rules apply to different countries), then there is no need to form a reconciling view.

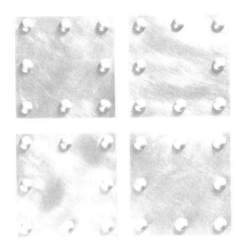

Appendix B:
The Data Management
Metamodel

The ATTRIBUTE entity

Definition

Each ENTITY is distinguished by a set of properties that are of interest, known as its ATTRIBUTEs. These have particular (but not necessarily unique) values for each instance of the ENTITY that is of interest. (Synonyms include RECORD FIELD and COLUMN.)

In common English, the ATTRIBUTEs of an ENTITY are a formal representation of those aspects that interest anyone who observes the ENTITY itself. ATTRIBUTEs only exist within the context of an ENTITY and are wholly dependent on it.

Where subtyping occurs, the SUBTYPE ENTITY may be considered to possess all attributes of its supertype, plus those specific to the subtype. Thus, all attributes common to the whole supertype will remain logically at that level. Any that are specific to a given subtype will be positioned within the said subtype instead.

Certain ATTRIBUTEs of an ENTITY can be used to identify each instance of the ENTITY. These attributes are known as KEY ATTRIBUTEs and form a subtype of the entity ATTRIBUTE. Figure B.1 shows a data context diagram for the ATTRIBUTE entity.

Basic relationships

ATTRIBUTE to ENTITY
The business rule for this entity is as follows: An ATTRIBUTE defines a property of one and only one ENTITY.

ATTRIBUTE to DATA MODEL ATTRIBUTE
The business rule for this entity is as follows: An ATTRIBUTE may be represented by zero, one, or many DATA MODEL ATTRIBUTEs.

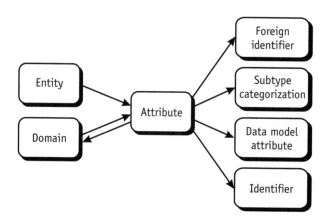

Figure B.1   Data context diagram.

ATTRIBUTE to DOMAIN (I)

The business rule for this entity is as follows: An ATTRIBUTE has the set of values it can take limited by one and only one DOMAIN.

ATTRIBUTE to DOMAIN (II)

The business rule for this entity is as follows: An ATTRIBUTE may constrain the values of zero, one, or many DOMAINs.

ATTRIBUTE to IDENTIFIER

The business rule for this entity is as follows: An ATTRIBUTE may form the component part of zero, one, or many IDENTIFIERs.

ATTRIBUTE to SUBTYPE CATEGORIzATION

The business rule for this entity is as follows: An ATTRIBUTE has its relevance to the operation of subtyping defined by zero, one, or many SUBTYPE CATEGORIzATIONs.

ATTRIBUTE to FOREIGN IDENTIFIER

The business rule for this entity is as follows: An ATTRIBUTE may contribute to zero, one, or many FOREIGN IDENTIFIER ATTRIBUTEs.

Basic attributes

- Entity identifier: This defines the ENTITY to which an ATTRIBUTE belongs and forms part of the primary identifier for that ATTRIBUTE. The entity identifier may be in the form of a descriptive name or a meaningless code. In this context, a meaningless code may be considered more appropriate, since it is less likely to be affected by changes in the business environment and is less open to misinterpretation. (See also ENTITY.)

- Attribute identifier: This completes the identifier for an ATTRIBUTE. The attribute identifier may be in the form of a descriptive name or a meaningless code. Once again, a meaningless code may be considered more appropriate, since it is less likely to be affected by changes in the business environment and is less open to misinterpretation.

- Global attribute description: The textual explanation for the context in which an ATTRIBUTE is used. This should be general enough to apply to the enterprise as a whole. More specific descriptions of the uses to which each ATTRIBUTE is put are stored within individual DATA MODELs. (See also DATA MODEL ATTRIBUTE.)

- Domain identifier: A nonidentifying, mandatory attribute that indicates the DOMAIN placing constraints on the values that may be taken by the ATTRIBUTE.

The DATA MODEL entity

Definition

A DATA MODEL is a bounded subset of the universe of ENTITYs, qualified by certain ATTRIBUTEs and connected by certain RELATIONSHIPs, as defined by the need for relevance to a particular set of activities within the enterprise.

The DATA MODEL provides a "view" of the data of relevance in a particular circumstance. Imagine a manufacturing company with an ENTITY RELATIONSHIP diagram representing the full scope of its activities (at least in principle). Each ENTITY will have a full set of ATTRIBUTEs, and the "model" as a whole can be referred to as the ENTERPRISE DATA MODEL.

For each department, activity chain, or loose context within that company, there will be a subset of the enterprise DATA MODEL (sometimes referred to as a *business area data model*) that contains only those ENTITYs, RELATIONSHIPs, and ATTRIBUTEs relevant to this tighter scope.

Each APPLICATION may also be said to have a DATA MODEL relevant to its scope. This will, in form, be closely related to the logical database for the APPLICATION in question, subset to specific technical constraints. This, of course, is known as the APPLICATION DATA

MODEL. (Note that for a properly controlled data environment all these DATA MODELs should form a pure subset of the enterprise model.) Figure B.2 shows a data context diagram for the DATA MODEL entity.

Basic relationships

DATA MODEL to DATA MODEL ENTITY
The business rule for this entity is as follows: A DATA MODEL defines a business context for zero, one, or many DATA MODEL ENTITYs.

DATA MODEL to DATA MODEL ATTRIBUTE
The business rule for this entity is as follows: A DATA MODEL defines a business context for zero, one, or many DATA MODEL ATTRIBUTEs.

Basic attributes

- Data model identifier: This attribute identifies the DATA MODEL and may be in the form of a descriptive name or a meaningless code. In most cases, a meaningless code is considered more appropriate, since it is less likely to be affected by changes in the business environment and is less open to misinterpretation.

- Data model description: The textual explanation for the context in which a DATA MODEL is used.

- Data model owner: A code, uniquely identifying the person, preferably with relevant line management responsibility, who will be the "owner" of this DATA MODEL and will be responsible for its general application throughout the entire enterprise.

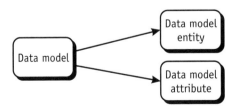

Figure B.2   Data context diagram.

The DATA MODEL ATTRIBUTE entity

Definition

> DATA MODEL ATTRIBUTEs describe the representation, interpretation, and use of ATTRIBUTEs within the context of a particular DATA MODEL, which in turn describes part of the business of an enterprise.

Whereas the ATTRIBUTE entity contains the data relevant to a global definition of a particular piece of data, the DATA MODEL ATTRIBUTE describes the use of that piece of data within the context of part of the business only. At its most fundamental, the relevance of data items to a particular part of the business is simply denoted by the existence or otherwise of a DATA MODEL ATTRIBUTE. Figure B.3 shows a data context diagram for the DATA MODEL ATTRIBUTE entity.

Basic relationships

DATA MODEL ATTRIBUTE to ATTRIBUTE
The business rule for this entity is as follows: A DATA MODEL ATTRIBUTE represents one and only one ATTRIBUTE.

DATA MODEL ATTRIBUTE to DATA MODEL
The business rule for this entity is as follows: A DATA MODEL ATTRIBUTE has its business context defined by one and only one DATA MODEL.

Basic attributes

- Data model identifier: See also DATA MODEL.

- Entity identifier: See also ENTITY.

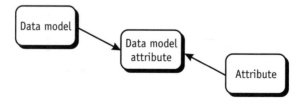

Figure B.3   Data context diagram.

■ Attribute identifier: See also ATTRIBUTE.

■ Data model attribute description: An optional attribute that provides a qualified perspective on the way in which a business attribute is captured, used, and interpreted within the context of a particular data model. This should be taken as further qualification of the generic attribute description within the ATTRIBUTE entity to provide a complete description of the business attribute.

The DATA MODEL ENTITY entity

Definition

DATA MODEL ENTITYs describe the representation, interpretation, and use of ENTITYs within the context of one DATA MODEL, covering part of the business of an enterprise.

Whereas the ENTITY entity contains the data relevant to a global definition of a particular type of data, the DATA MODEL ENTITY describes the use of that data in the context of part of the business only. At its most fundamental, the relevance of data items to a particular part of the business is denoted by the existence or otherwise of a DATA MODEL ENTITY. Figure B.4 shows a data context diagram for the DATA MODEL ENTITY entity.

Basic relationships

DATA MODEL ENTITY to ENTITY

The business rule for this entity is as follows: A DATA MODEL ENTITY represents one and only one ENTITY.

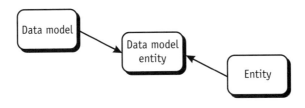

Figure B.4   Data context diagram.

DATA MODEL ENTITY to DATA MODEL

The business rule for this entity is as follows: A DATA MODEL ENTITY has its business context defined by one and only one DATA MODEL.

Basic attributes

- Data model identifier: See also DATA MODEL.

- Entity identifier: See also ENTITY.

- Data model entity description: An optional attribute that gives a qualified perspective on the way in which a particular entity is captured, used, and interpreted within the context of a particular data model. This should be taken in conjunction with the generic entity description provided by the ENTITY entity to form a complete description of the entity.

The DATA MODEL RELATIONSHIP entity

Definition

DATA MODEL RELATIONSHIPs describe the way in which ENTITYs behave in relation to each other, as seen from the context of a particular data model.

The behavior of the entities, as determined by the business rules constraining them, and as depicted by the ER concept can differ between the neutral view (the enterprise data model within the ENTITY and RELATIONSHIP entities) and the specific view of a DATA MODEL (subject area view, as defined within the DATA MODEL ENTITY and DATA MODEL RELATIONSHIP entities). This is not in itself a problem, provided the version with more limited scope (the subject area view) remains consistent with the enterprise view. Figure B.5 shows a data context diagram for the DATA MODEL RELATIONSHIP entity.

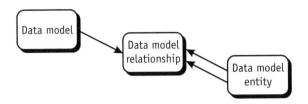

Figure B.5 Data context diagram.

Basic relationships

DATA MODEL RELATIONSHIP to DATA MODEL
The business rule for this entity is as follows: A DATA MODEL RELATIONSHIP exists in the context of one and only one DATA MODEL.

DATA MODEL RELATIONSHIP to DATA MODEL ENTITY (I)
The business rule for this entity is as follows: A DATA MODEL RELATIONSHIP has its dominant end represented by one and only one DATA MODEL ENTITY.

DATA MODEL RELATIONSHIP to DATA MODEL ENTITY (II)
The business rule for this entity is as follows: A DATA MODEL RELATIONSHIP has its dependent end represented by one and only one DATA MODEL ENTITY.

Basic attributes

- Data model identifier: See also DATA MODEL.

- Dominant entity identifier: See also ENTITY.

- Dependent entity identifier: See also ENTITY.

- Data model relationship description: This field should describe the role of the relationship, in specific terms relating to the context of the subject area covered by the DATA MODEL. This is an optional field to be used where there is value in further specifying or qualifying the general description held within the RELATIONSHIP entity.

The DATA MODEL SUBTYPING entity

Definition

> DATA MODEL SUBTYPINGs indicate the explicit relevance of a SUBTYPING instance to a particular DATA MODEL.

As with the DATA MODEL RELATIONSHIP entity, the behavior of business entities, as determined by the business rules constraining them (in this case what is assumed to be a sub- or superclass of what), and as depicted by the subtyping concept can differ between the neutral view (the Enterprise Data Model, within the ENTITY and SUBTYPING entities) and the specific view of a DATA MODEL (subject area view, as defined within the DATA MODEL ENTITY and DATA MODEL SUBTYPING entities). This is not in itself a problem, provided the version with more limited scope (the subject area view) does not contradict the enterprise view. Figure B.6 shows a data context diagram for the DATA MODEL SUBTYPING entity.

Basic relationships

DATA MODEL SUBTYPING to DATA MODEL

The business rule for this entity is as follows: A DATA MODEL SUBTYPING exists in the context of one and only one DATA MODEL.

DATA MODEL SUBTYPING to DATA MODEL ENTITY (I)

The business rule for this entity is as follows: A DATA MODEL SUBTYPING has its supertype end represented by one and only one DATA MODEL ENTITY.

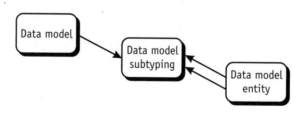

Figure B.6   Data context diagram.

DATA MODEL SUBTYPING to DATA MODEL ENTITY (II)

The business rule for this entity is as follows: A DATA MODEL SUB-TYPING has its subtype end represented by one and only one DATA MODEL ENTITY.

Basic attributes

■ Data model identifier: See also DATA MODEL.

■ Supertype entity identifier: See also ENTITY.

■ Subtype entity identifier: See also ENTITY.

■ Data model subtyping description: This field should describe the role of the subclassification, in specific terms relating to the context of the subject area covered by the DATA MODEL. This is an optional field to be used where there is value in further specifying or qualifying the general SUBTYPING description.

The ATTRIBUTE TYPE entity

Definition

ATTRIBUTEs that belong to a particular ATTRIBUTE TYPE are constrained in the format and values that they may take and the behavior they may exhibit.

The ATTRIBUTE TYPE provides a generic restriction on many ATTRIBUTEs but is not context-specific (in other words, these restrictions do not relate to the particular business uses to which the ATTRIBUTE is put—compare and contrast with DOMAIN).

As an example, the ATTRIBUTE EMPLOYEE DEPARTMENT may belong to the ATTRIBUTE TYPE TEXT, which merely constrains the contents of this field, in all the ENTITY INSTANCEs that it occurs, to consist entirely of printable characters and possibly to be of a fixed maximum length. Ensuring that this ATTRIBUTE is in fact a valid employee department is the primary role of the DOMAIN. Figure B.7 shows a data context diagram for the ATTRIBUTE TYPE entity.

Figure B.7 Data context diagram.

Basic relationships
ATTRIBUTE TYPE to DOMAIN
The business rule for this entity is as follows: An ATTRIBUTE TYPE constrains the generic nature of zero, one, or many DOMAINs.

ATTRIBUTE TYPE to ATTRIBUTE
The business rule for this entity is as follows: An ATTRIBUTE TYPE constrains the generic nature of zero, one, or many ATTRIBUTEs.

Basic attributes

- Attribute type identifier: A unique code identifying the attribute type. Although, as always, it would be preferable to use meaningless codes for this, a strong case can be built for allocating robustly defined and commonly understood names such as text, number, and date to this field, for the sake of simplicity.

- Attribute type description: This will provide the authoritative, universally agreed text describing the use of an instance of attribute type.

The DOMAIN entity
Definition

A representation of the set of possible values that may be taken by a particular ATTRIBUTE or group of ATTRIBUTEs. A particular DOMAIN may be "bounded" or "unbounded." A BOUNDED DOMAIN can be expressed explicitly as a list of values; an UNBOUNDED DOMAIN is usually expressed as a set of restrictions on the size, format, or character of a particular ATTRIBUTE TYPE. Strictly speaking, UNBOUNDED DOMAINs are not infinite, since it would be possible to list all permissible values.

The DOMAIN exerts a controlling influence over the values that may be taken by a particular attribute. It defines, either explicitly (in the case of BOUNDED DOMAINs) or implicitly (in the case of UNBOUNDED DOMAINs) which values may be taken by the ATTRIBUTE under a specific set of circumstances.

In the example of a ATTRIBUTE employee department code, the DOMAIN given will constrain its behavior and the behavior of other ATTRIBUTEs that belong to the same DOMAIN. Thus, the department code ATTRIBUTE within the ENTITY DEPARTMENT will be governed by the same set of rules as the employee department code within the ENTITY EMPLOYEE. The DOMAIN does not impose the ultimate constraint, namely which set of values are actually available to be used in the context of a given APPLICATION, which is defined by the CODESET for the ATTRIBUTE within the APPLICATION. Figure B.8 shows a data context diagram for the DOMAIN entity.

Basic relationships

DOMAIN to ATTRIBUTE TYPE
The business rule for this entity is as follows: A DOMAIN has its generic nature constrained by one and only one ATTRIBUTE TYPE.

DOMAIN to ATTRIBUTE (I)
The business rule for this entity is as follows: A DOMAIN constrains the specific behavior and nature of zero, one, or many ATTRIBUTEs.

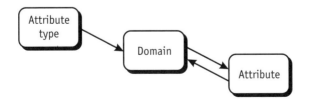

Figure B.8   Data context diagram.

DOMAIN to ATTRIBUTE (II)—value checking

The business rule for this entity is as follows: A DOMAIN has its set of values constrained by the values taken by zero or one ATTRIBUTE.

Basic attributes

- Domain identifier: A field that forms the primary identifier for the DOMAIN and that may take the form of a descriptive name or a meaningless code.

- Domain description: A textual description of the DOMAIN.

- Attribute type: A mandatory, nonidentifying field, indicating the ATTRIBUTE TYPE to which the DOMAIN as a whole belongs.

- Value checking attribute: An optional, nonidentifying attribute that indicates, where appropriate, the ATTRIBUTE that determines the set of permissible values for other ATTRIBUTEs constrained by the DOMAIN. In some cases, the simplest way in which a DOMAIN can be defined is as an explicit list of values. This attribute determines the place within a database that such values can be found for the DOMAIN under consideration.

The ENTITY entity

Definition

Any distinct class of things that can be associated together by a set of common characteristics. These things can be concrete, real items such as vehicles or people; they can be business events, such as purchase orders or deliveries. In some cases, they can be abstract, such as an opinion or a desire for a particular commodity. (Synonyms include RECORD TYPE, TABLE, and RELATION.)

The central role of the ENTITY entity can be seen from the following observations:

- All entities within the enterprise are subtypes of the ENTITY entity.

- All entities within the enterprise are represented by occurrences of the ENTITY entity.

- Most metadata entities are related directly to the ENTITY entity.

Figure B.9 shows a data context diagram for the ENTITY entity.

Basic relationships

ENTITY to ATTRIBUTE
The business rule for this entity is as follows: An ENTITY has its properties defined by one or many ATTRIBUTEs.

ENTITY to DATA MODEL ENTITY
The business rule for this entity is as follows: An ENTITY has its business context defined by zero, one, or many DATA MODEL ENTITYs.

ENTITY to SUBTYPING (I)
The business rule for this entity is as follows: An ENTITY may be partially represented by zero, one, or many SUBTYPINGs.

ENTITY to SUBTYPING (II)
The business rule for this entity is as follows: An ENTITY may be defined as part of another, by means of zero, one, or many SUBTYPINGs.

ENTITY to IDENTIFIER
The business rule for this entity is as follows: An ENTITY may be identified by one or many IDENTIFIERs.

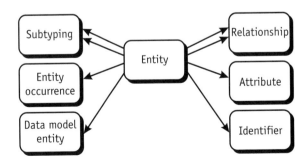

Figure B.9   Data context diagram.

ENTITY to ENTITY OCCURRENCE

The business rule for this entity is as follows: An ENTITY may manifest itself in the conduct of the business as zero, one, or many ENTITY OCCURRENCEs.

ENTITY to RELATIONSHIP (I)

The business rule for this entity is as follows: An ENTITY may represent the dominant end of zero, one, or many RELATIONSHIPs.

ENTITY to RELATIONSHIP (II)

The business rule for this entity is as follows: An ENTITY may represent the dependent end of zero, one, or many RELATIONSHIPs.

Basic attributes

- Entity identifier: This attribute identifies the ENTITY and may be in the form of a descriptive name or a meaningless code. In most cases, a meaningless code may be considered more appropriate, since it is less likely to be affected by changes in the business environment and is less open to misinterpretation.

- Global entity description: The textual explanation for the context in which an ENTITY is used. This should be general enough to apply to the enterprise as a whole. More specific descriptions of the uses to which each ENTITY is put are stored within individual DATA MODELs. (See also DATA MODEL ENTITY.)

The ENTITY OCCURRENCE entity
Definition

An individual member of a class defined by a particular ENTITY. (Synonyms include TUPLE and ROW.)

The ENTITY OCCURRENCE entity represents a level of abstraction lower than the ENTITY entity. Where types of things are identified in the ENTITY entity, the ENTITY OCCURRENCE entity will represent real instances of these things. Whereas the ENTITY entity possesses a series of ATTRIBUTEs that define its structure in the generic sense, the ENTITY OCCURRENCE entity is related to specific ATTRIBUTE VALUEs that have meaning in a real business context.

Most importantly, whereas the ENTITY entity represents the super-set of those concepts that are of importance to the data analysts, the ENTITY OCCURRENCE entity represents the superset of those things that are of interest to the business itself.

Therefore, it is unlikely that the ENTITY OCCURRENCE entity will ever be physically represented on a database. Its existence, as the superset of all "real tuples," is nevertheless of importance in the consid-eration of the metamodel as a whole. Figure B.10 shows a data context diagram for the ENTITY OCCURRENCE entity.

Basic relationships

ENTITY OCCURRENCE to ENTITY
The business rule for this entity is as follows: An ENTITY OCCURRENCE is a manifestation of one and only one ENTITY.

ENTITY OCCURRENCE to ATTRIBUTE VALUE
The business rule for this entity is as follows: An ENTITY OCCURRENCE is qualified by zero, one, or many ATTRIBUTE VALUEs.

Basic attributes

- Entity identifier: See also ENTITY.

- Entity occurrence identifier: In principle, this will be the same as the primary identifier of the entity under consideration, in terms of

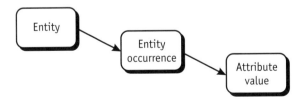

Figure B.10   Data context diagram.

format and value. In practice, it will seldom, if ever, be actually populated. (See also ongoing management principles.)

The IDENTIFIER entity

Definition

> An ATTRIBUTE or set of ATTRIBUTEs of a particular ENTITY that can be used to uniquely identify a particular ENTITY OCCURRENCE is known as an IDENTIFIER.

For every entity, there must be at least one way of uniquely identifying each of its INSTANCEs. It must be possible to take some combination of its attributes and use this as a unique tag that can be used thereafter as a means to "home in" on one particular record within the set in question.

The IDENTIFIER entity represents, for an ENTITY, those combinations of so-called KEY ATTRIBUTEs that fulfill this purpose. Figure B.11 shows a data context diagram for the IDENTIFIER entity.

Basic relationships

IDENTIFIER to KEY ATTRIBUTE
The business rule for this entity is as follows: An IDENTIFIER is composed of one or many KEY ATTRIBUTEs.

IDENTIFIER to ENTITY (I)
The business rule for this entity is as follows: An IDENTIFIER is used to distinguish between occurrences of one and only one ENTITY.

Figure B.11   Data context diagram.

IDENTIFIER to ENTITY (II)

The business rule for this entity is as follows: An IDENTIFIER may be the primary IDENTIFIER of zero or one ENTITY.

Basic attributes

- Entity identifier: See also ENTITY.

- Identifier code: A unique, preferably meaningless code that identifies the identifier. Effectively this separates out one possible combination of ATTRIBUTEs that can be used to identify an entity from another. If we take the example of a CAR entity, where it could be identified by its chassis number, its engine number, or a combination of its registration nationality and license plate number, then three such IDENTIFIER records would exist, each with a separate, unique identifier code.

- Identifier description: A textual explanation of the purpose and business context of the identifier.

The KEY ATTRIBUTE entity

Definition

An ATTRIBUTE of a particular ENTITY that can act either as a component or the whole of an IDENTIFIER and be used to uniquely identify a particular ENTITY OCCURRENCE is known as a KEY ATTRIBUTE.

Figure B.12 shows a data context diagram for the KEY ATTRIBUTE entity.

Basic relationships

KEY ATTRIBUTE to IDENTIFIER

The business rule for this entity is as follows: A KEY ATTRIBUTE may be a component of one or many IDENTIFIERs.

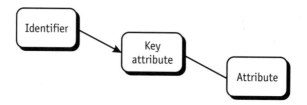

Figure B.12　Data context diagram.

KEY ATTRIBUTE to ATTRIBUTE
The business rule for this entity is as follows: A KEY ATTRIBUTE is one and only one ATTRIBUTE.

Basic attributes

- Attribute identifier: See also ATTRIBUTE.

The RELATIONSHIP entity
Definition

> A relationship describes the properties of one ENTITY as it acts upon, relates to, or restricts another.

All interactions between various types of things that are of interest to the enterprise can be represented as RELATIONSHIPs. In many senses, each relationship represents a business rule relevant to the enterprise, although the claims by some that all business rules can and should be defined in this form is open to debate.

In the sense that any RELATIONSHIP that is put in place between two ENTITYs represents a constraint on the way in which the business can operate, this is true. However, the systematic application of this technique to all constraints that the business feels it is under can result in contrived and often rather useless analysis.

Take as example the two ENTITYs CUSTOMER and ORDER. Without any explicit definition of the relationship between them, we can assume that they have nothing to do with each other. They can, in fact, exist independently, without any cross-reference being present.

If we impose the relationship "Each CUSTOMER places one or many ORDERs; Each ORDER is placed by exactly one CUSTOMER," then we are placing explicit restrictions on the way we do business by imposing rules that govern the behavior of these two ENTITIES. With this RELATIONSHIP, we have in fact implied the following:

1. That a CUSTOMER is not considered as such until he or she has placed at least one ORDER;

2. That a CUSTOMER is free to place more than one ORDER;

3. That an ORDER cannot be placed unless the CUSTOMER placing it is identified;

4. That no ORDER can be placed by more than one CUSTOMER.

In a different business context, not all of these constraints may apply, in which case the relationship should be changed.

It is worth noting that, like ENTITYs, some RELATIONSHIPs may only be relevant to a subset of the business. Thus, subject area or application DATA MODELs do not have to contain the same RELATIONSHIPs as the ENTERPRISE DATA MODEL. These "lower" DATA MODELs can be very different, in terms of the ER view, provided the business rules implied in them do not contradict those implied by the ENTERPRISE DATA MODEL. Consider the following examples, assuming that the ENTERPRISE DATA MODEL contains the relationship described above.

1. ORDER and CUSTOMER are both entities included in a DATA MODEL, and the relationship between them has restricted cardinality, implying that each CUSTOMER may only place FIVE ORDERs. While this is not necessarily sound business practice, it does not contradict the ENTERPRISE DATA MODEL at all and is therefore sound from the data analysis perspective.

2. ORDER and CUSTOMER are both entities included in a DATA MODEL, but the relationship between them is not included. This situation contradicts the ENTERPRISE DATA MODEL, since it

allows ORDERs without a defined CUSTOMER and CUSTOMERs who have placed no ORDER.

3. ORDER exists as an entity within a DATA MODEL, but CUSTOMER does not. As such, no relationship between the two can be recorded, and no business rule regarding their mutual behavior can be defined. Even so, no explicit contradiction with the ENTERPRISE DATA MODEL is implied, and the situation should be allowed.

Figure B.13 shows a data context diagram for the RELATIONSHIP entity.

Basic relationships

RELATIONSHIP to ENTITY (I)
The business rule for this entity is as follows: A RELATIONSHIP has its dominant end represented by one and only one ENTITY.

RELATIONSHIP to ENTITY (II)
The business rule for this entity is as follows: A RELATIONSHIP has its dependent end represented by one and only one ENTITY.

RELATIONSHIP to FOREIGN IDENTIFIER
The business rule for this entity is as follows: A RELATIONSHIP has its existence determined by one and only one FOREIGN IDENTIFIER.

Basic attributes

- Dominant entity: A RELATIONSHIP is described by a verbal phrase linking two ENTITYs. The ENTITY that forms the subject

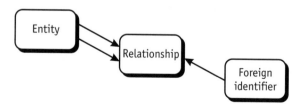

Figure B.13 Data context diagram.

of this phrase is known as the dominant entity and is recorded by means of an identifier within this field.

- Dependent entity: The ENTITY that forms the object of the verbal phrase is known as the dependent entity and is recorded by means of an identifier within this field.

- Relationship identification: It is possible for more than one RELATIONSHIP to exist between two ENTITYs, in the same direction. It is therefore necessary to include a further identifying attribute as part of the key to the RELATIONSHIP entity to ensure uniqueness.

- Relationship verbal phrase: A formal, descriptive phrase, indicating the nature of the relationship between the two ENTITYs.

- Relationship description: A looser description of the relationship between the two ENTITYs.

- Dependent cardinality minimum: An indication of the minimum number of INSTANCEs of the dependent ENTITY that can take part in a RELATIONSHIP with one instance of the dominant ENTITY.

- Dominant cardinality minimum: An indication of the minimum number of INSTANCEs of the dominant ENTITY that can take part in a RELATIONSHIP with one instance of the dependent ENTITY.

- Dependent cardinality maximum: An indication of the maximum number of INSTANCEs of the dependent ENTITY that can take part in a RELATIONSHIP with one instance of the dominant ENTITY.

The SUBTYPING entity

Definition

An ENTITY that wholly encompasses several other ENTITYs, each of which are distinguished one from the other by means of a categorizing ATTRIBUTE is referred to as a SUPERTYPE ENTITY. Conversely, an ENTITY that defines a bounded subset of the INSTANCEs of another ENTITY is referred to as a SUBTYPE ENTITY. The noncategorizing ATTRIBUTEs of a particular subtype ENTITY may be shared with some or all other "sibling" subtype ENTITYs or may be unique to itself. In general, the ATTRIBUTEs (including categorizing ATTRIBUTEs) that are shared by all subtype ENTITYs will be kept at the SUPERTYPE ENTITY level. The subtype relationship between one entity and another is recorded in a SUBTYPING entity.

Figure B.14 shows a data context diagram for the SUBTYPING entity.

Basic relationships

SUBTYPING to ENTITY (I)

The business rule for this entity is as follows: A SUBTYPING denotes a partition of the scope of one and only one ENTITY.

SUBTYPING to ENTITY (II)

The business rule for this entity is as follows: A SUBTYPING denotes the inclusion of the scope of one and only one ENTITY in the scope of another.

SUBTYPING to SUBTYPE

The business rule for this entity is as follows: A SUBTYPING has its applicability defined by one or many SUBTYPE CATEGORIZATIONs.

Basic attributes

- Supertype entity: A mandatory attribute containing the identifier for the ENTITY that is being partitioned by the operation of subtyping.

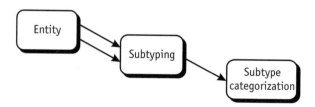

Figure B.14 Data context diagram.

- Subtype entity: A mandatory attribute containing the identifier for the ENTITY that is the result of the operation of subtyping.

- Subtype description/text: Optional descriptive text, explaining the concept embodied in the SUBTYPING operation.

The SUBTYPE CATEGORIZATION entity
Definition

The manner in which a single ATTRIBUTE acts as a categorizing agent for a single SUBTYPING operation.

Any ATTRIBUTE of an ENTITY can act as a categorizer for that ENTITY, determining how and into what subtypes it will be partitioned. Each ATTRIBUTE can act in many different ways to subtype its ENTITY. For instance, an INDIVIDUAL's address can be used to subtype the set of INDIVIDUALs between DOMESTIC RESIDENTs and FOREIGN RESI-DENTs. In this spurious example, the same ATTRIBUTE can be used for a different subtyping exercise, such as splitting those with a house number greater than 10 from the others.

Also, a single SUBTYPING operation may involve the examination of many categorizing ATTRIBUTEs. There is, thus, a many-to-many relationship between the SUBTYPING entity and the ATTRIBUTE entity, which is resolved by inclusion in our metamodel of the SUBTYPE CATEGORIZATION entity. Figure B.15 shows a data context diagram for the SUBTYPE CATEGORIZATION entity.

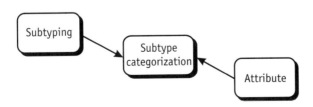

Figure B.15   Data context diagram.

Basic relationships

SUBTYPE CATEGORIZATION to SUBTYPING

The business rule for this entity is as follows: A SUBTYPE CATE-GORIZATION defines the applicability rules for one and only one SUBTYPING.

SUBTYPE CATEGORIZATION to ATTRIBUTE

The business rule for this entity is as follows: A SUBTYPE CATE-GORIZATION defines the relevance within the context of one type of subtyping, of one ATTRIBUTE.

Basic attributes

- Supertype entity identifier: A mandatory attribute, containing the identifier for the ENTITY that is being partitioned by the operation of subtyping. In this context, it is used as a partial identifier for the "parent" SUBTYPING record.

- Subtype entity identifier: A mandatory attribute, containing the identifier for the ENTITY that is the result of the operation of subtyping. In this context, it is used as a partial identifier for the "parent" SUBTYPING record.

- Attribute identifier: A mandatory attribute, identifying the ATTRIBUTE whose value is being tested to determine the subtype category into which the supertype entity should be placed.

- Formal notation for attribute test: A mandatory attribute indicating some interpretable pseudologic that formally specifies the nature of the test to be made on the attribute that, if determined to be true, will result in the supertype ENTITY being considered a member of the subtype under consideration.

- Textual description for attribute test: A plain language description of the test to be performed, with accompanying explanation if necessary.

The FOREIGN IDENTIFIER entity

Definition

A FOREIGN IDENTIFIER is an ATTRIBUTE or set of ATTRIBUTEs belonging to an ENTITY that together define a related instance of another ENTITY by forming sufficient components for a primary IDENTIFIER of that second ENTITY.

Figure B.16 shows a data context diagram for the FOREIGN IDENTIFIER entity.

Basic relationships

FOREIGN IDENTIFIER to FOREIGN IDENTIFIER ATTRIBUTE

The business rule for this entity is as follows: A FOREIGN IDENTIFIER is made up of one or many FOREIGN IDENTIFIER ATTRIBUTEs.

FOREIGN IDENTIFIER to RELATIONSHIP

The business rule for this entity is as follows: A FOREIGN IDENTIFIER provides the path by which to identify each instance of a RELATIONSHIP.

Basic attributes

- Foreign identifier code: An identifier, uniquely denoting the foreign key identifier. As usual, a meaningless code is generally more appropriate and safer in this context.

Figure B.16   Data context diagram.

- Foreign identifier description: A textual definition of the operation and business relevance of the FOREIGN IDENTIFIER.

- Foreign identifier source entity: See also RELATIONSHIP.

- Foreign identifier destination entity: See also RELATIONSHIP.

- Foreign identifier relationship: See also RELATIONSHIP.

The FOREIGN IDENTIFIER ATTRIBUTE Entity

Definition

An ATTRIBUTE that forms part or all of the structure of a FOREIGN IDENTIFIER, linking a source and destination ENTITY.

ATTRIBUTEs may form part of several different foreign keys within the same entity. For instance, within a DRIVER entity a COUNTRY attribute may be used as a foreign key onto the COUNTRY entity itself, together with the car registration number as a validity check on the vehicle the individual drives and with his or her zip code as a validity check on the location of the driver's address.

As there is an implied many-to-many relationship between ATTRIBUTE and FOREIGN KEY, it is necessary to introduce a resolving entity. Figure B.17 shows a data context diagram for the FOREIGN IDENTIFIER ATTRIBUTE entity.

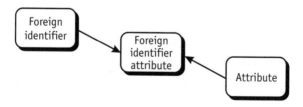

Figure B.17 Data context diagram.

Basic relationships

FOREIGN IDENTIFIER ATTRIBUTE to FOREIGN IDENTIFIER

The business rule for this entity is as follows: A FOREIGN IDENTIFIER ATTRIBUTE forms a structural part of one and only one FOREIGN IDENTIFIER.

FOREIGN IDENTIFIER ATTRIBUTE to ATTRIBUTE

The business rule for this entity is as follows: A FOREIGN IDENTIFIER ATTRIBUTE defines the foreign key role of one and only one ATTRIBUTE.

Basic attributes

- Foreign identifier code: See also FOREIGN IDENTIFIER.

- Entity identifier: See also ATTRIBUTE.

- Attribute identifier: See also ATTRIBUTE.

- Referential integrity flag: A Boolean value, indicating whether the referential integrity should be checked or not. In other words, if this flag is set, the assumption is that the existence of records on the destination ENTITY corresponding to the values stored in the foreign key attributes on the source entity is guaranteed and enforced over time.

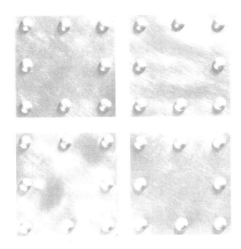

Appendix C:
The Application
Management Metamodel

The APPLICATION entity
Definition

An APPLICATION is a set of objects that are generically related by virtue of their use to automate an area of the enterprises business. An APPLICATION may consist of program logic directed at the end user or at its own operation together with the data required for its effective execution over which it fulfills the function of ownership.

An APPLICATION is a deliberately loose concept, since its main purpose is to group things together that are required to be managed as a consistent unit. In some cases, the bounds of a particular APPLICATION are very clearly set. If it has been defined, developed, and used within a strict set of constraints and has not fundamentally changed its nature over time, then it will be clear to those with an interest just what is meant by "the X application."

However, more often an APPLICATION will have evolved over time to encompass others, or its basic technology may have changed. Figure C.1 shows a data context diagram for the APPLICATION entity.

Basic relationships

APPLICATION to APPLICATION INSTALLATION

The business rule for this entity is as follows: An APPLICATION is represented by zero, one, or many physical instances of APPLICATION INSTALLATION.

APPLICATION to APPLICATION DEVELOPMENT MODULE

The business rule for this entity is as follows: An APPLICATION is divided, for the purposes of its own development and evolution, into one or many APPLICATION DEVELOPMENT MODULEs.

APPLICATION to APPLICATION SECURITY MODULE

The business rule for this entity is as follows: An APPLICATION is divided, for the purposes of managing the legitimate use of its

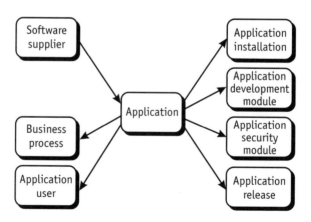

Figure C.1 Data context diagram.

constituent parts, into one or many APPLICATION SECURITY MODULEs.

APPLICATION to APPLICATION RELEASE

The business rule for this entity is as follows: An APPLICATION evolves in a controlled fashion by means of zero, one, or many APPLICATION RELEASEs.

APPLICATION to APPLICATION USER

The business rule for this entity is as follows: An APPLICATION is used by zero, one, or many APPLICATION USERs.

APPLICATION to SOFTWARE SUPPLIER

The business rule for this entity is as follows: An APPLICATION is provided by one and only one SOFTWARE SUPPLIER.

APPLICATION to BUSINESS

The business rule for this entity is as follows: An APPLICATION is designed to automate zero, one, or many BUSINESS PROCESSes.

Basic attributes

- Application identifier: A mandatory, identifying attribute, preferably meaningless, used to denote a single application.

- Application description: A textual description of the business context in which a particular application is used.

- Application software supplier: An identifier for the organization responsible for the development and further enhancement of the application at the present time. Effectively, these are the people who will be delivering the next release, whoever they are (internal or third-party). This will form a nondiscrete subset of the general business entity "SUPPLIER."

- Current application release: The code for the currently completed and deployed evolutionary step in the life of the application.

- Application first-installed date: Self-explanatory.

- Application status: Indicates whether the APPLICATION is planned, under development, partially deployed, under prototype, fully deployed, scheduled for decommissioning, decommissioned, etc.

- Application owner: The person with overall responsibility for the way in which the APPLICATION is developed, used, and evolved within the mainstream business.

- Application manager: The person with responsibility within the IT function for the evolution of the APPLICATION as a whole.

The APPLICATION INSTALLATION entity
Definition

A distinct example of an APPLICATION, installed at a particular point of the technical infrastructure, managed as such and capable of independent existence, is known as an APPLICATION INSTALLATION.

In many cases, a particular APPLICATION may have been developed and then deployed as multiple, identical copies across several computers. For certain purposes once this deployment has taken place, it is important to regard these systems as distinct, and therefore the notion of an APPLICATION INSTALLATION has been defined. The main areas for which this distinct management is relevant are the following:

- Control over divergence in logic (if the responsibility for evolution of logic is dispersed, or if the logic is heavily parameter-driven);

- Control over data shared between APPLICATION INSTALLATIONs;

- Management of application usage;

- Management of application changes (if responsibility for evolution of the logic is centralized);

- Management of hardware resources used by the application.

Figure C.2 shows a data context diagram for the APPLICATION INSTALLATION entity.

Basic relationships

APPLICATION INSTALLATION to APPLICATION
The business rule for this entity is as follows: An APPLICATION INSTALLATION represents the real-world manifestation of one and only one APPLICATION.

APPLICATION INSTALLATION to APPLICATION DEVELOPMENT MODULE
The business rule for this entity is as follows: An APPLICATION INSTALLATION includes copies of zero, one, or many APPLICATION DEVELOPMENT MODULEs.

APPLICATION INSTALLATION to APPLICATION MODULE RELEASE
The business rule for this entity is as follows: An APPLICATION INSTALLATION hosts, at a point in time, representations of zero, one, or many APPLICATION MODULE RELEASEs.

APPLICATION INSTALLATION to APPLICATION RELEASE
The business rule for this entity is as follows: An APPLICATION INSTALLATION hosts, at a point in time, operational representations of one and only one APPLICATION RELEASE.

APPLICATION INSTALLATION to NETWORK NODE
The business rule for this entity is as follows: An APPLICATION INSTALLATION is resident on one and only one NETWORK NODE.

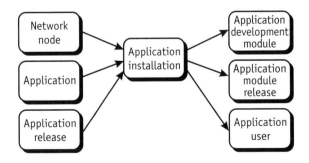

Figure C.2   Data context diagram.

APPLICATION INSTALLATION to APPLICATION USER

The business rule for this entity is as follows: An APPLICATION INSTALLATION is accessible to zero, one, or many APPLICATION USERs.

Basic attributes

- Application identifier: See also APPLICATION.

- Network node identifier: A mandatory attribute indicating logical location upon which the APPLICATION INSTALLATION resides. See also NETWORK NODE.

- Application installation identifier: A unique, mandatory attribute, indicating the specific installation of an APPLICATION.

- Application installation description: A textual reference for the APPLICATION INSTALLATION, offering a more meaningful way of naming the software in question.

- Application current release: The release level currently used at the APPLICATION INSTALLATION. Together with application identifier forms a foreign key reference to the APPLICATION RELEASE entity.

- Application installation date: Self-explanatory.

The APPLICATION MODULE entity

Definition

Any distinctly defined portion of an APPLICATION that can, from an IT perspective, be managed separately from the APPLICATION as a whole.

Figure C.3 shows a data context diagram for the APPLICATION MODULE entity.

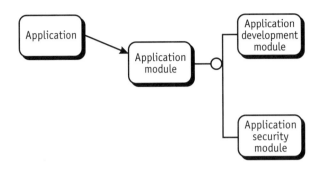

Figure C.3   Data context diagram.

Basic relationships

APPLICATION MODULE to APPLICATION

The business rule for this entity is as follows: An APPLICATION MODULE represents a generic logical subset of one and only one APPLICATION.

APPLICATION MODULE to APPLICATION SECURITY MODULE

The business rule for this entity is as follows: An APPLICA-TION MODULE may be zero or one APPLICATION SECURITY MODULE.

APPLICATION MODULE to APPLICATION DEVELOPMENT MODULE

The business rule for this entity is as follows: An APPLICA-TION MODULE may be zero or one APPLICATION DEVELOPMENT MODULE.

Basic attributes

- Application identifier: See also APPLICATION.

- Application identifier: Forms the primary identifier of an application module. As usual, it is preferable to keep this meaningless to avoid potential problems in the future due to the volatility of the environment.

- Application module description: A textual, nonidentifying attribute aimed at providing a plain language explanation of the nature of an APPLICATION MODULE.

- Application module type: Denotes whether the modularization has been performed for security or application development purposes (or otherwise).

The APPLICATION SECURITY MODULE entity
Definition

Any distinctly defined portion of an APPLICATION that can, from an application security perspective, be managed separately from the APPLICATION as a whole.

Figure C.4 shows a data context diagram for the APPLICATION SECURITY MODULE entity.

Basic relationships

APPLICATION SECURITY MODULE to APPLICATION MODULE
The business rule for this entity is as follows: An APPLICATION SECURITY MODULE is one and only one APPLICATION MODULE.

APPLICATION SECURITY MODULE to APPLICATION USER
The business rule for this entity is as follows: An APPLICATION SECURITY MODULE is legitimately accessed by zero, one, or many APPLICATION USERs.

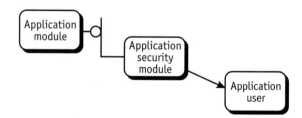

Figure C.4   Data context diagram.

Basic attributes

- Application identifier: See also APPLICATION.

- Application security module identifier: Together with the APPLICA-
  TION IDENTIFIER, forms the primary identifier of an
  APPLICATION SECURITY MODULE. As usual, it is preferable to
  keep this meaningless to avoid potential problems in future due to the
  volatility of the environment. See also APPLICATION MODULE.

- Application module security coordinator: An identifier for the
  person who has responsibility for ensuring that an individual
  APPLICATION SECURITY MODULE is correctly and legitimately accessed. This is an optional field, since it is not always
  appropriate to manage application security at this level. See also
  INDIVIDUAL.

The APPLICATION DEVELOPMENT MODULE entity

Definition

> Any distinctly defined portion of an APPLICATION that can, from an
> application development perspective, be managed separately from the
> APPLICATION as a whole.

Once again, the precise meaning of this concept will vary according to
circumstances. Indeed, the intention is that any such split of APPLICA-
TIONs will be made for the convenience of those who develop, maintain,
and use it. As such, the scope and complexity of each MODULE, relative
to the APPLICATION as a whole, will vary considerably.

One important factor to consider is the relationship between
APPLICATION DEVELOPMENT MODULE and APPLICATION
MODULE RELEASE. This tends to emphasize the importance of mak-
ing a split that reflects the work of developing and evolving the
APPLICATION, possibly at the expense of the management or user
view. Figure C.5 shows a data context diagram for the APPLICATION
DEVELOPMENT MODULE entity.

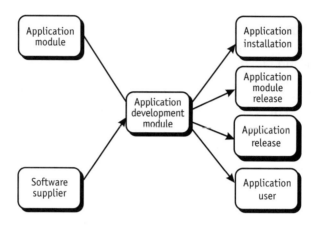

Figure C.5 Data context diagram.

Basic relationships

APPLICATION DEVELOPMENT MODULE to APPLICATION MODULE

The business rule for this entity is as follows: An APPLICATION DEVELOPMENT MODULE is one and only one APPLICATION MODULE.

APPLICATION DEVELOPMENT MODULE to APPLICATION INSTALLATION

The business rule for this entity is as follows: An APPLICATION DEVELOPMENT MODULE may be physically installed at zero, one, or many APPLICATION INSTALLATIONs.

APPLICATION DEVELOPMENT MODULE to APPLICATION MODULE RELEASE

The business rule for this entity is as follows: An APPLICATION DEVELOPMENT MODULE is evolved over time by means of zero, one, or many APPLICATION MODULE RELEASEs.

APPLICATION DEVELOPMENT MODULE to APPLICATION RELEASE

The business rule for this entity is as follows: An APPLICATION DEVELOPMENT MODULE forms a constituent part of zero, one, or many APPLICATION RELEASEs.

APPLICATION DEVELOPMENT MODULE to APPLICATION USER

The business rule for this entity is as follows: An APPLICATION DEVELOPMENT MODULE fulfills the business needs of zero, one, or many APPLICATION USERs.

APPLICATION DEVELOPMENT MODULE to SOFTWARE SUPPLIER

The business rule for this entity is as follows: An APPLICATION DEVELOPMENT MODULE is supplied by one and only one SOFTWARE SUPPLIER.

Basic attributes

- Application identifier: See also APPLICATION.

- Application development module identifier: Together with the APPLICATION IDENTIFIER, this forms the primary identifier of an APPLICATION DEVELOPMENT MODULE . As usual, it is preferable to keep this meaningless to avoid potential problems in future due to the volatility of the environment.

- Application development module coordinator: The person with responsibility for the evolution of an APPLICATION DEVELOPMENT MODULE. This is generally an IT responsibility, reporting to the application manager and/or the application owner. It forms a foreign key reference to the INDIVIDUAL entity. See also APPLICATION.

- Application development module subowner: The person with responsibility for the business use of a self-contained portion of the application, across the relevant scope of its usage. This is analogous to the role of, and should be responsible to, the application owner. Forms a foreign key reference to the INDIVIDUAL entity. See also APPLICATION.

- Application development module current release: An indication of the currently installed and operational version of the APPLICATION DEVELOPMENT MODULE. Together with the APPLICATION IDENTIFIER and the APPLICATION DEVELOPMENT MODULE identifier, this forms a foreign key reference to an instance of the APPLICATION MODULE RELEASE entity.

The APPLICATION MODULE RELEASE entity
Definition

> An APPLICATION MODULE RELEASE is a time series element, defining the state of a particular APPLICATION DEVELOPMENT MODULE at a point in time. This reflects the evolution of the APPLICATION DEVELOPMENT MODULE and the deployment of related changes across the various APPLICATION INSTALLATIONs.

The purpose of this entity is to record each stage in the evolution of an APPLICATION DEVELOPMENT MODULE. Within an application support environment, each APPLICATION MODULE RELEASE will represent a major unit of work, being done on an APPLICATION DEVELOPMENT MODULE. The components of this work need not necessarily be related to one another, but they must all be on the same APPLICATION DEVELOPMENT MODULE, and they must be implemented as a single unit.

Thus, although all the APPLICATION INSTALLATIONs within the enterprise need not have the same release level for each module, the changes that take place must represent whole APPLICATION MODULE RELEASE units. If the concept is implemented correctly, it should not be possible for a single APPLICATION INSTALLATION to play host to only a part of one release. Figure C.6 shows a data context diagram for the APPLICATION MODULE RELEASE entity.

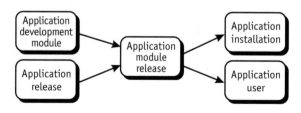

Figure C.6 Data context diagram.

Basic relationships

APPLICATION MODULE RELEASE to APPLICATION DEVELOPMENT MODULE

The business rule for this entity is as follows: An APPLICATION MODULE RELEASE represents an evolutionary state of one and only one APPLICATION DEVELOPMENT MODULE.

APPLICATION MODULE RELEASE to APPLICATION RELEASE

The business rule for this entity is as follows: An APPLICATION MODULE RELEASE forms a constituent part of zero or one APPLICATION RELEASE.

APPLICATION MODULE RELEASE to APPLICATION INSTALLATION

The business rule for this entity is as follows: An APPLICATION MODULE RELEASE is physically manifested at zero, one, or many APPLICATION INSTALLATIONS.

APPLICATION MODULE RELEASE to APPLICATION USER

The business rule for this entity is as follows: An APPLICATION MODULE RELEASE is used by zero, one, or many APPLICATION USERs.

Basic attributes

- Application identifier: See also APPLICATION.

- Application development module identifier: See also APPLICATION DEVELOPMENT MODULE.

- Application module release identifier: A mandatory identifying attribute, indicating a particular evolutionary stage of an APPLICATION MODULE.

- Application module release description: A textual description, if appropriate, of the business context in which a particular APPLICATION MODULE RELEASE will be used, the enhancements it brings, etc.

- Application module release definition: An optional formal code that identifies the release level of the APPLICATION MODULE. This code can be used in addition to the formal identifier, where an external form is required that does not meet the standards for rigor imply by use as a primary key.

- Application module release planned deployment date: Self-explanatory.

- Application module release actual deployment date: Self-explanatory.

The APPLICATION RELEASE entity
Definition

Where an APPLICATION is managed as a whole or where major evolutionary steps are made that aim to consolidate previous APPLICATION MODULE RELEASEs, the concept of APPLICATION RELEASE is used.

The APPLICATION RELEASE represents a more major evolutionary step than the APPLICATION MODULE RELEASE. It will typically correspond to units of work within the application support group on the level of PROJECTs, rather than TASKs.

The APPLICATION RELEASE is, of course, APPLICATION DEVELOPMENT MODULE-independent. As such, all APPLICATION INSTALLATIONs for a particular APPLICATION, while not necessarily being on the same release level, will nevertheless be on one and only one APPLICATION RELEASE level for their entire scope. Technically, any partial implementations should be represented by the previous APPLICATION RELEASE, selectively enhanced with a subset of the APPLICATION MODULE RELEASEs that make up the new APPLICATION RELEASE.

Also, an APPLICATION RELEASE can be made up of a set of APPLICATION MODULE RELEASEs. This can take the form of a "catch-up" evolution, where some APPLICATION INSTALLATIONs have evolved ahead of others at the MODULE level, the laggards being brought into line at the time of a new APPLICATION RELEASE. Figure C.7 shows a data context diagram for the APPLICATION RELEASE entity.

Basic relationships

APPLICATION RELEASE to APPLICATION MODULE RELEASE
The business rule for this entity is as follows: An APPLICATION RELEASE is made up of zero, one, or many APPLICATION MODULE RELEASEs.

APPLICATION RELEASE to APPLICATION
The business rule for this entity is as follows: An APPLICATION RELEASE represents an evolutionary step for one and only one APPLICATION.

APPLICATION RELEASE to APPLICATION INSTALLATION
The business rule for this entity is as follows: An APPLICATION RELEASE is physically manifested at zero, one, or many APPLICATION INSTALLATIONs.

Basic attributes

- Application identifier: See also APPLICATION.

- Application release identifier: A mandatory identifying attribute, indicating a particular evolutionary stage of an APPLICATION.

Figure C.7 Data context diagram.

- Application release description: An optional textual description of the business context in which a particular APPLICATION RELEASE will be used, the enhancements it brings, etc.

- Application module release definition: An optional formal coding that identifies the release level of the APPLICATION. This code can be used in addition to the identifier, where an external form is required that does not meet the standards for rigor impled by use as a primary key.

- Application release planned deployment date: Self-explanatory.

- Application release actual deployment date: Self-explanatory.

The APPLICATION USER entity
Definition

An individual, who is permitted, by virtue of his or her role within the enterprise, to make use of an APPLICATION and who does so by means of access to one or more APPLICATION INSTALLATIONs.

Figure C.8 shows a data context diagram for the APPLICATION USER entity.

Basic relationships
APPLICATION USER to APPLICATION
The business rule for this entity is as follows: An APPLICATION USER makes use of one and only one APPLICATION.

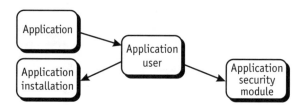

Figure C.8   Data context diagram.

APPLICATION USER to APPLICATION INSTALLATION

The business rule for this entity is as follows: An APPLICATION USER has access to zero, one, or many APPLICATION INSTALLATIONs.

APPLICATION USER to APPLICATION SECURITY MODULE

The business rule for this entity is as follows: An APPLICATION USER is permitted access to zero, one, or many APPLICATION SECURITY MODULEs.

Basic attributes

- Application identifier: See also APPLICATION.

- Application user code: A meaningless (see also application userid, below) code identifying an individuals use of a particular APPLICATION, by means of a single channel of access (userid).

- Application userid: A code that defines the technical channel of access available by a particular individual (or group of individuals) to a particular APPLICATION. Note that this is deliberately not used as part of the identifier since technical changes can force amendments to the userid, without altering the nature of the system usage itself.

- Application use description: A free format description of the way in which an INDIVIDUAL will make use of an APPLICATION and the reason behind allowing such use to take place.

- Validity date (from): Self-explanatory.

- Validity date (to): Self-explanatory.

The BUSINESS EVENT entity
Definition

A happening, or series of happenings, that changes either the STATE or the CONDITION of a particular ENTITY.

A state change occurs when an ENTITY occurrence is transformed into an occurrence of a different ENTITY occurrence, a condition change when the value of one or more ATTRIBUTEs of an ENTITY is altered. Figure C.9 shows a data context diagram for the BUSINESS EVENT entity.

Basic relationships

BUSINESS EVENT to BUSINESS PROCESS
The business rule for this entity is as follows: A BUSINESS EVENT acts as a trigger to zero, one, or many BUSINESS PROCESSes.

BUSINESS EVENT to APPLICATION USER
The business rule for this entity is as follows: A BUSINESS EVENT is initiated by zero, one, or many APPLICATION USERs.

BUSINESS EVENT to APPLICATION
The business rule for this entity is as follows: A BUSINESS EVENT falls within the scope of zero, one, or many APPLICATIONs.

Basic attributes

- Business event identifier: A meaningless, mandatory attribute, identifying the BUSINESS EVENT.

- Business event description: A textual description of the meaning, context, and other details pertaining to a BUSINESS EVENT.

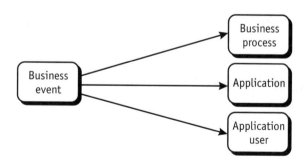

Figure C.9   Data context diagram.

The BUSINESS PROCESS entity

Definition

A course of EVENTs occurring in accordance with a planned objective.

In practice, a BUSINESS PROCESS represents a logical partition of the activities of an enterprise. Generally, this partition is capable of further decomposition (see also PROCESS DECOMPOSITION) and is executed, as indicated in the definition, in pursuit of some recognizable objective. Figure C.10 shows a data context diagram for the BUSINESS PROCESS entity.

Basic relationships

BUSINESS PROCESS to BUSINESS EVENT
The business rule for this entity is as follows: A BUSINESS PROCESS is triggered by one and only one BUSINESS EVENT.

BUSINESS PROCESS to PROCESS DECOMPOSITION (I)
The business rule for this entity is as follows: A BUSINESS PROCESS may represent the parent in zero, one, or many PROCESS DECOMPOSITIONs.

BUSINESS PROCESS to PROCESS DECOMPOSITION (II)
The business rule for this entity is as follows: A BUSINESS PROCESS may represent the child in zero, one, or many PROCESS DECOMPOSITIONs.

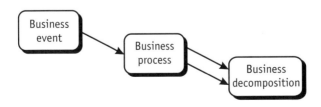

Figure C.10   Data context diagram.

Basic attributes

- Process identifier: A meaningless, mandatory identifying attribute, defining the primary key for a particular BUSINESS PROCESS.

- Process description: A formal textual label to be applied to the BUSINESS PROCESS.

- Process text: A free-format attribute, enabling a more detailed description of the BUSINESS PROCESS and its business context to be made.

- Triggering event identifier: An attribute, forming a foreign key identifier of an instance of the EVENT entity, indicating the triggering event for a particular BUSINESS PROCESS.

The PROCESS DECOMPOSITION entity

Definition

The act of partitioning a BUSINESS PROCESS, known as the parent, into one or more subprocesses, known as the children, in accordance with a particular view of the enterprise's operation.

In practice, a BUSINESS PROCESS may be divided in many different ways, which represent logical, sensible partitions, according to a particular view of the way an organization operates. Also, a particular process can be considered as a subprocess of many different parent BUSINESS PROCESSes. The resolution of this complex relationship is achieved by definition of an "artificial" entity, the PROCESS DECOMPOSITION, which represents one single "parent-child" couple. Figure C.11 shows a data context diagram for the PROCESS DECOMPOSITION entity.

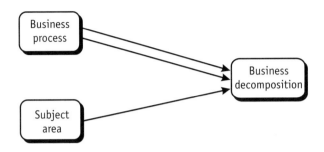

Figure C.11   Data context diagram.

Basic relationships

PROCESS DECOMPOSITION to BUSINESS PROCESS (I)
The business rule for this entity is as follows: A PROCESS DECOM-POSITION has, as the parent, one and only one BUSINESS PROCESS.

PROCESS DECOMPOSITION to BUSINESS PROCESS (II)
The business rule for this entity is as follows: A PROCESS DECOMPO-SITION has, as the child, one, and only one BUSINESS PROCESS.

PROCESS DECOMPOSITION to SUBJECT AREA
The business rule for this entity is as follows: A PROCESS DECOMPO-SITION represent a partitioning of enterprise activities relevant to one and only one SUBJECT AREA.

Basic attributes

- Parent process identifier: A mandatory, identifying foreign key attribute referring to the process that is being decomposed.

- Child process identifier: A mandatory, identifying foreign key attribute referring to the process that is being aggregated.

- Subject area context identifier: A foreign key attribute, identifying the subject area within which the context of this decomposition is defined.

The SOFTWARE SUPPLIER entity

Definition

An individual or corporate concern, either within the enterprise or a third party, who is responsible for the provision of program logic to be used in support of the enterprise activities.

Figure C.12 shows a data context diagram of the SOFTWARE SUPPLIER entity.

Basic relationships

SOFTWARE SUPPLIER to APPLICATION

The business rule for this entity is as follows: A SOFTWARE SUPPLIER may be the originator of zero, one, or many APPLICATIONs.

SOFTWARE SUPPLIER to APPLICATION DEVELOPMENT MODULE

The business rule for this entity is as follows: A SOFTWARE SUPPLIER may be the originator of zero, one, or many APPLICATION DEVELOPMENT MODULEs.

Basic attributes

- Software supplier identifier: A mandatory code identifying the SOFTWARE SUPPLIER .

- Software supplier description: A textual attribute describing the SOFTWARE SUPPLIER.

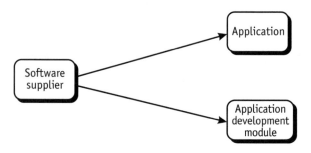

Figure C.12   Data context diagram.

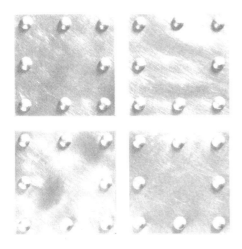

Appendix D:
The Activity Management
Metamodel

The ASSIGNMENT entity
Definition

An ASSIGNMENT is the specific work performed by one INDIVIDUAL, in the context of one JOB ROLE.

It is possible, of course, to have several people within an organization doing the same job. In such a case, each person has a separate ASSIGNMENT to the JOB ROLE in question.

Conversely, it is possible for one person to have several distinct purposes within an organization. In this case, he or she will have

269

ownership of several coexistent ASSIGNMENTs. Each INDIVIDUAL will build a series of ASSIGNMENTs over time, as his or her career progresses. A separate time series of ASSIGNMENTs can be defined that expresses the holders of a particular job, over time. Figure D.1 shows a data context diagram for the ASSIGNMENT entity.

Basic relationships

ASSIGNMENT to INDIVIDUAL
The business rule for this entity is as follows: An ASSIGNMENT is performed by one and only one INDIVIDUAL.

ASSIGNMENT to JOB ROLE
The business rule for this entity is as follows: An ASSIGNMENT represents the performance of one and only one JOB ROLE.

Basic attributes

- Individual identifier: A mandatory, identifying attribute, forming part of the primary key to the ASSIGNMENT entity and indicating the person to whom the work has been assigned. This attribute forms a foreign key reference to the INDIVIDUAL entity. See also INDIVIDUAL.

- Job role identifier: A mandatory, identifying attribute, forming part of the primary key to the ASSIGNMENT entity and defining the job role being assigned. This attribute forms a foreign key reference to the JOB ROLE entity. See also JOB ROLE.

- Assignment description: A textual definition of the ASSIGNMENT.

- Actual start date: Self-explanatory. This should form part of the identifier for this entity, since it is possible for the same

Figure D.1 Data context diagram.

INDIVIDUAL to perform the same JOB ROLE on more than one occasion.

- Planned start date: Self-explanatory.

- Actual end date: Self-explanatory.

- Planned end date: Self-explanatory.

The IT EMPLOYEE entity
Definition

An INDIVIDUAL under the contract of employment to the enterprise who is charged with fulfilling one or more of the JOB ROLEs that support the BUSINESS PROCESSes of the IT METAMODELs.

Figure D.2 shows a data context diagram for the IT EMPLOYEE entity.

Basic relationships
IT EMPLOYEE to INDIVIDUAL
The business rule for this entity is as follows: An IT EMPLOYEE is one and only one INDIVIDUAL.

IT EMPLOYEE to ASSIGNMENT
The business rule for this entity is as follows: An IT EMPLOYEE may perform zero, one, or many ASSIGNMENTs.

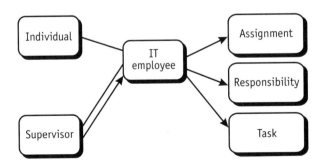

Figure D.2 Data context diagram.

IT EMPLOYEE to RESPONSIBILITY

The business rule for this entity is as follows: An IT EMPLOYEE may be entrusted with zero, one, or many RESPONSIBILITYs.

IT EMPLOYEE to SUPERVISOR (I)

The business rule for this entity is as follows: An IT EMPLOYEE may have zero or one immediate SUPERVISOR.

IT EMPLOYEE to SUPERVISOR (II)

The business rule for this entity is as follows: An IT EMPLOYEE may be zero or one SUPERVISOR.

IT EMPLOYEE to TASK

The business rule for this entity is as follows: An IT EMPLOYEE may have prime responsibility for the execution of zero, one, or many TASKs.

Basic attributes

- IT employee identifier (internal): A mandatory identifying attribute, forming the primary key of the IT EMPLOYEE entity.

- Supervisor employee identifier: A foreign key reference to the INDIVIDUAL entity, indicating the immediate supervisor of a particular instance of the IT EMPLOYEE entity.

- Supervisor flag: A Boolean, indicating whether or not the IT EMPLOYEE is also a SUPERVISOR and will hence be represented by an instance of that entity also.

The JOB ROLE entity

Definition

A distinct, bounded set of ACTIVITYs in support of the enterprise.

A key facet of the behavior of a JOB ROLE is the capability of a single INDIVIDUAL to perform one instance of it, at any point in time. Therefore, if an activity requires more than one person, acting in a nonhomogeneous fashion for its successful completion, then the components, rather than the activity as a whole, should correspond to the JOB ROLEs. Figure D.3 shows a data context diagram for the JOB ROLE entity.

Basic relationships

JOB ROLE to ASSIGNMENT

The business rule for this entity is as follows: A JOB ROLE is fulfilled by zero, one, or many ASSIGNMENTs.

JOB ROLE to TASK

The business rule for this entity is as follows: A JOB ROLE encompasses zero, one, or many TASKs.

JOB ROLE to RESPONSIBILITY

The business rule for this entity is as follows: A JOB ROLE encompasses zero, one, or many RESPONSIBILITYs.

JOB ROLE to SUPERVISOR

The business rule for this entity is as follows: A JOB ROLE is supervised by zero or one SUPERVISOR.

JOB ROLE to PROJECT

The business rule for this entity is as follows: A JOB ROLE may be defined as part of zero or one PROJECT.

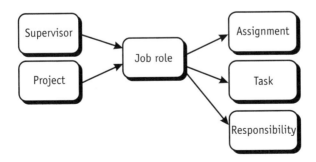

Figure D.3   Data context diagram.

Basic attributes

- Job role identifier: A mandatory, preferably meaningless, identifying attribute, forming the primary key of the JOB ROLE entity.

- Job role description: A short, textual description of the JOB ROLE and its context within the operation of the business.

- Job role project identifier: Where a JOB ROLE is an identified subset of the activities of a single PROJECT, this attribute identifies the project in question.

- Job role supervisor employee identifier: This attribute identifies the individual within the enterprise who has direct supervisory responsibility for the JOB ROLE in question, regardless of who is actually performing it. This forms a foreign key reference to the INDIVIDUAL entity. See also INDIVIDUAL.

- Job role employee identifier: This attribute identifies the INDIVIDUAL who was responsible for the definition of the JOB ROLE. It forms a foreign key reference to the INDIVIDUAL entity. See also INDIVIDUAL.

- Job role specification date: Self-explanatory.

- Job role amendment date: Self-explanatory.

The PROJECT entity

Definition

A distinct set of activities, in support of the enterprise, characterized by a defined and agreed product, start date, and resource usage.

The actual nature of what is considered to be a PROJECT will vary considerably according to the context. The general need is to determine the appropriate scope of self-contained activities and the resulting product. Figure D.4 shows a data context diagram for the PROJECT entity.

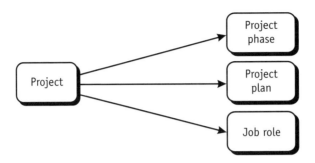

Figure D.4 Data context diagram.

Basic relationships

PROJECT to PROJECT PHASE
The business rule for this entity is as follows: A PROJECT can be logically split into zero, one, or many PROJECT PHASEs.

PROJECT to PROJECT PLAN
The business rule for this entity is as follows: A PROJECT has its progress defined over time by zero, one, or many PROJECT PLANs.

PROJECT to JOB ROLE
The business rule for this entity is as follows: A PROJECT may encompass zero, one, or many JOB ROLEs.

Basic attributes

- Project identifier: A mandatory, identifying attribute, defining the primary key for an instance of the PROJECT entity.

- Project description: A textual attribute, describing the nature and form of the PROJECT.

- Project plan identifier: An attribute, forming a foreign key reference to the instance of the PROJECT PLAN entity relevant to the PROJECT.

- Project planned start date: Self-explanatory.

- Project actual start date: Self-explanatory.

- Project planned end date: Self-explanatory.
- Project actual end date: Self-explanatory.

The PROJECT PHASE entity

Definition

A partition of a project in any way suitable to the management thereof.

The actual definition of project phases will depend largely on the project management methodology used, the nature of the project, and the progress reporting requirements within a particular enterprise. Figure D.5 shows a data context diagram for the PROJECT PHASE entity.

Basic relationships

PROJECT PHASE to PROJECT
The business rule for this entity is as follows: A PROJECT PHASE forms part of one and only one PROJECT.

PROJECT PHASE to PROJECT PLAN
The business rule for this entity is as follows: A PROJECT PHASE may be included in zero or one PROJECT PLAN.

PROJECT PHASE to TASK
The business rule for this entity is as follows: A PROJECT PHASE may be composed of zero, one, or many TASKs.

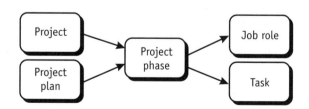

Figure D.5 Data context diagram.

PROJECT PHASE to JOB ROLE
The business rule for this entity is as follows: A PROJECT PHASE may define a need for zero, one, or many JOB ROLEs.

Basic attributes

- Project phase identifier: A mandatory, identifying attribute providing the significant part of the primary key for an instance of the PROJECT PHASE entity.

- Project identifier: An attribute identifying the PROJECT of which the PROJECT PHASE forms a part. See also PROJECT.

- Project phase description: A textual attribute, describing the PROJECT PHASE, and defining its context within the PROJECT and the work of the enterprise as a whole.

- Project phase planned start date: Self-explanatory.

- Project phase planned end date: Self-explanatory.

- Project phase actual start date: Self-explanatory.

- Project phase actual end date: Self-explanatory.

The PROJECT PLAN entity
Definition

A dynamic representation of the organization and structure of the component parts of a project and any interdependence that may exist between them.

Figure D.6 shows a data context diagram for the PROJECT PLAN entity.

Basic relationships
PROJECT PLAN to PROJECT
The business rule for this entity is as follows: A PROJECT PLAN structurally defines the progress of one and only one PROJECT.

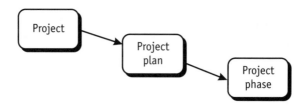

Figure D.6 Data context diagram.

PROJECT PLAN to PROJECT PHASE

The business rule for this entity is as follows: A PROJECT PLAN structurally defines the progress of zero, one, or many PROJECT PHASEs.

Basic attributes

- Project identifier: A mandatory, attribute, preferably meaningless, being the primary means of identifying a PROJECT. This will form a foreign key reference to the PROJECT entity, for the purposes of checking referential integrity. (See also PROJECT.)

- Project plan revision identifier: A mandatory, attribute that, together with the project identifier, forms the full identifier for this entity. This enables multiple generations of the project plan to be referenced from the metadata-base.

- Planned budget: A monetary representation of work effort quantity indicating the original intended cost of the PROJECT.

- Planned start date: Self-explanatory.

- Planned end date: Self-explanatory.

The RESPONSIBILITY entity

Definition

A RESPONSIBILITY defines a set of professional obligations undertaken by one or more individuals, in fulfillment of a particular JOB ROLE.

Figure D.7 shows a data context diagram for the RESPONSIBILITY entity.

Basic relationships

RESPONSIBILITY to SUPERVISOR

The business rule for this entity is as follows: A RESPONSIBILITY is under the control of zero or one SUPERVISOR.

RESPONSIBILITY to IT EMPLOYEE

The business rule for this entity is as follows: A RESPONSIBILITY is carried out by zero, one, or many IT EMPLOYEEs.

RESPONSIBILITY to JOB ROLE

The business rule for this entity is as follows: A RESPONSIBILITY forms part of the scope of one and only one JOB ROLE.

Basic attributes

- Job role identifier: This attribute defines the JOB ROLE within which the RESPONSIBILITY in question is defined and forms a foreign key reference to that entity. See also JOB ROLE.

- Responsibility identifier: This is a mandatory, identifying attribute that, with the job role identifier, forms the primary key of the RESPONSIBILITY entity.

- Responsibility description: A textual description of the RESPONSIBILITY, its context within the JOB ROLE, and the work of the organization as a whole.

Figure D.7 Data context diagram.

■ Supervisor identifier: A foreign key reference to an instance of the INDIVIDUAL entity, whose general responsibility is for supervision of the activities that form the RESPONSIBILITY, regardless of who is actually executing them.

The SUPERVISOR entity

Definition

A SUPERVISOR is an INDIVIDUAL with responsibility for the conduct of work actually performed by others, within the context of an organizational entity.

Figure D.8 shows a data context diagram for the SUPERVISOR entity.

Basic relationships

SUPERVISOR to IT EMPLOYEE (I)
The business rule for this entity is as follows: A SUPERVISOR supervises zero, one, or many IT EMPLOYEEs.

SUPERVISOR to IT EMPLOYEE (II)
The business rule for this entity is as follows: A SUPERVISOR is one and only one IT EMPLOYEE.

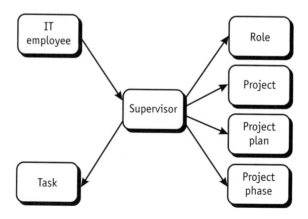

Figure D.8   Data context diagram.

SUPERVISOR to RESPONSIBILITY

The business rule for this entity is as follows: A SUPERVISOR has control over zero, one, or many RESPONSIBILITYs.

SUPERVISOR to TASK

The business rule for this entity is as follows: A SUPERVISOR has control over zero, one, or many TASKs.

SUPERVISOR to PROJECT PLAN

The business rule for this entity is as follows: A SUPERVISOR has ownership of zero, one, or many PROJECT PLANs.

SUPERVISOR to PROJECT PHASE

The business rule for this entity is as follows: A SUPERVISOR has control over zero, one, or many PROJECT PHASEs.

SUPERVISOR to PROJECT

The business rule for this entity is as follows: A SUPERVISOR has control over zero, one, or many PROJECTs.

Basic attributes

- Supervisor individual identifier: The mandatory attribute identifying the INDIVIDUAL who has supervisory responsibility. All instances of the INDIVIDUAL entity for which the supervisor flag have been set will have a corresponding entry in the SUPERVISOR entity, with the same primary key. See also INDIVIDUAL.

- Supervisor role description: Self-explanatory.

The TASK entity

Definition

The lowest level of controllable activity within the scope of a particular JOB ROLE.

Whereas the JOB ROLE entity described the intended activities to be performed, the ASSIGNMENT entity defined which person was identified as having the responsibility for its execution and the RESPONSIBILITY entity gave explicit details of what was involved, the TASK entity gives a planner's view of what actually should be done. Figure D.9 shows a data context diagram for the TASK entity.

Basic relationships

TASK to JOB ROLE
The business rule for this entity is as follows: A TASK is encompassed by one and only one JOB ROLE.

TASK to IT EMPLOYEE
The business rule for this entity is as follows: A TASK is performed by one and only one IT EMPLOYEE.

TASK to SUPERVISOR
The business rule for this entity is as follows: A TASK is controlled by one and only one SUPERVISOR.

Basic attributes

- Job role identifier: A mandatory, unique and preferably meaningless code forming the significant part of the primary identifier for the TASK. (See also JOB ROLE.)

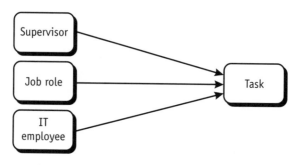

Figure D.9   Data context diagram.

- Task identifier: A mandatory, unique and preferably meaningless code forming the less significant part (with the job role identifier) of the identifier for this entity.

- Task description: A textual representation definition of the nature and scope of the TASK in question.

- IT employee individual identifier: A foreign key identifier for the person responsible for execution of the TASK.

- Supervisor individual identifier: A foreign key identifier for the person responsible for the supervision of the TASK and ultimately responsible for ensuring that it is concluded successfully.

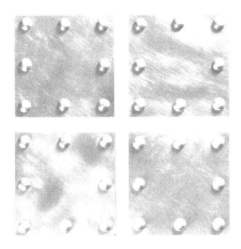

Appendix E:
The Infrastructure
Management Metamodel

The COMPUTER entity

Definition

A COMPUTER defines a physical processing facility capable of independent use for the purpose of data manipulation.

Figure E.1 shows a data context diagram for the COMPUTER entity.

Basic relationships

COMPUTER to NETWORK (I)

The business rule for this entity is as follows: A COMPUTER may be physically connected to zero, one, or many NETWORKs.

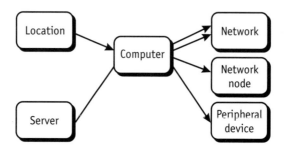

Figure E.1 Data context diagram.

COMPUTER to NETWORK (II)
The business rule for this entity is as follows: A COMPUTER may represent the server for zero, one, or many NETWORKs.

COMPUTER to LOCATION
The business rule for this entity is as follows: A COMPUTER has its physical position defined by one and only one LOCATION.

COMPUTER to NETWORK NODE
The business rule for this entity is as follows: A COMPUTER is virtually represented by one or many NETWORK NODEs.

COMPUTER to SERVER
The business rule for this entity is as follows: A COMPUTER may be zero or one SERVER.

COMPUTER to PERIPHERAL DEVICE
The business rule for this entity is as follows: A COMPUTER may be connected to zero, one, or many PERIPHERAL DEVICEs.

Basic attributes

- Computer identifier: A mandatory, meaningless identifying attribute used to define the primary key for the COMPUTER instance under consideration.

- Computer-coded identifier: An alternative identifier, providing more meaningful, but still coded, references to the computer (e.g., LONDON-3090-2), which may satisfy the need for some form of human-identifiable shorthand for the machines.

- Serial number: Another alternative identifying mechanism, being the serial number allocated to the machine by the manufacturer.

- Computer description: A textual description of the COMPUTER, including such factors as manufacturer, model and submodel designation, indication of the location, departmental ownership, and usage of the machine.

- Server flag: A Boolean flag, indicating whether the machine is a uses as a network server, it which case, it will appear as an instance on the SERVER entity.

- Computer location identifier: A foreign key reference to an instance of the LOCATION entity, indicating the physical position of the machine in question. See also LOCATION.

- Commission date: Self-explanatory.

- Decommission date: Self-explanatory.

The NETWORK entity
Definition

A set of COMPUTERs linked bidirectionally and capable of intercommunication, operating over a limited or wide geographical area.

Figure E.2 shows a data context diagram for the NETWORK entity.

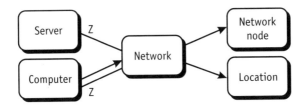

Figure E.2   Data context diagram.

Basic relationships

NETWORK to COMPUTER (I)

The business rule for this entity is as follows: A NETWORK may connect many COMPUTERs.

NETWORK to COMPUTER (II)

The business rule for this entity is as follows: A NETWORK has, as its server, zero or one COMPUTER.

NETWORK to SERVER

The business rule for this entity is as follows: A NETWORK has zero or one SERVER.

NETWORK to NETWORK NODE

The business rule for this entity is as follows: A NETWORK may connect many NETWORK NODEs.

NETWORK to LOCATION

The business rule for this entity is as follows: A NETWORK is accessible from zero, one, or many LOCATIONs.

Basic attributes

- Network identifier: A mandatory, identifying (preferably meaningless) attribute, forming the primary key to the NETWORK entity.

- Network code: An alternative identifier, coded, that may provide a meaningful reference in addition to the primary key.

- Network type: A coded indication of the mechanisms (both software and hardware) used to operate the NETWORK.

- Network architecture: A coded indication of the technical structure of the NETWORK (e.g., STAR or Token Ring).

- Network description: A textual description of the NETWORK, its function and type, and its use within the context of the enterprise.

- Server identifier: An attribute forming a foreign key reference to the SERVER controlling traffic on the NETWORK, where appropriate.

- Commissioning date: Self-explanatory.
- Decommissioning date: Self-explanatory.

The LOCATION entity
Definition

A bounded, identifiable place of interest to the enterprise.

The interest in the concept of LOCATION is not restricted to the IT department, of course. It is represented in the same manner as LOCA-TIONs for storage points, customer addresses, office buildings, etc. As usual, where there are a significant number of attributes that are unique to a particular logical subtype of the entity, then an explicit entity may be drawn out to represent it. Figure E.3 shows a data context diagram for the LOCATION entity.

Basic relationships
LOCATION to COMPUTER
The business rule for this entity is as follows: A LOCATION defines the physical position of zero, one, or many COMPUTERs.

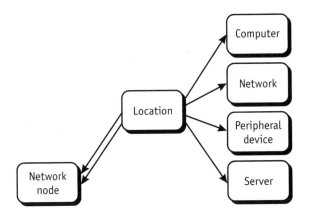

Figure E.3   Data context diagram.

LOCATION to NETWORK
The business rule for this entity is as follows: A LOCATION may be able to access of zero, one, or many LANs.

LOCATION to NETWORK NODE (I)
The business rule for this entity is as follows: A LOCATION defines the physical position of zero, one, or many NETWORK NODEs.

LOCATION to NETWORK NODE (II)
The business rule for this entity is as follows: A LOCATION may be able to access zero, one, or many NETWORK NODEs.

LOCATION to SERVER
The business rule for this entity is as follows: A LOCATION defines the physical position of zero, one, or many SERVERs.

LOCATION to PERIPHERAL DEVICE
The business rule for this entity is as follows: A LOCATION defines the physical position of zero, one, or many PERIPHERAL DEVICEs.

Basic attributes

- Location identifier: A mandatory, identifying attribute, preferably meaningless, defining the primary key to the LOCATION entity. (Note that although being considered for this purpose as part of the infrastructure metamodel, this entity is in fact far more widespread.)

- Location code: An alternative identifier, allowing a more meaningful coding to be used for the LOCATION in question.

- Location description: A textual description of the LOCATION, including a reference to the "plain language" version of its physical/geographical position (e.g., third floor, Bullock building).

- Physical address identifier : A foreign key reference to the physical address (e.g., postal address) of the LOCATION.

The NETWORK NODE entity

Definition

A logically defined, uniquely identifiable point within the network topography of an enterprise.

Figure E.4 shows a data context diagram for the NETWORK NODE entity.

Basic relationships

NETWORK NODE to COMPUTER
The business rule for this entity is as follows: A NETWORK NODE will be hosted by one and only one COMPUTER.

NETWORK NODE to NETWORK
The business rule for this entity is as follows: A NETWORK NODE will form a component part of one and only one NETWORK.

NETWORK NODE to LOCATION (I)
The business rule for this entity is as follows: A NETWORK NODE will have its physical position defined by one and only one LOCATION.

NETWORK NODE to LOCATION (II)
The business rule for this entity is as follows: A NETWORK NODE will be accessible from zero, one, or many LOCATIONs.

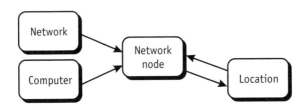

Figure E.4 Data context diagram.

Basic attributes

- Network node code: An identifying, mandatory attribute, defining the primary key for the NETWORK NODE entity.

- Network node description: A textual attribute, describing the NETWORK NODE in plain language terms.

- Network node location identifier: A foreign key reference to the LOCATION entity, being the physical/geographical position of the NETWORK NODE. See also LOCATION.

- Network node NETWORK identifier: A foreign key reference to the NETWORK entity, being the network of which the instance in question forms a node. See also NETWORK.

- Network node computer identifier: A foreign key reference to the COMPUTER entity, being the instance representing the physical machine upon which the NETWORK NODE is hosted. See also COMPUTER.

The SERVER entity

Definition

A uniquely defined computing facility, providing a specific service within the context of a particular network.

Figure E.5 shows a data context diagram for the SERVER entity.

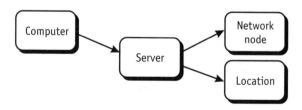

Figure E.5   Data context diagram.

Basic relationships

SERVER to COMPUTER

The business rule for this entity is as follows: A SERVER may be hosted by one and only one COMPUTER.

SERVER to NETWORK NODE

The business rule for this entity is as follows: A SERVER may be connected to zero, one, or many NETWORK NODEs.

SERVER to LOCATION

The business rule for this entity is as follows: A SERVER may be accessible from zero, one, or many LOCATIONs.

Basic attributes

- Server identifier: A mandatory, identifying attribute, providing the primary key to the SERVER entity. Preference should be given to allocation of meaningless values to this attribute.

- Server code: A coded, alternative identifier for the SERVER entity, providing a more natural language means of reference.

- Server description: A textual description of the SERVER and its technical and business context.

The PERIPHERAL DEVICE entity

Definition

A device designed to perform an operation auxiliary to the main function of a COMPUTER, to which it is connected.

Figure E.6 shows a data context diagram for the PERIPHERAL DEVICE entity.

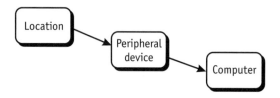

Figure E.6 Data context diagram.

Basic relationships

PERIPHERAL DEVICE to COMPUTER

The business rule for this entity is as follows: A PERIPHERAL DEVICE is connected to zero, one, or many COMPUTERs.

PERIPHERAL DEVICE to LOCATION

The business rule for this entity is as follows: A PERIPHERAL DEVICE is physically present at one and only one LOCATION.

Basic attributes

- Peripheral device identifier: A mandatory, identifying attribute, uniquely indicating the PERIPHERAL DEVICE under consideration. Preference should once again be given to the use of meaningless codes for this purpose to avoid misunderstanding and complexity as the business usage evolves.

- Peripheral device code: An alternative identifying attribute that can be coded in a more meaningful manner than the PERIPHERAL DEVICE identifier, to allow for a plain language name to be used for each PERIPHERAL DEVICE.

- Peripheral device description: A textual description of the PERIPHERAL DEVICE, its type and use in the context of business activities.

- Peripheral device supplier: A foreign key reference to the SUPPLIER entity, indicating the party responsible for supplying the PERIPHERAL DEVICE.

- Commissioning date: Self-explanatory.

- Decommissioning date: Self-explanatory.

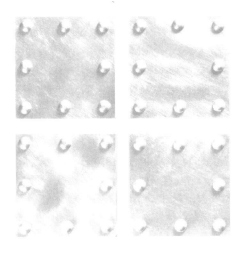

Glossary

Application architecture A representation and formalization of the computer applications in use within the enterprise, their interactions, and their control mechanisms.

CASE tool A computer-aided software engineering tool. Effectively a software application designed to automate the process of systems analysis—definition of data and process models, etc. They are often coupled with downstream facilities for schema and code generation.

CORBA Common object request broker architecture. A middleware architecture, defined by the OMG, designed to provide neutral structure for communication of objects between processes running on diverse platforms.

Data behavior The manner in which particular data evolves as it passes through its business life cycle, together with any formal or informal constraints that affect that evolution.

Data dictionary   A formally controlled data store containing meta-data used to control and constrain data within a database management system (DBMS). Such data dictionaries are usually embedded within the DBMS itself and often in a proprietary structure.

Data management metamodel   A representation of the structure of metadata used to manage the data within an enterprise.

Data mart   A subset of the data warehouse, physically distinct and representing a defined portion of the enterprises activity; often described as a "departmental" warehouse, although the organizational split is not the only representation of a mart.

Data ownership   The responsibility for defining and administering the rules that govern the behavior of a bounded set of data.

Data stewardship   Responsibility for the inherent quality and integrity of the contents of a particular data entity.

Data warehouse   A large-scale, centralized database covering enterprise-wide scope and typically feeding OLAP style applications.

Database management system (DBMS)   A set of software designed to maintain the availability, accuracy, and integrity of a database.

DCOM   A standard for object request brokerage defined by Microsoft; currently in a competitive situation with CORBA, although some moves are being made toward convergence.

Decision support system (DSS)   Large-scope reporting systems designed to address specific needs within the enterprise, typically to assist the decision-making process for strategic level management; tends to be passive and static in format (compare and contrast with OLAP).

Enterprise   For this purpose, any bounded organization for which the entire base of data is recognized. The implication is generally that this represents the ultimate breadth of vision for those with strategic steering responsibilities for a corporation or other organization.

Enterprise data model   A high-level ER model defining the data of interest to an enterprise.

Enterprise resource planning systems   Wide-scope, integrated application system, generally supplied and supported by third parties, rather than developed in-house. Examples include SAP R/3, PeopleSoft, Baan, Oracle Financials, and J. D. Edwards.

Entity classification   The process of developing a classification system (hierarchical or "matrix") for entities, recognizing the ways in which characteristics of one entity can be inherited by its subclasses.

ERP   See enterprise resource planning systems.

Information consumers   Anyone within an enterprise who has a requirement for information.

Information management (IM)   Those portions of an enterprise whose role it is to satisfy the needs of all information consumers; alternatively, the activities performed to fulfill this role.

Information technology (IT)   Those portions of an enterprise whose role it is to deploy and support the technical infrastructure required to satisfy the needs of information consumers (compare and contrast with information management); alternatively, used to denote the infrastructure itself or its component parts.

Informational metadata   Metadata within a data warehouse environment that is adding to the end users' understanding of the data within the enterprise. This implies that it should be structured and presented in a user-friendly and comprehensive fashion, while preserving the robustness and universality of the operational metadata.

ISO   International Standards Organization.

Legacy systems   Applications that are in a stable state, generally considered to be nearing the end of their useful life within the enterprise; used more loosely to describe systems that have been deployed in the past without regard for the overall application architecture.

Mart exclusive   An architecture employed in the deployment of data warehouses, where all user access is via marts, rather than directly on the warehouse itself. This method has significant advantages with regard to performance, security, and cost justification of OLAP applications.

Metamodel   A representation of the constraints and business rules that act upon a portion of the metadata.

MOLAP   Multidimensional OLAP. These tools use a nonrelational, proprietary structure, often represented as a multidimensional hypercube, rather than the relational model. This enables faster response to complex analytical queries on data sourced from a data warehouse environment.

Normalization   A set of refinement techniques designed to ensure that a database is structured to eliminate the redundancy of the data it contains and to ensure that the referential integrity may be preserved explicitly by the operations of the DBMS.

OLAP   Online analytical processing. Typified by statistical analysis performed on very high-volume databases extracted from a data warehouse. Characterized by being low-selectivity (looking at large numbers of transactions at any one time) and low-volatility (history is preserved). Also characterized by the high degree of flexibility and sophistication required by end users when examining the contents of the data warehouse.

OLTP   Online transaction processing. Typified by standard "capture and process" business applications such as sales order processing and financial transaction systems; characterized by being accessed with high selectivity and containing dynamically changing data.

OMG   The Object Management Group. An industry standards body represented by IBM, Oracle, and Unisys inter alia; sponsors of the CORBA middleware standard.

Operational metadata   Metadata within a data warehouse environment that represent the formal, complete, and accurate behavior of the data, from a technical perspective.

ORB   Object request broker.

RDBMS   Relational database management system.

Referential integrity   The quality of data, expressed in terms of conformance to the referential constraints that are applied by the metadata and enforced by the DBMS; in other words, the adherence to those rules that define the behavior of data entities, with respect to the existence of other, reference entities (e.g., implying that a CUSTOMER must exist before SALES ORDERs are taken for them and that the CUSTOMER cannot be deleted if such SALES ORDERs remain outstanding).

Repository An enterprise-wide mechanism for capturing and storing metadata. Intended to be a platform-neutral, universal point of reference for operational metadata. Compare and contrast with data dictionary.

ROLAP Relational OLAP. Data analysis mechanism based upon relational DBMSs.

SAP R/3 An ERP.

Staging area A distinct area for storing data at the entry point to a data warehouse environment. Within the staging area, the quality and integrity of the data arriving from multiple sources is checked and, where necessary, improved; effectively a quarantine area, protecting the data warehouse environment from poor-quality data.

Subject Area A bounded subset of the activities of the enterprise; used to limit the scope, and therefore the impact, of data analysis activities.

W3C The World Wide Web Consortium.

XML Extensible mark-up language.

XSL Extensible style-sheet language. Complementary to XML, this provides formal definition of the content of XML pages, providing it with its inherent extensibility.

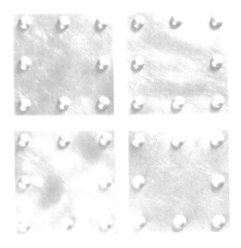

About the Author

Guy Tozer is an independent consultant, lecturer, and author on the subject of corporate information management. During his eighteen years experience in IT within software house and corporate environments, he has been responsible for the definition and management of data architecture in large, multinational companies.

In recent years, Tozer has become involved with defining strategies for the deployment of data warehouse technology. His consideration of large, complex business intelligence (BI) environments has led to an emphasis on clear, robust, and universal control of business rules. The necessity to achieve this control through metadata has led him to recognize and formally define the architectural management principles embodied in this book.

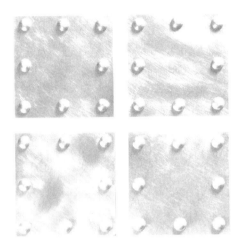

Index

Recent Titles in the Artech House Computing Library

Authentication Systems for Secure Networks, Rolf Oppliger

Business Process Implementation for IT Professionals and Managers, Robert B. Walford

Client/Server Computing: Architecture, Applications, and Distributed Sytems Management, Bruce Elbert and Bobby Martyna

Computer-Mediated Communications: Multimedia Applications, Rob Walters

Computer Telephony Integration, Second Edition, Rob Walters

Data Modeling and Design for Today's Architectures, Angelo Bobak

Data Quality for the Information Age, Thomas C. Redman

Data Warehousing and Data Mining for Telecommunications, Rob Mattison

Designing Web Software, Stan Magee and Leonard L. Tripp

Distributed and Multi-Database Systems, Angelo R. Bobak

Electronic Payment Systems, Donal O'Mahony, Michael Peirce, and Hitesh Tewari

Future Codes: Essays in Advanced Computer Technology and the Law, Curtis E.A. Karnow

A Guide to Programming Languages: Overview and Comparison, Ruknet Cezzar

Guide to Software Engineering Standards and Specifications, Stan Magee and Leonard L. Tripp

Internet and Intranet Security, Rolf Oppliger

Internet Digital Libraries: The International Dimension, Jack Kessler

Managing Computer Networks: A Case-Based Reasoning Approach, Lundy Lewis

Metadata Management for Information Control and Business Success, Guy Tozer

Practical Guide to Software Quality Management, John W. Horch

Practical Process Simulation Using Object-Oriented Techniques and C++, José Garrido

Risk Management Processes for Software Engineering Models, Marian Myerson

Secure Electronic Transactions: Introduction and Technical Reference, Larry Loeb

Software Process Improvement With CMM, Joseph Raynus

Software Verification and Validation: A Practitioner's Guide, Steven R. Rakitin

Solving the Year 2000 Crisis, Patrick McDermott

User-Centered Information Design for Improved Software Usability, Pradeep Henry

For further information on these and other Artech House titles, including previously considered out-of-print books now available through our In-Print-Forever® (IPF®) program, contact:

Artech House
685 Canton Street
Norwood, MA 02062
Phone: 781-769-9750
Fax: 781-769-6334
e-mail: artech@artechhouse.com

Artech House
46 Gillingham Street
London SW1V 1AH UK
Phone: +44 (0)20 7596-8750
Fax: +44 (0)20 7630-0166
e-mail: artech-uk@artechhouse.com

Find us on the World Wide Web at:
www.artechhouse.com